Learning NHibernate 4

Explore the full potential of NHibernate to build robust
data access code

Suhas Chatekar

BIRMINGHAM - MUMBAI

Learning NHibernate 4

First published: July 2015

Production reference: 1280715

Published by Packt Publishing Ltd.
Livery Place
35 Livery Street
Birmingham B3 2PB, UK.

ISBN 978-1-78439-356-4

www.packtpub.com

Credits

Author
Suhas Chatekar

Reviewers
Fabio Maulo

Ricardo Peres

Alexander Zaytsev

Commissioning Editor
Usha Iyer

Acquisition Editor
Meeta Rajani

Content Development Editor
Anish Sukumaran

Technical Editor
Tanmayee Patil

Copy Editors
Tani Kothari

Kausambhi Majumdar

Alpha Singh

Angad Singh

Project Coordinator
Mary Alex

Proofreader
Safis Editing

Indexer
Rekha Nair

Graphics
Jason Monteiro

Production Coordinator
Aparna Bhagat

Cover Work
Aparna Bhagat

About the Author

Suhas Chatekar has been in the business of building software for 12 years. He has mainly worked on .NET but possesses the skills of a full-stack developer. He started his career as a software developer, working on a trading platform. Since then, he has worked in several different domains, building both desktop and web-based applications. He is very passionate about coding and learning. He believes that practices such as test-driven development, automated testing, continuous deployment, and Agile are at the heart of quality software development. He currently works as a technical architect and mentor for a London-based company, working in the fields of loyalty, assistance, and insurance.

He has used NHibernate in various commercial projects, including both greenfield and brownfield. He also has experience in using NHibernate along with other ORMs and data retrieval techniques in large code bases. He is especially fond of clean code and following the right architectural guidelines. Through years of experience of working with NHibernate, he believes he has acquired some knowledge about best architectural principles that help in building resilient data access code using NHibernate, which he can share with readers.

In his spare time, he explores new technologies and writes a blog. He lives in London with his wife, Snehal, and daughter, Ovee. You can reach out to Suhas on Twitter using his handle at `suhas_chatekar`.

I would like to thank my wife, Snehal, without whose love, inspiration, and support, this book would never have been written. I would also like to thank everyone in my big family who supported me through the busy process of writing this book.

I would like to dedicate this book to my father, who would have been very proud if he was still with us.

Special thanks to my editors at Packt Publishing, who helped me at every stage of the book and had more patience than I would have had. And, how can I miss out on the expert reviewers, without whose input, the book would have never been complete. Thanks a lot.

About the Reviewers

Ricardo Peres is a Portuguese developer who has been working with .NET since 2001. He's a technology enthusiast and has worked in many areas, from games to enterprise applications. His main interests nowadays are enterprise application integration and web technologies. He is a contributor to the NHibernate community, writes a blog on technical subjects at `http://weblogs.asp.net/ricardoperes`, and can be followed on Twitter at `@rjperes75`. Ricardo has been declared a Microsoft Most Valuable Professional (MVP) in ASP.NET/IIS.

He is currently working as technical evangelist for a London-based company called Simplifydigital.

Ricardo Peres has authored *Entity Framework Code First Succinctly*, *NHibernate Succinctly*, *Microsoft Unity Succinctly*, and *ASP.NET Multitenant Applications Succinctly*, for the Succinctly series of books by Syncfusion.

I'd like to thank my family, Zézinha, Francisco, and Madalena, for all their support and patience.

Alexander Zaytsev discovered his passion for IT when he was a small kid, and since then, he has dedicated his life to becoming an excellent software developer. He has over 10 years of experience in the IT field, analyzing, designing, and developing .NET-based enterprise applications, using cutting-edge technologies. He works as an independent consultant in the .NET space, providing technical expertise to all kinds of software development companies. He is an active member of open source and local development communities. He writes a blog at `http://alexzaytsev.me`. He is also one of the main contributors to the NHibernate project and one of the few people who really know NHibernate's internals.

He considers himself a highly qualified expert in the C# language and the Microsoft .NET platform. He is an expert in technologies such as ASP.NET, web services, ASP. NET MVC, ASP.NET Web API, NServiceBus, NHibernate, Entity Framework, LINQ, Windows Forms (including related technologies such as HTML), JavaScript, and CSS/Less.

In his work, Alexander uses the principles of Agile, extreme programming, and scrum. In day-to-day tasks, he uses test-driven development (TDD) and pair programming.

I would like to thank my family(em dash)my wife, Olga, and my son, Stepan, for all their support and love.

www.PacktPub.com

Support files, eBooks, discount offers, and more

For support files and downloads related to your book, please visit www.PacktPub.com.

Did you know that Packt offers eBook versions of every book published, with PDF and ePub files available? You can upgrade to the eBook version at www.PacktPub.com and as a print book customer, you are entitled to a discount on the eBook copy. Get in touch with us at service@packtpub.com for more details.

At www.PacktPub.com, you can also read a collection of free technical articles, sign up for a range of free newsletters and receive exclusive discounts and offers on Packt books and eBooks.

https://www2.packtpub.com/books/subscription/packtlib

Do you need instant solutions to your IT questions? PacktLib is Packt's online digital book library. Here, you can search, access, and read Packt's entire library of books.

Why subscribe?

- Fully searchable across every book published by Packt
- Copy and paste, print, and bookmark content
- On demand and accessible via a web browser

Free access for Packt account holders

If you have an account with Packt at www.PacktPub.com, you can use this to access PacktLib today and view 9 entirely free books. Simply use your login credentials for immediate access.

Table of Contents

Preface

Connecting the object-oriented world of .NET to the relational world of databases has always been a fiddly issue. With the onset of ORMs, such as NHibernate, developers have got some relief in this area. However, using NHibernate without understanding its core features, and how they work, can always lead to more fiddly code and frustration. Learning how to use NHibernate in practical scenarios with the help of proven patterns and techniques goes a long way to building a robust data access layer. Knowing the best practices of designing a data access layer with NHibernate, before you start your next project, will help you to avoid any problems and deliver a successful project.

What this book covers

Chapter 1, Introduction to NHibernate, provides a view of NHibernate from 10,000 feet above and touches upon topics such as what an ORM is and why developers should use it. New features of NHibernate 4.0 are examined in this chapter along with the basic building blocks of NHibernate.

Chapter 2, Let's Build a Simple Application, describes a problem statement and builds a very simple domain model, so that we have a set of known business requirements to refer to in the rest of the book. This chapter also covers different software and tools that we will use throughout the book.

Chapter 3, Let's Tell NHibernate About Our Database, takes a deep dive into one of the building blocks of NHibernate -- mapping. The chapter starts with a brief introduction to the different mechanisms of mapping supported by NHibernate. The rest of the chapter goes into the details of mapping classes, properties, identifiers, associations, and inheritance hierarchies. In this chapter, the domain model defined in *Chapter 2, Let's Build a Simple Application,* is mapped to an appropriate database schema.

Chapter 4, NHibernate Warm-up, walks through the configuration of NHibernate. The chapter starts with a discussion on the different ways of configuring NHibernate and the minimal configurations required to get it up and running. Many important, but optional, configurations that include caching, session context, batch size, and so on, are covered next. The chapter ends with a discussion on generating database creation and updating scripts using NHibernate mappings.

Chapter 5, Let's Store Some Data into the Database, in a nutshell covers the NHibernate API that saves data in database. Beyond this, this chapter covers important concepts such as transactions, flush modes, cascades, and inverse collections. This chapter explains how transitive persistence works in different scenarios. Entity equality and its implementation in the context of NHibernate is provided in this chapter.

Chapter 6, Let's Retrieve Some Data from the Database, as the name suggests, talks about retrieving data from the database using the different querying methods supported by NHibernate. The book stresses using LINQ but other methods, namely native SQL, HQL, Criteria API and QueryOver, are also introduced and covered in detail wherever required. The chapter goes into the details of important concepts such as joins, lazy loading, eager fetching, and polymorphic queries. Basic querying requirements such as sorting and ordering the results are explained in this chapter.

Chapter 7, Optimizing the Data Access Layer, talks about making the NHibernate code more efficient by making use of techniques such as batching, different fetching strategies, and avoiding "select N+1" and eager fetching.

Chapter 8, Using NHibernate in a Real-world Application, introduces some architectural principles such as onion architecture and dependency injection that will help in building a robust data access layer using NHibernate in production code. This chapter covers important concepts, such as unit of work and session per request along with their implementation in NHibernate. Repository pattern, the most commonly used pattern for abstracting the low level details of data access code, is also covered in this chapter.

Chapter 9, Advanced Data Access Patterns, begins with a discussion on the shortcomings of repository pattern. The chapter then introduces two data access patterns, namely specification pattern and query object pattern, which address the shortcomings of repository pattern.

Chapter 10, Working with Legacy Database, goes into the NHibernate features that come handy in legacy database situations -- where database schema is not ideal for the domain model at hand. The chapter talks about composite IDs, components, working with database views, stored procedures, and custom DTOs. Custom lazy loading retention is introduced, so that it can be used with DTOs when there is a chance that NHibernate's lazy loading is rendered ineffective.

Chapter 11, A Whirlwind Tour of Other NHibernate Features, talks about the features of NHibernate that are slightly advanced and are not touched upon in any of the previous chapters. Important features such as concurrency control, event system, caching, and user-defined types are covered along with practical examples of their usage.

What you need for this book

Though this book is code heavy, readers should be able to follow this book, if they have, at least, any version of Visual Studio and MS SQL Server. The book makes use of the following pieces of software:

- Visual Studio 2013
- SQL Server 2012 Express
- NuGet
- NUnit
- SQLite
- NHProfiler
- ReSharper

If you are using Visual Studio 2010 or higher, you should be able to run the sample code of the book. SQL Server 2012 Express is used in the book, but any version of SQL Server up to SQL Server 2008 should work. NuGet is used to download NHibernate, NUnit and SQLite. NHProfiler is used to capture the SQL generated by NHibernate but SQL Profiler or NHibernate logging should do, if NHProfiler is not available. ReSharper is the author's favorite code refactoring companion for Visual Studio, but it's strictly optional.

Who this book is for

This book is intended for three types of developers:

- You are a .NET developer and have never used an ORM before
- You have used an ORM before, but are new to NHibernate
- You have used NHibernate sparingly and believe that you have more to learn about NHibernate

Conventions

In this book, you will find a number of text styles that distinguish between different kinds of information. Here are some examples of these styles and an explanation of their meaning.

Code words in text, database table names, folder names, filenames, file extensions, pathnames, dummy URLs, user input, and Twitter handles are shown as follows: "Once all of this is in place, you can just tell your ORM to save an instance of the `Customer` class."

A block of code is set as follows:

```
SELECT a_.FirstName,
  a_.LastName,
  a_.EmailAddress,
  a_.Age
FROM tblCustomer a_
WHERE a_.Age > 28 AND a_.Age < 35
```

When we wish to draw your attention to a particular part of a code block, the relevant lines or items are set in bold:

```
public interface IRepository<T> where T : EntityBase<T>
{
  void Save(T entity);
  void Update(int id, Employee employee);
  T GetById(int id);
  IEnumerable<T> Apply(ISpecification<T> specification);
}
```

New terms and important words are shown in bold. Words that you see on the screen, for example, in menus or dialog boxes, appear in the text like this: "Next, we click on the Install button that appears next to NUnit."

Warnings or important notes appear in a box like this.

Tips and tricks appear like this.

Reader feedback

Feedback from our readers is always welcome. Let us know what you think about this book—what you liked or disliked. Reader feedback is important for us as it helps us develop titles that you will really get the most out of.

To send us general feedback, simply e-mail feedback@packtpub.com, and mention the book's title in the subject of your message.

If there is a topic that you have expertise in and you are interested in either writing or contributing to a book, see our author guide at www.packtpub.com/authors.

Customer support

Now that you are the proud owner of a Packt book, we have a number of things to help you to get the most from your purchase.

Downloading the example code

You can download the example code files from your account at http://www. packtpub.com for all the Packt Publishing books you have purchased. If you purchased this book elsewhere, you can visit http://www.packtpub.com/support and register to have the files e-mailed directly to you.

Errata

Although we have taken every care to ensure the accuracy of our content, mistakes do happen. If you find a mistake in one of our books—maybe a mistake in the text or the code—we would be grateful if you could report this to us. By doing so, you can save other readers from frustration and help us improve subsequent versions of this book. If you find any errata, please report them by visiting http://www.packtpub. com/submit-errata, selecting your book, clicking on the **Errata Submission Form** link, and entering the details of your errata. Once your errata are verified, your submission will be accepted and the errata will be uploaded to our website or added to any list of existing errata under the Errata section of that title.

To view the previously submitted errata, go to https://www.packtpub.com/books/content/support and enter the name of the book in the search field. The required information will appear under the **Errata** section.

Piracy

Piracy of copyrighted material on the Internet is an ongoing problem across all media. At Packt, we take the protection of our copyright and licenses very seriously. If you come across any illegal copies of our works in any form on the Internet, please provide us with the location address or website name immediately so that we can pursue a remedy.

Please contact us at copyright@packtpub.com with a link to the suspected pirated material.

We appreciate your help in protecting our authors and our ability to bring you valuable content.

Questions

If you have a problem with any aspect of this book, you can contact us at questions@packtpub.com, and we will do our best to address the problem.

1

Introduction to NHibernate

In this chapter, we will go over a very brief introduction to NHibernate. This chapter is mainly aimed at absolute beginners to either NHibernate or ORMs. Therefore, we will begin with a discussion around what is an ORM and what kind of problems it solves. We will then dive into NHibernate and talk about what NHibernate offers in specific. Next, we would talk about the latest version of NHibernate and what new features are added in the latest version. While I am introducing NHibernate to you, I will also touch upon the important building blocks of NHibernate. In the end, I would try to answer the question of whether it is a bad idea to use ORM, as portrayed by some experts.

For those of you who have used or read about **Entity Framework (EF)**, I have added a section talking about features in NHibernate that are missing in the current version of EF. This is no way tries to present a picture that NHibernate is superior that EF. Rather, this information will help you to choose the right tool for the job.

What is ORM?

ORM stands for **Object Relational Mapping**. It is a technique that lets you map objects to relational databases and vice versa. Here, the term "object" mostly means an instance of a class. Tools that make use of ORM techniques are also referred to as ORM, which stands for Object Relational Mapper. NHibernate is one such tool. Let's take a look at a very simple example in order to understand what exactly this technique does. Suppose that you have the following Customer class:

```
public class Customer
{
  public string FirstName {get; set;}
  public string LastName {get; set;}
  public string EmailAddress {get; set;}
  public int Age {get; set;}
}
```

Downloading the example code

You can download the example code files from your account at http://www.packtpub.com for all the Packt Publishing books that you have purchased. If you have purchased this book elsewhere, you can visit http://www.packtpub.com/support and register to have the files e-mailed directly to you.

Every customer will be represented by an instance of the preceding class in the memory. Every such instance will also be persisted in the database. Suppose that the following database table is used to store customer instances:

```
CREATE TABLE tblCustomer
(
FirstName NVARCHAR(100),
LastName NVARCHAR(100),
EmailAddress NVARCHAR(100),
Age INT
);
```

The preceding syntax is for the MS SQL Server database. If you are using a different RDMBS, then the syntax may differ.

Depending on which ORM you are using, you will have a way to tell your ORM that the Customer class corresponds to the tblCustomer table in your database. Similarly, you can tell that the FirstName, LastName, EmailAddress, and Age properties map to columns with the same names in the tblCustomer table. Once all of this is in place, you can just tell your ORM to save an instance of the Customer class; it will ensure that a record is inserted into the tblCustomer table with the appropriate values for all the columns.

In a nutshell, that is ORM for you. ORM will handle all your database CRUD operations for you without you having to write a single line of SQL script. However, the most important principle to understand around an ORM is that it tries to bridge the gap between the OO world and the relational world. Programs written using the object-oriented principles adhere to a set of rules and support a particular set of data types. On the other hand, most RDBMSs follow rules derived from the set theory and support a set of data types that may not all be compatible with the corresponding data type on the OO side of the world. Besides this, there are differences in how new objects are constructed, how they associate with each other, what kind of operations are permitted on them, and so on.

All these differences make working with databases difficult when viewed from the perspective of the OO program. These differences are also called **impedance mismatch**, a term taken from electrical engineering. Impedance gives a measure of how easily the current can flow through an electrical circuit. For two electrical circuits to work in coherence with each other when connected, their impedances should match. In the same way, for a program written in OOP to work with an RDBMS in coherence, the impedance between them has to be matched. An ORM does this job.

What is NHibernate?

Obviously, it is an ORM. If I may quote from the NHibernate website:

> "*NHibernate is a mature, open source object-relational mapper for the .NET framework. It's actively developed, fully featured and used in thousands of successful projects.*"

NHibernate is a .NET port of a very famous ORM from the Java land called Hibernate. Now, Hibernate is quite old and is used by thousands of production applications. NHibernate has not only inherited most of the good features from its Java ancestor but has also been enriched with features from .NET, such as LINQ queries. To understand how powerful it can be, let's take a very simple example. If you have the `Customer` class from the previous section, mapped to a database table called `tblCustomer`, and you want to fetch all customers between 28 and 35 years of age, then with NHibernate, you can write something as follows:

```
var customers  = from c in session.Query<Customer>()
   where c.Age > 28 && c.Age < 35
   select c;
```

This is an LINQ query written in C#. **LINQ** stands for **Language-Integrated Query**. This is a feature introduced in C# and Visual Basic that offers data query and update syntax, which is similar to SQL. LINQ works against a variety of data sources but within the constraints of the C# language; further, it works nicely with the `IQueryable` types. If you are not familiar with LINQ, then do not worry too much as we will cover them in the coming chapters. You must be wondering what is `session.Query<Customer>()`? This is an NHibernate API that we will use extensively throughout this book. For now, `session.Query<Customer>()` returns `IQueryable<Customer>`. It is this queryable type that makes writing the previous LINQ query possible.

NHibernate then processes the previous LINQ query and generates the following SQL:

```
SELECT a_.FirstName,
  a_.LastName,
  a_.EmailAddress,
  a_.Age
FROM tblCustomer a_
WHERE a_.Age > 28 AND a_.Age < 35
```

As you can see, all you wrote was a simple C# LINQ expression against a C# class. You did not have to think about what the database table name is and how to form the correct SQL query; NHibernate has handled all of that for you. NHibernate has a lot of such features that will make writing database interaction code a breeze. We are going to cover these features of NHibernate throughout this book.

NHibernate is an open source project which prospers entirely on community contributions. As with any open source project, this gives a lot of transparency to every aspect of NHibernate. You can download the source code from their GitHub repository at `https://github.com/nhibernate/nhibernate-core/` and check out how things are implemented. You can raise bugs on their official JIRA board, contribute to discussions around the right fixes for the defects, development of new features, and the future roadmap. All these activities are mostly led by a few top contributors, but transparency and community inclusion are what keep NHibernate going. You can access the NHibernate JIRA board by navigating to `http://nhibernate.jira.com`. I will not spend too much space talking about NHibernate here. Besides the fact that the whole book covers all important aspects of NHibernate anyway, I am now going to peek into some interesting NHibernate features in the remaining sections of this chapter.

Before I move onto the next section, I would like to mention that the latest stable version of NHibernate is 4.0.3.400 as of the time of writing of this book. The latest version of NHibernate can be confirmed by visiting the NuGet page of NHibernate at `https://www.nuget.org/packages/NHibernate/`. The latest version is an important milestone since this a major release that has come about 3 years after the previous major release 3.0. There were several minor releases in these 3 years. All these releases have collectively added a lot of great features to version 4.0 of NHibernate. Let's take a brief tour of these features.

What is new in NHibernate 4.0?

The General Availability release of NHibernate 4.0.3.400 was released on August 17 2014. This is the latest release of NHibernate as of the time of writing of this book. This release is quite important from a lot of perspectives. This is a major release of NHibernate that has come almost after three and a half years, so it contains a lot of interesting features and bug fixes.

If you are new to the ORM land or have never used NHibernate before, then you may not find this section very interesting. But hey, why not keep reading and you might find something that strikes a chord with you:

- NH 4.0 is built for .NET 4.0. This may not mean much for the users of NHibernate 4.0 as you can still use older versions of NHibernate on a project that is built on .NET 4.0. However, this is a major move for NHibernate since it now gives NHibernate developers the ability to utilize new features of .NET 4.0. An immediate consequence of this was that NHibernate 4.0 now does not depend on the `Iesi.Collection` library to support sets (`Iesi.Collections.Generic.ISet<T>`) because .NET 4.0 has native support for sets, in the form of `ISet<T>`, and implementations such as `HashSet<T>`. Back in the days when the old versions of .NET did not have support for sets, the `Iesi.Collections` library offered a mature set functionality. NHibernate had a dependency on this external library as NHibernate uses sets to represent collections.

- Support for SQL Server 2012 has improved with the implementation of the native `IIF` function, query paging, and SQL Server 2012 sequences.

- "Mapping by code" rids you of having to write and maintain cumbersome XML mapping files. However, the general audience was never happy with this feature as it was buggy till recent times. NHibernate 4.0 has several defects in this area fixed, thus giving *Mapping by code* a facelift.

- We all love LINQ and we all hated the fact that NH's LINQ support never matched that of Criteria or QueryOver. There has been great community contribution in this area with over 140 issues fixed. LINQ support in NHibernate 4.0 has matched that of other query providers in a lot of respects. We will be using this feature a lot in the coming chapters of this book.

NHibernate for users of Entity Framework

If you are using or have used Entity Framework (EF), then chances are you know about NHibernate. While EF has been in business for a few years now, it is only in the last couple of years that it has got some serious attention, thanks to the performance improvements brought about in EF 6.x and the implementation of some features that are at the core of any ORM. In spite of the recent popularity of EF, a natural question to ask is why you should be taking a look at NHibernate? Well, for starters, NHibernate is probably the oldest ORM in existence. The NHibernate code base has been used in thousands of production applications over the years and is quite sturdy. However, this sounds very subjective to you, so let me give you a list of features that NHibernate has but EF does not.

- NHibernate has a stable and sophisticated support for second-level cache. The caching implementation of NHibernate is supported by more than one caching provider ranging from in-memory hash tables to distributed caching solutions such as NCache.

- NHibernate has native support for mapping dictionaries. Dictionary mapping comes in handy in various different situations but one interesting situation that comes to my mind is building a multi-tenant system. In a multi-tenant system, multiple tenants are served from the same instance of the application and their data is stored in a single database instance. If a particular tenant has a requirement that needs to have additional properties on some entity to handle additional data about that entity, then this additional data can be stored in a dictionary of key-value pairs. This dictionary is declared as a property on the entity. NHibernate can then map these dictionaries directly to a suitable table schema.

- In situations where you need to update a large number of database records as part of batch jobs, the usual session object of NHibernate may be too slow as it tracks every change made to the entities and enforces all the database relations/constraints before the changes are saved to the database. However, the stateless sessions of NHibernate speed things up manifold at the cost of losing features such as change tracking and in-memory enforcement of database constraints. EF has some support for such a behavior through an extension method called `AsNoTracking` or through specific options in the `DbContextConfiguration` class. However, in my opinion, both of these options are not as intuitive as the stateless sessions of NHibernate.

- NH, in general, supports more number of databases than EF does. EF is built, tested, and most commonly used for MS SQL Server. A lot of people also use it for Oracle, but the level of support for databases such as MySQL, Sybase ASE, PostgreSQL, and DB2 is not at par with that for the other databases. If you use one of these databases, then chances are that you will face fewer problems if you are using NHibernate.

- Identity generation is one of the important features offered by an ORM. Every database table must have an identity column that uniquely identifies a particular record from the other records. We skipped this part in the introduction section for the sake of simplicity. Corresponding to the identity column in the database table, you will have a class property that holds the identity value. You can then generate a unique identity value for every new instance of this class or you can ask your ORM to generate one for you. If used wisely, identity generation can save a few database trips and improve performance. A particular identity generation strategy may not work well for all situations, so having more than one strategy always helps. NHibernate comes bundled with several identity generation strategies, while EF is still catching up.

- NHibernate's support for managing concurrency is far better. Concurrency is when two sessions (usually representing two different end users connecting to the database) try to update the same database record. The last session to update the record is usually working on a stale copy of data. Data is called stale when there is a latest updated version of the data present in the database than the one that you have loaded in the memory. In such a situation, in the absence of proper checks, it is possible that the session working with stale data ends up overwriting a legitimate record with some old value. NHibernate has at least three different models of concurrency management wherein NHibernate detects updates on stale data, aborts the update, and lets the application know of the same. We are going to look at these concurrency models in one of the upcoming chapters in detail, but it is worth mentioning that EF has a limited support for concurrency and it works most effectively only when used with the MS SQL Server database.

- NHibernate supports global filters. Global filters let you define dynamic SQL filters once and apply them to every database query or selectively apply them to some of the database queries. One situation where this feature comes in very handy is when you are working with a multi-tenant database. Another situation that I can think of is when you are storing the localized versions of strings in the database and you filter out the correct version by using a culture filter based on the current thread culture.

- NHibernate supports four different mechanisms for querying data. While LINQ is the easiest and is supported by both NHibernate and EF, the other three, namely, HQL, Criteria, and QueryOver, are only available in NHibernate. One of the useful things that you can do with these is the tuning of the final SQL generated for your code. With these different query mechanisms, you get a better control over the final SQL generated. Most DBAs would want this ability.

Is using ORM a bad idea?

ORMs offer a frictionless development experience when working with relational databases. Still, some minds in the industry feel that using an ORM is not a good idea. Of all the reasons presented against using ORMs, the two most commonly given are as follows:

- ORMs abstract away databases, and hence, the important database concepts that are essential for any developer to master usually get ignored

- The use of ORMs results in a performance degradation of the application

It will be interesting to drill deeper into these reasons. It is true that ORMs abstract away databases and handle almost all database interactions for you in a transparent way. You do not need to bother yourself with a deeper understanding of how an ORM is fetching data from the database. If you master APIs offered by the ORM, you will do just good to interact with a moderately complex database through the most commonly used queries. Further, since this almost always works, you never need to figure out what the ORM is doing under the hood for you. So, you indeed miss out on learning how to work with databases. If you are using your ORM to generate a database schema, then chances are that you are missing out on important database building blocks such as keys, associations, relations, and indexes. So, there is an element of truth in the first reasoning. If you do fall into this category of developers, then this lack of database knowledge will hit you the hardest when least expected.

Talking about the performance degradation caused by ORMs, I can only say that this has an element of truth but it is very subjective. I say subjective because the word "performance" cannot stand on its own. When we talk about performance, we usually refer to a benchmark. This benchmark can be the expected performance of a system or the performance of a similar system used for the purpose of comparison. The performance argument against ORMs is usually in the context of a comparison with other ways of interacting with databases, which include, but are not limited to, the use of plain SQL with ADO.NET or the use of micro-ORMs. While micro-ORMs do offer the best performance, the situation with ADO.NET is slightly different. ADO.NET offers barebones, and you need to write most of the code around reading data from datasets/data readers and hydrating objects. Depending on your experience with building performant systems, you may be able to squeeze more performance out of ADO.NET than is offered by ORMs. However, the key phrase is "experience with building a performant system." If you do not have such experience, then it may be better to stick to an ORM as you will tend to not make the common mistakes made while working with databases.

Why ORM is a better bet?

So, why should we use an ORM then? Let's take a step back and think about our options when we do not use any ORM. In the absence of an ORM, you can either use a micro-ORM or put together your own data access layer implemented using something such as ADO.NET. Micro-ORMs take a minimalist approach towards object relational mapping. Some of them use advanced language features and conventions to automatically map classes to a database schema, while others explicitly make use of custom SQL.

Micro-ORM can be called the little brother of ORMs and is an entirely different topic, so I am not going to consider this option for the sake of this discussion. So, we are left with building our own data access layer. Now what does this mean? First and foremost, this means that you are going to spend a significant amount of time in building something that lets you interact with relational data stores. Further, you are going to do this along with numerous other fellow developers from the "No-ORM" camp. Can you imagine how many times this wheel is going to be reinvented? If you are working in an environment where everyone values "code reuse," then chances are that you would try to reuse this data access layer in more than one project, thus limiting the duplication. However, in reality, this rarely happens for two reasons. One, most of the time, we are so busy delivering our own stuff that we tend to ignore work by other teams, work that you can potentially use as is in your project. The second reason is the realization of the fact that the first team that built the original data access layer did it to tailor to their needs and it does not quite fit your own needs. So, you decide to roll your own. So, all of this leads to countless developers building the similar thing all over again for every new project that they start working on.

Next is the challenge of maintaining the quality of such a data access layer. For simple applications, you can write a complete data access layer in a single class, but such an approach usually does not work for complex applications. When requirements from a data store become complex, it becomes challenging to implement a data access layer that can cope with all the requirements. Without proper experience and knowledge of different experience patterns, you are bound to build a data access layer whose quality cannot be guaranteed.

Every data access layer follows a particular pattern to interact with the database. While some data access patterns have stood the test of time, there are others that should be avoided at any cost. Rolling out a home-grown data access layer means having knowledge of what has worked for others and what has not. It also means having a gut feeling about what will work for your project depending on how the project turns out in the future. These things are not easy to come by and people who are usually good at these things have years of experience in dealing with such problems. It is not possible to have such people onboard every time you are building a data access layer. So, chances are that things may go wrong and you would invest time in fixing things. ORMs, most notably NHibernate, have been around for years. The data access patterns implemented in NHibernate are proven to be the best. At the same time, a care has been taken to avoid designs that are considered harmful for database interactions. Being an open source project, NHibernate welcomes contributions and defect reports from the general public. So, NHibernate has become richer and more stable over time. Contributions from the general public mean that NHibernate is built by learning from the mistakes of hundreds of developers and by listening to the needs of a large community of developers around the world. Not using NHibernate or any mature, open source ORM for that matter would only mean shunting out such a huge source of common knowledge from your system and reinventing the wheel.

Non-functional features required by the data access layer

Besides the above, there are some non-functional requirements that every data access layer would need to offer sooner or later. The following is a representative list of such features:

- **Logging**: Logging probably is one of the most important non-functional requirements. You would need to log not only the errors and exceptions but also important information such as details of the SQL query sent to the database and the data returned from the database.

- **Caching**: Caching may sound a simple thing to implement but as your domain grows complex so do the data querying patterns. Such complex data query patterns have very different caching requirements, which are not trivial to implement.

- **Connection management**: You might think that ADO.NET offers connection management and connection pooling. Indeed, it does. But there are more features around connection management that we need. In real-life applications, you need the ability to reuse connections across multiple queries, be able to make new connections, disconnect the existing connections at the right time, and so on.

- **Transaction management**: As with connection management, ADO.NET does offer basic transaction management but the needs of most of the real-life software around this area can soon grow complex.

- **Concurrency management**: Concurrent updates to the same data from multiple users may result in defects that are difficult to find out. Being able to know whether you are working on stale data or not is critical to building robust applications.

- **Lazy loading**: Lazy loading is when you load only the part of an object that is needed at the moment. We will cover lazy loading in greater detail in the coming chapters. For now, it is worthwhile to note that lazy loading is not a simple feature to implement.

- **Security**: Your data access layer is the primary gateway to the critical data that you store in your database. The security of this data is paramount, and hence, any data access layer needs to be secured and should be hardened against attacks such as SQL injection attacks.

- **Batching of queries**: Some queries can be batched with other queries and executed at a later time. This improves the throughput of the SQL connection and hence improves the performance. Not all data access layers are intelligent to batch and execute queries at a later time.

It is unlikely that your home-grown data access layer will have all of these features. You might manage to build some of these features, but getting all of the features in would practically not be possible. This can mainly be driven by the fact that your main objective on the project is to deliver business functionality and not build a fully featured data access layer. Even if you do manage to put together a decent data access layer that has most of the above features, what are the odds of you having tested every edge case and fixed most defects?

On the other hand, any mature ORM would offer most of these features. Since this book is about NHibernate, I will concentrate on NHibernate here. NHibernate has all of these features built into it from the beginning. These features have not only been timely tested but have also taken shape according to the real needs of the developers. Because it is an open source project, a lot of community feedback and contribution has gone into shaping these features. So, you are guaranteed to see superior implementations of most of these features.

Given all of the preceding advantages, would I consider using an ORM a bad idea? I think not. On the contrary, I would consider using an ORM to be a good idea.

Building blocks of NHibernate

Now that we know that using an ORM is not essentially a bad idea but can actually be a very productive way of writing code that interacts with the database, let's turn our attention back to NHibernate.

NHibernate stands on three important building blocks. To understand these building blocks is essential to understand and use NHibernate effectively. We are going to explore these building blocks in detail in the coming chapters, but I would like to give you a brief introduction to these now.

Mappings

NHibernate uses mappings to find out which class maps to which database table and which property on the class maps to which column on the table. Every time your application tries to interact with the database, NHibernate refers to the mappings in order to generate the appropriate SQL to be sent to the database for execution.

There are three different ways that you can tell NHibernate about the mappings. One of the ways is based on traditional XML, whereas the other two are based on the code and provide a fluent API to express the mappings. In *Chapter 3, Let's Tell NHibernate About Our Database*, I will talk about these ways in enough detail. However, mappings that we will use in the other chapters will only be explained using a code-based API, also called mapping by code.

I have simplified mappings for the sake of introduction, but mappings offer a lot of advanced features that go beyond the basics such as mapping tables and columns. These advanced features impact the generation of SQL, performance of the application, and resilience of the data access layer. Hence, it is important to understand and master the mappings in order to use NHibernate most effectively.

Configuration

NHibernate lets you specify via configuration a lot of details that it uses at runtime. These details affect what NHibernate does and how NHibernate does a particular thing. Although configuration is a small thing, it is important to master it. On most projects, you will deal with configuration in the initial phase, and once everything is settled, you will rarely come back to it. The only times that you will come back to it are when you need to turn on or off something and knowing how to do this will save you some time. The NHibernate configuration lets you control the following:

- which database you want to connect to (MS SQL Server, Oracle, and so on)
- where is that database (read connection strings)

- which SQL driver to use (or which SQL client library should NHibernate use)
- where are the class mappings
- should NHibernate log important information
- should NHibernate cache entities by default
- how should NHibernate manage sessions
- should NHibernate use second-level cache
- where is the second-level cache

As you can see, there are some useful configuration options there. We will see the details of these options and how to configure them in *Chapter 4, NHibernate Warmup*.

Configuration is not just about providing the defaults for a few NHibernate settings. Configuration can be loaded in the memory, and you can do some amazing things with it. One of such commonly done things is the use of the configuration to generate database scripts. Once you define your mappings and build your configuration, you can generate a SQL script to build all database schemas, tables, relations, constraints, indexes and so on. We are going to cover this in detail in *Chapter 4, NHibernate Warmup*. For now, it is worth noting how important and powerful the NHibernate configuration is.

Session

Session is the most commonly used object from NHibernate. Any database interaction that your application needs to do using NHibernate, it must do so by using a Session object. Think of a Session object as a wrapper around the pipe to the database, which is an SQL connection. The Session object not only manages the connection to the database but also exposes methods (some directly and the others indirectly through extension methods) that let you write code to interact with the database in the form of queries and create, update, and delete operations. The Session object also exposes the API for transaction management. Further, the Session object implements a form of caching that boosts the performance of queries. This list can go on as there are so many features that the Session object offers. However, let's leave those features to later chapters where we will look at them in detail.

Because of the rich set of features that the Session object offers, the Session object is the most commonly used NHibernate type. Since Session is so commonly used, NHibernate has implemented it in such a way that creating a new Session object is a very cheap operation. However, this does not mean that you should freely create new instances of the Session object. There is some penalty that you will have to pay directly or indirectly when you create a large number of session objects randomly. There are some rules that if you play with, you can gain all the benefits of cheap Session objects. We will cover all of these rules at appropriate times in different chapters of this book.

Summary

Most people choose to skip the introduction chapter of any book. If you are not one of them and have actually gone through my attempt at introducing you to the world of ORMs and NHibernate in particular, then congratulations, you have had a very good start. You now know briefly what NHibernate is and what kind of problems it solves for you. You may also have an idea of some of the advanced features of NHibernate. Last, but not least, I hope that now, you have an answer to the question "Whether using an ORM is a bad idea?," and I hope that the answer is a resounding "No."

In next chapter, I am going to present a business problem. The aim is to use NHibernate to build the data access layer as one of the parts of the solution to this problem. We will build the data access layer incrementally as we go over each chapter. In the next chapter, I will also talk about how to set up your development environment and how to get ready for some NHibernate action. Just flip over when you are ready.

2

Let's Build a Simple Application

The title of the chapter says *Let's Build a Simple Application*, but that is not entirely true. What is true is that we are going to start building an application. This chapter sets the foundation for that. So, in this chapter, I am going to introduce you to the application that we are going to build as we progress through the book.

However, just knowing the application is not enough in my opinion. In order to make sure that you make most out of this book and stay on track while your training shoes are still on, I am going to take you through my development setup and talk about various tools that I will be using. If you try out the sample code from this book and stick to the versions of tools mentioned in this chapter, then you can be assured that things will go smoothly. However, this does not mean that you must use the tools that I am using and the versions that I have installed in my environment. Most tools in the .NET ecosystem these days are backward compatible, so if you happen to have a lower version of some tool, never mind. As long as you know how to use the tool, we are in business.

Besides tools, I will also give you a brief introduction to the methodologies, particularly **Test-driven Development (TDD)**, that we will be using throughout the book. If you are new to TDD, then do not worry because I am not going to use any knowledge beyond what can be called basic.

So, let's get started!

Explaining the approach used in learning NHibernate

Before we actually talk about the application, I thought I will write about the overall approach that I will take to teach you NHibernate.

In this chapter, we will define a simple problem statement. The aim is to implement an efficient data access layer for our problem using NHibernate as we progress through the chapters in this book. In this process, you will learn about important NHibernate features and apply them to an actual software problem at the same time. When we finish the book, we may not have addressed the complete data access requirements of our problem, but we will have implemented the solutions for important aspects of the problem with a certain level of detail. This level of understanding and some experience should set up to build any kind of data access solution using NHibernate.

It may seem disconnected to jump from the problem statement to the data access layer directly, so my first step is to come up with a domain model that captures the core concepts of our problem domain. I will try to follow the guidelines from **Object-oriented Analysis and Design (OOAD)** and **Domain-driven Design (DDD)**. Both are much specialized areas of software design and explaining them in detail will be another book in itself. So, I will try to keep it to a level sufficient to build a simple domain model for our problem in the right way.

As we go on building our data access layer, we also need a way to validate the correctness of our implementation. Since we are going to build it brick by brick, a lot of times, we will need to go back and change something that was previously implemented as we learn more about NHibernate. While we change things, we need a way to make sure that our changes have not altered the outcomes or have broken a feature that was working previously. We will use TDD to implement our solution. If you have already used TDD, then you will know what I am talking about. If you are new to TDD, then do not worry. TDD is not very difficult to master, and for the kind of work that we are going to do around TDD, you do not need to master the art. We are going to write simple tests that validate the behavior of our data access layer. We will then use NHibernate to build the missing pieces and make our tests pass. I will make sure that I give you enough explanation of the code that I am going to present.

For most part of this book, the solution will be implemented in the form of a class library supported by unit tests to validate the correctness of the code. Towards the end of the book, we should be able to look at the complete solution and understand how NHibernate is used in real-life applications.

The problem statement

The problem that we are going to solve is related to an employee benefit management system. This is a system where the employees of an organization can log in and see the benefits that they are entitled to and utilize the benefits. A very simple example of an employee benefit is leave. Every employee of an organization is entitled to get paid or unpaid leave. Employees have the right to take days off when they need by using their leave entitlement, but there are rules around how many leaves a particular employee is entitled to and how he/she can utilize his/her leave.

There are two main actors or end users of this system. The first is evidently an employee, and the second is an administrator user. An employee can see only his/her benefits. An administrator user on the other hand can see everyone else's benefits and can add/delete benefits. An administrator can be an employee himself/herself.

This is a brief of our problem statement. As you can see, this can be a quite big and complex problem. There is a boatload of benefits that employers offer these days. There are complex rules about who is eligible for which benefits, in what circumstances can the employees utilize the benefits, how exactly does the utilization works, who approves the employee requests for the utilization of a particular benefit, and so on. The aim of this book is to learn NHibernate and not build a sophisticated employee benefit management system, so I am going to use a subset of the requirements of this system that will help us navigate through the chapters of this book with a common understanding of the business problem that we are working with. I am going to be careful to choose only those requirements that let me demonstrate most of the features of NHibernate without having to invest time in trying to understand the problem at hand. With that clear, here are main highlights of the problem subset that we will try to address:

- There are only two actors in this system. One is an employee, and the other is an administrator user.

- An administrator user can be an employee and is entitled to some benefits of his/her own.

- An administrator can add new benefits into the system or can update the existing benefits.

- For auditing and legal reasons, a benefit cannot be deleted from the system.

- Some benefits may have entitlements associated with them. For example, an employee gets 20 paid leaves every year. Our system holds the available entitlements for every employee, but the management of leave happens outside of our system. For example, the organization has a different leave management system where employees can apply for their leave, which are approved by their line managers.

- Since the utilization of the benefits happens outside of this system, it needs to import data from those systems in order to reflect the correct benefits and their entitlements. This import can be a batch job run every night.
- This system supports the following benefits:
  - **Leave**: Paid, sick, and unpaid leave
  - **Season ticket loan**: Employer pays you for an annual public transport pass to commute to work and you repay the employer in monthly payments
  - **Skill enhancement allowance (or training allowance)**: All employees are eligible to go for trainings paid for by the employer

There are additional system requirements that I am going to look into later in the book. However, it is worthwhile to mention them now. These requirements give us an opportunity to explore some interesting features of built into NHibernate. Without NHibernate, these features would require a significant time investment to get implemented correctly.

- It is possible that two administrator users could update the same record at the same time. The results of such operations are unpredictable, and usually only the first update is on the correct version of data; the rest are all on a stale copy of the data. Our data access layer needs to be able to detect when an update is happening on a stale copy of data and abandon it.
- Systems like these hold important information. Further, when there are multiple users acting on the data, chances are things would go wrong for one reason or the other. Organizations usually do not like to be in a situation where their employees get agitated because the system is not reflecting the correct information about the benefits that they are entitled to. If such a thing happens, organizations need to know how the data came to be in that state. This not only helps with understanding what went wrong but also gives an opportunity to fix any system defects quickly. For this reason, we would like to maintain a data audit for every change made to any data via this system.

You do not have to worry about the last three requirements just now. We will visit this in the later chapters of this book. I have presented these here for the sake of completeness of the problem.

If you are wondering whether this is a web-based system or a desktop application, I would suggest that you do not bother yourself. Our aim is only to build a suitable data access layer for this system that can be used by any kind of application. With this clear, let's proceed to our development setup to know more about the tools that I will be using to implement this solution.

The development setup

In order to learn NHibernate most effectively, it is important that you follow the concepts and code samples from this book and try them yourself. While the code from this book should work on any general development environment, it would be prudent to mention which tools I am going to use in particular. If any of the code samples from this book does not work for you, you can always confirm first if it is due to tooling incompatibility. There are a couple of optional tools that I will be referring to in some chapters. These tools help working with NHibernate but are not necessary as there are alternatives available. These tools are not listed here. I will introduce them when they are referred to for the first time in this book.

So, here is the list of tools that we will use:

Visual Studio 2013

I will primarily be using Visual Studio as my code editor. I will be using VS 2013, which is the latest version of Visual Studio at the time of writing of this book. Lately, Visual Studio has had both backward and forward compatibility. This means that you can open a Visual Studio 2013 solution in Visual Studio 2012 and vice versa. So, even if you are on a slightly older or possibly a newer version of Visual Studio, things should work just fine.

SQL Server 2012 Express

We will be using the free Express version of SQL Server 2012. The latest version of SQL Server is 2014. However, the latest stable version of NHibernate officially supports SQL Server versions only till 2012. This does not mean that NHibernate will not support SQL Server 2014. Everything except the newly added features of SQL Server 2014 will work just fine. You can download SQL Server 2012 Express from here: `http://www.microsoft.com/en-gb/download/details.aspx?id=29062`.

Note that the SQL Server download page has multiple downloads available. You can choose the right one for your hardware and operating system by going through the details on the same page.

ReSharper

ReSharper is a code inspection and refactoring tool that fully integrates with Visual Studio. ReSharper makes it very easy to add new code, refactor the existing code, and so on, and increases your productivity greatly. Although ReSharper has no role to play in learning NHibernate, I think that it is worth mentioning as I have used it extensively while preparing the samples for the book. ReSharper is a paid tool, but you can download a free trial version from here: `https://www.jetbrains.com/resharper/download/`.

NUnit

We will use NUnit to write our unit tests. There are two ways of running the unit tests. If you have ReSharper or a similar code refactoring tool available, then you can run your NUnit tests right from within Visual Studio. For others, you can use the NUnit GUI runner. The NUnit GUI runner is a Windows application that does not integrate with Visual Studio but is capable of detecting and running unit tests from loaded assemblies. I will be using ReSharper to run the tests as it is the most productive in my experience.

You can download NUnit GUI runner from here: `http://www.nunit.org/index.php?p=download`.

NuGet

In order to use NHibernate and any other dependent libraries, we will use NuGet. NuGet is a package manager for .NET. Think of NuGet as a repository of the third-party packages and libraries that you would like to reference in your project. NuGet makes it very easy to add new libraries to a project, manage versions of the references libraries, and so on. The latest version of Visual Studio supports NuGet out of the box and there is no configuration that you need to change to enable NuGet. For older versions, you would need to install the NuGet extension. Instructions for installing the NuGet extension can be found here: `https://docs.nuget.org/consume/installing-nuget`.

SQLite

SQLite is a lightweight relational database that we are going to use during our unit tests. If I can quote the SQLite website here, then here is what it says about SQLite:

> "*SQLite is a software library that implements a self-contained, serverless, zero-configuration, transactional SQL database engine.*"

So, as the website says, SQLite is self-contained, meaning minimal or no dependency on external libraries. It is also serverless, so it does not require a server that needs to be running all the time in order to serve our data requests. It absolutely does not require any configuration for the setup. You just add a reference to a DLL and that is it. Further, most importantly, it is a transactional and relational database engine that supports SQL. These attributes along with its ability to run in the in-memory mode make it suitable for use within unit tests.

However, you have to remember that this is a light implementation of a relational database, so it does not support all features of an SQL server. However, it does support the most commonly used features. For what it does not support, there are workarounds available that we are going to look into as we encounter them.

The domain model

Now that our development environment is in place, let's put together a domain model for our problem. A domain model describes the important concepts in the problem domain in a way that can be implemented in software. There are different techniques of preparing a domain model and there are different ways of representing a domain model. The most commonly used representation of a domain model is a class diagram. We will prepare a class diagram and define our classes and their attributes and relations on the basis of the knowledge that we have so far about our problem. I am going to take a slightly agile approach at this. What I mean by this is that I am not going to overly analyze anything here. We will prepare a very simple domain model that covers most of my requirements to a certain degree of comfort. As I go on implementing the features, I will uncover a lot of hidden domain knowledge, which will help me shape my domain model better.

Classes in a class diagram will have attributes, associations, and methods. At this stage, we are more interested in attributes and associations. This is because attributes and associations tell us what kind of data the class holds, while methods tell us what kind of operations the class supports. In order to persist a class in an appropriate database table, all you need to know is what kind of data the class holds. For this reason, I will concentrate on detailing the attributes and associations of the classes in our domain model.

Let's start building our class diagram. Let's start with a class representing an employee.

Employee

The Employee class represents an employee and should hold the following information at the very least:

- First name
- Last name
- E-mail address
- Date of birth
- Date of joining
- Address
- Password

Leave

The Leave class represents a leave benefit that the employees receive. The Leave class can hold the following information:

- Name
- Description
- Entitlement
- Remaining
- Type of leave (paid, sick, or unpaid)

SeasonTicketLoan

This is another employee benefit. This class can hold the following information:

- Name
- Description
- Amount
- Start date
- End date
- Monthly installment

SkillEnhancementAllowance

A skill enhancement allowance benefit. This class should have the following information:

- Name
- Description
- Entitlement
- Remaining entitlement

Next, we can start thinking about the relationships or associations between these classes. The following associations can be derived from the knowledge that we have:

- Every employee is entitled to a number of leaves of different types
- Every employee can avail the season ticket loan
- Every employee is eligible to get paid for skills enhancement training
- All three benefit classes have the name and description attributes, which can be moved into a common base class
- The address of an employee is not a primitive type and can be represented by a class
- Leave types (paid, unpaid, sick) can be represented by an enumeration

This mostly covers what we need to begin our journey. The following class diagram puts together all of the previous information:

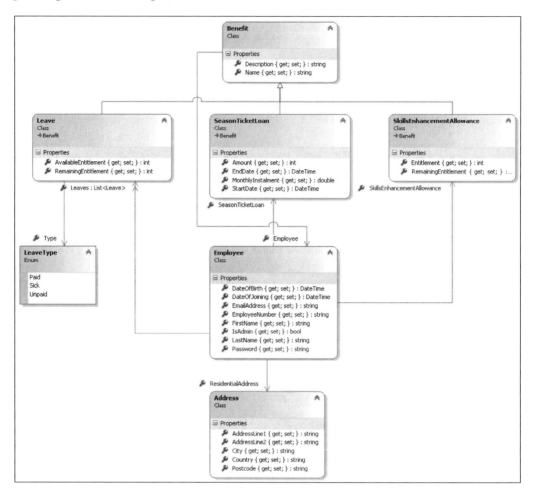

If you look closely, I have added some attributes on the Address class to give it some shape. I have also added an attribute named IsAdmin to the Employee class. This attribute identifies an employee with admin rights.

One more thing that I have added is the association from the Benefit class back to the Employee class. This makes the association between the two classes a bidirectional one. An advantage of this bidirectional association is that for a given instance of the Benefit class, it is easy to find which employee this instance belongs to.

Adding some code

It is time to implement all the classes from the preceding class diagram and look at our overall source and project structure.

Let's open Visual Studio and create a blank solution named `EmployeeBeneftis.sln`. In this solution, let's add a project of the **Class Library** type named `Domain`.

> To add a blank solution, you need to go to **File | New | Project**. On the **New Project** dialog that opens, inside the pane on the left side, locate a tree node named **Other Project Types**. Inside this node, you will find an item named **Visual Studio Solutions**. Click on this item, and then, you can choose **Blank Solution** in the middle pane.

We will now add all the classes to the `Domain` project. In order to minimize the compilation errors, we will start with the class that does not refer to other classes. Right-click on the `Domain` project in Visual Studio and add a class named `Address`. Use the following code for the body of the class:

```
namespace Domain
{
  public class Address
  {
    public string AddressLine1 { get; set; }
    public string AddressLine2 { get; set; }
    public string Postcode { get; set; }
    public string City { get; set; }
    public string Country { get; set; }
  }
}
```

> For the sake of brevity, I am skipping the `using namespace` statements from these code snippets. I intend to do so unless the mention of namespace is critical to the piece of code at hand. Other times, you should be able to proceed with whatever namespaces Visual Studio adds for you automatically.

Let's add a second class named `Benefit` and use the following code snippet: This class acts as a base class for any class that represents an employee benefit:

```
namespace Domain
{
  public class Benefit
  {
    public string Name { get; set; }
```

```csharp
        public string Description { get; set; }
        public Employee Employee { get; set; }
    }
}
```

Next, we can add classes representing our three benefits. Before this, let's define the enumeration that will be used by the leave benefit as follows:

```csharp
namespace Domain
{
  public enum LeaveType
  {
    Casual,
    Sick,
    Unpaid
  }
}
```

With the enumeration in place, here is the code snippet for our three employee benefit classes:

```csharp
namespace Domain
{
  public class SkillsEnhancementAllowance : Benefit
  {
    public int RemainingEntitlement { get; set; }
    public int Entitlement { get; set; }
  }
}


namespace Domain
{
  public class SeasonTicketLoan : Benefit
  {
    public int Amount { get; set; }
    public double MonthlyInstalment { get; set; }
    public DateTime StartDate { get; set; }
    public DateTime EndDate { get; set; }
  }
}

namespace Domain
```

```
{
  public class Leave : Benefit
  {
    public LeaveType Type { get; set; }
    public int AvailableEntitlement { get; set; }
    public int RemainingEntitlement { get; set; }
  }
}
```

We have all the classes in place except the class that represents an employee. Let's add one more classes named `Employee` and use the following code snippet:

```
namespace Domain
{
  public class Employee
  {
    public string EmployeeNumber { get; set; }
    public string Firstname { get; set; }
    public string Lastname { get; set; }
    public string EmailAddress { get; set; }
    public DateTime DateOfBirth { get; set; }
    public DateTime DateOfJoining { get; set; }

    public Address ResidentialAddress { get; set; }
    public bool IsAdmin { get; set; }
    public string Password { get; set; }
    public ICollection<Benefit> Benefits { get; set; }
  }
}
```

Note that we have a collection of `Benefit` classes in the `Employee` class. Not every employee may be eligible for every type of benefit. So, we cannot have an association to every benefit type in `Employee`. A collection of benefits helps with such a situation when you do not know in advance which benefits a particular employee is eligible for. Our code should compile at this point. If not, just fix whatever errors come up.

Next, we are going to add one more project for our unit tests. So, let's add another project of the **Class Library** type and name it `Tests.Unit`. This project needs to reference the `Domain` project because we will be calling into the classes defined in the `Domain` project from our tests. We are going to use NUnit to write our tests. So, let's go and grab NUnit by using NuGet.

Adding the NuGet packages to projects

There are two ways in which you can add NuGet packages to your projects. The first one uses the **Manage NuGet Packages** menu of Visual Studio. This is an easy-to-follow option in which you do not need to leave Visual Studio. The second uses the **Package Manager Console** feature of Visual Studio. This is slightly involved but gives you better control over the packages that you are installing. We will look at the first option here. I will leave the second option for you to explore:

1. Right-click on the project to which you want to add a NuGet package. In our case that would be the project named `Tests.Unit`. You would see the following menu pop out:

2. In the above menu, click on **Manage NuGet Packages...** highlighted with the yellow rectangle in the preceding screenshot. This will bring out the **Manage NuGet Packages** dialog for the `Tests.Unit` project. This is how the dialog looks:

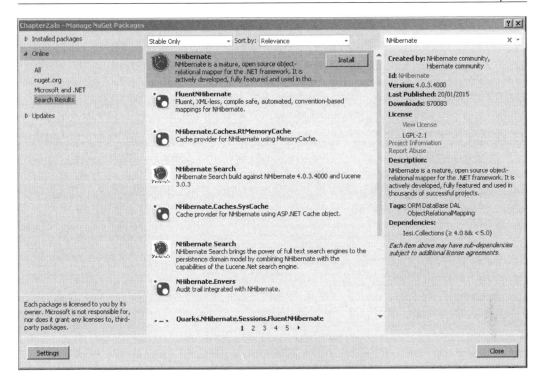

On this dialog, there is a search box in the top-right corner. We can enter here the names of the packages that we want to search.

The search functionality is activated as you start typing, so there is no need to hit the enter key. Rather do not hit the enter key as doing do will start installing whatever NuGet package is currently selected.

In the left-hand pane, you can see various options. I do not intend to go into the details of these, but one thing worth noting is that **nuget.org** is selected. This means that we are using **nuget.org** as our source of NuGet packages. If you are using a different source, then you can change this from the settings, but you will rarely need to do so.

3. Next, we enter NUnit into the search box and NUnit appears in the result list at the top:

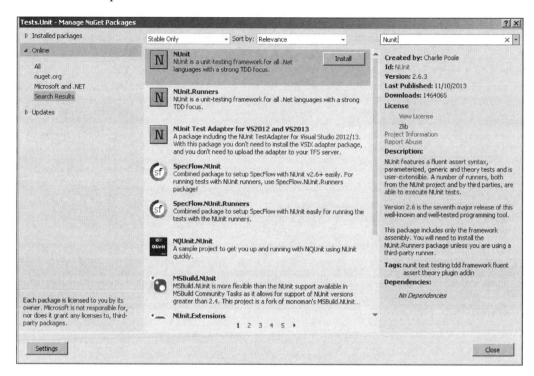

4. Next, we click on the **Install** button that appears next to **NUnit**. This will install NUnit in our `Tests.Unit` project. After NUnit is successfully installed, the **Manage NuGet Packages** dialog changes to look as shown in the following screenshot:

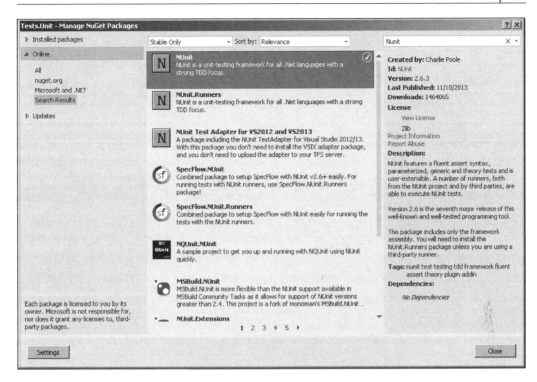

5. Notice the green tick next to **NUnit**, which tells us that this package is installed in the `Tests.Unit` project.

Back to our test

If you have never used NUnit, here is a brief primer for you:

1. Every unit test is written as a method.

2. An attribute `[Test]` is added to a test method. This is how NUnit distinguishes between a test method and a normal method.

3. Any class that has one or more test methods can optionally have an attribute `[TestFixture]` added to it. That is how the NUnit GUI runner (or other NUnit runners) finds all the test classes/fixtures to be run. However, with the latest versions of ReSharper, this attribute is not required.

4. The last and the most important, an `using` statement to reference the `NUnit.Framework` namespace should be added to any class that has test methods in it.

Here is a how a test looks:

```
using NUnit.Framework

namespace Tests.Unit
{
  [TestFixture]
  public class EmployeeTests
  {
    [Test]
    public void EmployeeIsEntitledToPaidLeaves()
    {
      //Arrange
      var employee = new Employee();

      //Act
      employee.Leaves = new List<Leave>();
      employee.Leaves.Add(new Leave
      {
        Type = LeaveType.Paid,
        AvailableEntitlement = 15
      });

      //Assert
      var paidLeave = employee.Leaves.FirstOrDefault(l => l.Type
      == LeaveType.Paid);
      Assert.That(paidLeave, Is.Not.Null);
      Assert.That(paidLeave.AvailableEntitlement, Is.EqualTo(15));
    }
  }
}
```

This is not a meaningful test. The purpose is to show you an example of how tests are written in NUnit. Let me walk you through this test in order to understand it better. A unit test usually has three parts – Arrange, Act, and Assert. You can see these commented in the preceding test.

In the Arrange part, you set up everything that is required to run the test. In our example, we create a new instance of the Employee class.

In the Act part, we execute the code that is to be tested. In the preceding test, we add a Leave object to the Leaves collection of the Employee class. This Leave object is of the Paid type having an entitlement of 15.

In the `Assert` part, we verify that the code that we wanted to test has behaved correctly. In the preceding test, we verify this by finding the `Leave` object from the list of `Leaves` whose type is `Paid`. We confirm that such an object is present in the list and that `AvailableEntitlement` has a value of `15`.

This was simple, wasn't it? If this is first time you are seeing tests, don't worry. We are going to see lot of these and we will get there together.

Summary

When you are learning about a vast software library like NHibernate, it is very easy to get lost reading the pages of the manual. Using a library to build an application end to end is a lot more engaging and offers a different level of learning experience. Although the problem statement that I have presented in this chapter does not sound very modern, it does give us an opportunity to learn some important NHibernate features. It is important that you spend some time distilling the problem in your head.

A developer's true friend at work is his/her development environment, the tools that he/she uses, and the methodologies that he/she follows. While agile has become commonplace, I understand that TDD is not. We are going to use both to some extent in this book. However, as I said earlier, I will keep the TDD aspect to a level required to finish the job at hand. Our focus is to build the data access layer using NHibernate.

We looked at what NHibernate is capable of already and I hope that you are excited to know more. Well, we are on the verge of starting our NHibernate tour. Turn the page over to learn more about the most important and most basic feature NHibernate, which lets us map the domain model that we defined in this chapter with a suitable database schema.

3
Let's Tell NHibernate About Our Database

You must be excited to start your NHibernate learning tour. Well, we are just about to do that. In this chapter, we are going to talk about declaring mappings for your domain model. You declare mappings to tell NHibernate how classes in your domain model match to database tables. If you have built your database to suit to the domain model then mappings would look very simple. But if database and domain models are not compatible with each other, then mappings start getting complex. Having a thorough knowledge of mappings would help in such situations. There are multiple ways of declaring mappings, from XML-based ones to code-based ones. We will cover three most widely used methods, namely, XML mappings, mapping by code, and fluent mappings.

Mapping is the most important concept in NHibernate. The way NHibernate interacts with database largely depends on how mappings are written. In this chapter, we will cover the basics of mapping. As we go deeper into the other NHibernate features in the upcoming chapters, we would revisit mappings to see how slightly tweaking a mapping can bring about big changes in the way NHibernate interacts with your database. This chapter should give you a basic understanding of how to declare mappings and make you ready for taking the plunge into the more advanced NHibernate topics.

Important NHibernate terminology

From this chapter onwards, we will be using some terms. These terms have special meanings when used in context of NHibernate or data access layers of applications. It would help to know what these terms mean and how we are going to use them in this chapter and in rest of the book. It is possible that some of these terms are already known to you.

POCO, Plain Old CLR Object. An alternate term for a class in C# which:

- Does not inherit from classes defined in any framework
- Does not implement interfaces defined in any framework
- Does not use any attributes defined in any framework

We will just use the word class most of the time in this book but if I may have to use POCO in a few places, you will know what I mean.

- **Entity**: A class having an identifier that identifies an instance at least in the entity graph maintained by NHibernate. This may be slightly confusing, but as we progress through the chapter you will know more about NHibernate to understand this clearly. Till that time, whenever I say entity, assume that I am referring to a class/POCO.
- **Persistent Class**: Any class which NHibernate is able to persist in one or more database tables using the mappings defined.
- **Attribute/property**: When used in reference to POCO/class, this means getter/setter properties or fields on the class. When used in reference to XML, this would mean usual XML attributes. I may refer to class attributes as properties in some places to avoid confusion.

Mapping the prerequisites

Classes, as we defined in the previous chapter, cannot be used with NHibernate as is. There are some prerequisites that every class must satisfy before NHibernate is able to persist that class to database. Persistent classes must satisfy at least following two requirements:

- Every attribute on class that NHibernate should save in the database has to be declared as one of `public virtual`, `protected virtual`, and `protected internal virtual`. This is to make the **lazy loading** feature work. Lazy loading is an important feature. We will look into it in detail in *Chapter 6, Let's Retrieve Some Data from the Database*, where we learn about retrieving entities from database. For now, it is worth mentioning that lazy loading only works with virtual attributes of persistent classes. Having said that, let me also tell you that NHibernate is capable of working with private attributes as well, if the need be and we will look into that. But in most cases, you would not need to declare private attributes unless you are working with legacy databases. In order for lazy loading to work, every non-private method on the entity must also be declared as `virtual`.

- Every entity that is persisted to its own table in database must have an identifier attribute. Identifiers are used to distinguish two instances of the same entity. Identifier maps to primary key of database table. Traditionally, databases have generated the identifier/primary key values automatically. But there could be some pitfalls to this approach. On the other hand, NHibernate is capable of generating identifiers using multitude of different strategies. We would examine these in some detail in the *Identifier generation* section of this chapter.

The first prerequisite is quite straightforward. We just need to add the `virtual` keyword to all the attributes and methods in our domain model. For the second prerequisite, we have multiple options really, but I want to keep this change simple for now. We would add an identifier attribute of type integer to all entities in our domain model. Since this is an attribute that appears on every domain class, we can refactor this into a common base class. Here is how that class looks:

```
public abstract class EntityBase
{
   public virtual int Id { get; set; }
}
```

Note that we have marked this class as `abstract`. We do not want this class to be used directly by any code. The purpose of this class is only to provide a common base class for domain entities. And here is what our `Employee` class changes to:

```
public class Employee : EntityBase
{
   public virtual string EmployeeNumber { get; set; }
   public virtual string Firstname { get; set; }
   public virtual string Lastname { get; set; }
   public virtual string EmailAddress { get; set; }
   public virtual DateTime DateOfBirth { get; set; }
   public virtual DateTime DateOfJoining { get; set; }
   public virtual Address ResidentialAddress { get; set; }
   public virtual bool IsAdmin { get; set; }
   public virtual string Password { get; set; }
   public virtual ICollection<Benefit> Benefits { get; set; }
}
```

For brevity, I have omitted other classes here but you get the crux, I hope. With the preceding code change, we are now ready to write mappings for our domain model. We will begin with a quick introduction to different mechanisms offered by NHibernate to write mappings.

Different mechanisms to write the mappings

NHibernate has at least three different mechanisms for mapping persistent classes to database tables. This is both good and bad. While you can choose the one that you are most comfortable with, this can also leave you confused at times. Two of the mechanisms are natively supported by NHibernate library and one is an external implementation. In this section, we would look at all the three mechanisms briefly, before proceeding to implement mapping for our employee benefits problem. Though there are three different ways of expressing entity mappings, keep in mind that the core of the mapping engine is same, no matter which way you express your mappings. For all the mapping discussions in this chapter, I plan to express mappings using all the three methods in most of the cases. That way you will get a feel of how expressive each method is. It would not harm to stick to one method and ignore the others but remember that XML mappings are most complete and knowing them would always help in tricky situations.

There is also a fourth mechanism which uses attributes. Here, attribute refers to the .NET construct and not the properties on entity. We will not be covering attribute-based mappings in this book. The main reason for this decision is that attribute-based approach adds NHibernate dependency to domain layer. As we will see in *Chapter 8, Using NHibernate in a Real-world Application*, domain layer should not depend on any infrastructure layer or code. We would prefer not to reference any NHibernate type from the domain model. This way we can prevent domain model from any accidental dependency on infrastructure code. But remember that this is in the context of a particular architectural principle I am choosing to follow. You might want to explore the attribute-based mappings on your own.

XML mappings

Mapping persistent classes to database using XML file is the oldest and original method of writing mapping. This is what was first supported by Hibernate and NHibernate ported it as is. In this method, you write mapping information in an XML file using custom elements and attributes made available by NHibernate.

As we will see in this chapter and in the coming chapters, mappings can become quite detailed and intricate as your business requirements grow in complexity. The biggest advantage of XML mappings is that you can express mappings for every feature that NHibernate supports. Other two mechanisms have some limitations in supporting every feature of NHibernate. For instance, mapping of a protected attribute is no different than mapping of a public attribute when it comes to XML mappings. For the other two mechanisms, the same is not true. Think of XML mappings as superset of all mapping features.

While there are some clear advantages of using XML mappings, there are some disadvantages too. Most frowned upon is that XML mappings are not refactoring friendly. As we will see in this chapter, XML mappings use lot of magic strings to refer to classes and attributes. This may lead to subtle defects when you rename a class or attribute but forget to update the magic strings XML mappings. I personally do not see that as much of a problem if you have well written unit tests that warn you of failing code every time you change something. You still have to manually update the XML files but at least it saves you the embarrassment of a broken feature after your commit.

Fluent mapping

XML was the hero of its time but soon the fame was waning and the development community was looking at non-XML options for everything. NHibernate was still only supporting XML mappings. Some enthusiastic developers decided to build a new mechanism for mapping persistent classes. They built a library named **Fluent NHibernate (FNH)**. If I could quote from FNH's website (`http://www.fluentnhibernate.org/`), this is how they describe FNH:

> *"Fluent, XML-less, compile safe, automated, convention-based mappings for NHibernate."*

With FNH, you do not need to write a single line of XML. All you use is their fluent API. So far, this is the most famous non-XML mechanism for writing mappings.

FNH manages to avoid magic strings to refer to classes and attributes by using lambda expressions. But that adds constraints as lambdas only have access to public properties. If you want to map protected/private properties then FNH offers a few ways, but none are as elegant. Another thing to note about FNH is their choice of naming. Developers of FNH chose to use different names from the ones used in XML to represent mappings. For instance, to map an attribute, XML uses *property* whereas FNH uses *map*. This may cause confusion in the beginning if you are going from FNH to XML or vice versa.

Mapping by code

FNH became so famous that authors of NHibernate felt a need to support FNH natively in NH. But the fact that FNH API deviated significantly from XML conventions was an issue. NHibernate team wanted an API that is closer to XML conventions. Another open source library called **ConfORM** was able to achieve this and authors of NHibernate took inspiration from ConfORM's style to build support for mapping by code. Version 3.2 is the first version released with such support but implementation was not finished and hence it never got the level of adoption that other methods have got. Latest release of NHibernate has number of fixes in the area of mapping by code, making it quite stable.

API of mapping by code conforms to the naming convention and structure of XML mappings. The names of the methods used to declare mappings match with corresponding XML element names. All API methods fundamentally accept two parameters (with several overloads to accommodate for edge cases). The first one is attribute being mapped and second one is a lambda that can be used to declare additional mapping information. This closely follows the way XML mappings are declared.

I must say that this is not the better API in comparison to FNH as it is very XML-like and you cannot write mapping code without thorough understanding of XML mappings. One good thing about mapping by code is that it lets you map private properties/fields through specifically provided overrides and some lambda tricks. While this seems to fix a problem, remember that it also makes the mappings less refactor-friendly. But if you are unable to use FNH for any reason and do not want to use XML mappings for their refactor unfriendly nature, then mapping by code can be a good choice.

We will look at mapping our employee benefits domain using all the three methods. We will begin with XML mappings first where we would deep dive into understanding how to write mappings for different scenarios. We will then go on to rewrite the same mappings using the other two techniques.

XML mappings for the Employee class

Learning mapping through documentation may not be the best experience for beginners. What can work better is using one of the classes from our domain model as an example and guiding you through the mapping exercise. That is exactly what we are going to do in this section. We will begin our journey with writing XML mapping for the `Employee` class.

The `Employee` class has some attributes of primitive type as well as collections and associations to other classes. To keep things simple in the beginning, we will first look at mappings of the primitive attributes of the `Employee` class and not the associations to the other classes. The objective is to understand how to declare simple mappings before we start handling complex scenarios.

Before we start mapping, I would like to talk about making the development environment ready for XML mapping and NHibernate in general. What I mean by that is ensuring that we have projects in place, third-party libraries installed, and any Visual Studio configuration done. We are going to use unit tests to verify mappings. Any VS configuration needed to write and run unit tests will also be discussed.

Getting the development environment ready

In our Visual Studio solution, we already have a project named `Domain` that holds all our domain entities. Let's create another project of type **Class Library** named `Persistence`. We will add our XML mappings in this project. Follow the steps listed next to set yourself up for your XML mappings tour:

1. In the `Persistence` project, add reference to the `Domain` project.
2. Add the NuGet package `NHibernate` to the `Persistence` project.
3. Add a folder named `Mappings` to the newly created `Persistence` project.
4. Add another folder named `Xml` under the newly added `Mappings` folder. We are going to add our XML mappings into this folder.

The `Persistence` project has referenced the `Domain` project. So `Persistence` has knowledge of `Domain` but `Domain` does not have any knowledge of `Persistence`. This is inspired from *Onion Architecture* principle. As we will learn in *Chapter 8, Using NHibernate in a Real-world Application*, `Domain` usually holds and should hold all the business logic. This business logic should not be dependent on a particular database or a particular software library being used. Presentation layers, data access layers are all specific details which are needed to make business logic work but business logic should not depend on these. Business logic should plainly be dependent on your domain model, which in our case is defined inside the `Domain` project. Uncle Bob Martin calls this *The Clean Architecture* which he has explained in his blog at `http://blog.8thlight.com/uncle-bob/2012/08/13/the-clean-architecture.html`.

Every mapping must be named such that the name ends with `.hbm.xml`. Lot of developers follow a convention to name the files as `<Entity name>.hbm.xml` for simplicity and readability. For instance, XML mapping file for the `Employee` class would be named `Employee.hbm.xml`. But this is not a prerequisite and you are free to name your mapping files whatever you like, as long as they end with `.hbm.xml`.

Getting IntelliSense to work with the XML mapping files

One of the greatest powers of Visual Studio comes from its IntelliSense feature. As a long time user of Visual Studio (and ReSharper), I find it uncomfortable when IntelliSense does not work for some non-standard files. Fortunately for XML mappings, NH's authors have provided XSD files that will enable IntelliSense. Follow the steps listed next to enable IntelliSense for your XML mapping files. For these instructions, I am assuming that a file named `Employee.hbm.xml` is added to your project.

1. Open `Employee.hbm.xml` by double clicking on the file in **Solution Explorer**.

2. Once the file is open, right-click anywhere within the file.

3. On the menu that appears, choose the **Properties** option.

4. This will open properties dialog for **Xml Document**, as shown in the following image. Click on the **Schemas** property and a button with ellipsis becomes visible:

5. Click on the ellipsis button, which will bring up the **XML Schemas** dialog, as shown in the next screenshot:

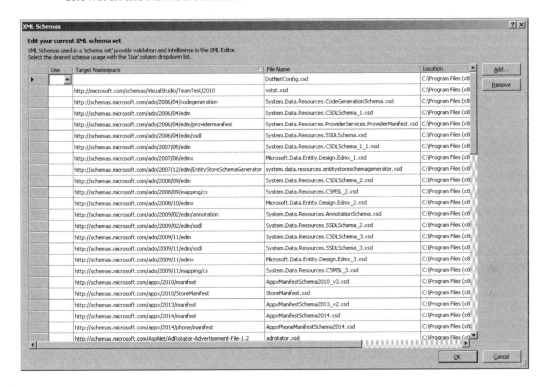

6. Click on the **Add...** button which will open a browse file dialog.

7. Browse to where your NuGet packages are downloaded. This is usually inside a folder named `packages` at solution folder level. Locate the folder of NHibernate package inside this folder, you would find two XSD files named `nhibernate-configuration.xsd` and `nhibernate-mapping.xsd`. Choose both these files.

8. Click **OK** on the **XML Schemas** dialog.

9. Congratulations, you have successfully enabled IntelliSense for mapping files.

With that, your development environment should be ready for working with XML mappings. So let's start with mapping the `Employee` class.

Unit tests to verify the Employee mappings

To verify that mappings are correct and they map to the database table as per our expectations, we will create an instance of the `Employee` class and save it to an in-memory database. We will then retrieve the instance we just saved and confirm that all the attribute values we had saved are retrieved from the database. Add a new class to project `Tests.Unit` and call it `InMemoryDatabaseForXmlMappings`. Use the following code snipped to define the class:

```
using System;
using NHibernate;
using NHibernate.Cfg;
using NHibernate.Dialect;
using NHibernate.Driver;
using NHibernate.Tool.hbm2ddl;
using Environment = NHibernate.Cfg.Environment;

namespace Tests.Unit
{
  public class InMemoryDatabaseForXmlMappings : IDisposable
  {
    protected Configuration config;
    protected ISessionFactory sessionFactory;

    public InMemoryDatabaseForXmlMappings()
    {
      config = new Configuration()
      .SetProperty(Environment.ReleaseConnections, "on_close")
      .SetProperty(Environment.Dialect, typeof
      (SQLiteDialect).AssemblyQualifiedName)
      .SetProperty(Environment.ConnectionDriver, typeof
      (SQLite20Driver).AssemblyQualifiedName)
      .SetProperty(Environment.ConnectionString, "data
      source=:memory:")
      .AddFile("Mappings/Xml/Employee.hbm.xml");

      sessionFactory = config.BuildSessionFactory();

      Session = sessionFactory.OpenSession();
```

```
        new SchemaExport(config).Execute(true, true, false,
        Session.Connection, Console.Out);
    }

    public ISession Session { get; set; }

    public void Dispose()
    {
        Session.Dispose();
        SessionFactory.Dispose();
    }
  }
}
```

As you can see, there is a lot going on here. Let me give you a brief explanation of what the preceding code is doing. In the constructor of the class, we have created an instance of NH `Configuration` object and have set different configuration values. These properties tell NHibernate what kind of database we are going to use and where NHibernate can find this database. An important point to note is that we are using an in-memory version of SQLite database. We then add the `Employee.hbm.xml` file to configuration to let NHibernate know that this file contains the mappings for the `Employee` entity. Note that adding the mapping XML file directly to configuration file is one of the ways of configuring mappings. NHibernate supports several different ways which we will cover in more detail in the next chapter. We then create an instance of session object. If you remember from *Chapter 1, Introduction to NHibernate*, session object is what lets us connect to the database. The last line which uses the `SchemaExport` class, will use the mappings supplied to configuration and build database schema into the in-memory database. This database schema is built based on the mappings we would declare. I am sure this is information overload for you at this time but feel free to ignore all the details and just remember that this class lets us use an in-memory database for our tests. In the next chapter, we are going to take a look at NHibernate configuration in detail.

With the configuration sorted out, let's look at our first test. Since we are only going to map primitive properties on the `Employee` class, our first test is going to be about verifying that primitive properties of the `Employee` class are saved correctly in the database. Add a new folder named `Mappings` to the project `Test.Unit`. In this folder, add a new class named `EmployeeMappingsTests`. Add a method named `MapsPrimitiveProperties` to this class, as shown next:

```
using System;
using Domain;
using NHibernate;
using NUnit.Framework;
```

```
namespace Tests.Unit.Mappings.Xml
{
  [TestFixture]
  public class EmployeeMappingsTests
  {
    private InMemoryDatabaseForXmlMappings database;
    private ISession session;

    [TestFixtureSetUp]
    public void Setup()
    {
      database = new InMemoryDatabaseForXmlMappings();
      session = database.Session;
    }

    [Test]
    public void MapsPrimitiveProperties()
    {
      object id = 0;
      using (var transaction = session.BeginTransaction())
      {
        id = session.Save(new Employee
          {
            EmployeeNumber = "5987123",
            Firstname = "Hillary",
            Lastname = "Gamble",
            EmailAddress = "hillary.gamble@corporate.com",
            DateOfBirth = new DateTime(1980, 4, 23),
            DateOfJoining = new DateTime(2010, 7, 12),
            IsAdmin = true,
            Password = "Password"
          });
          transaction.Commit();
      }

      session.Clear();

      using (var transaction = session.BeginTransaction())
      {
        var employee = session.Get<Employee>(id);
        Assert.That(employee.EmployeeNumber,
                  Is.EqualTo("5987123"));
        Assert.That(employee.Firstname, Is.EqualTo("Hillary"));
        Assert.That(employee.Lastname, Is.EqualTo("Gamble"));
```

```
        Assert.That(employee.EmailAddress,
                    Is.EqualTo("hillary.gamble@corporate.com"));
        Assert.That(employee.DateOfBirth.Year, Is.EqualTo(1980));
        Assert.That(employee.DateOfBirth.Month, Is.EqualTo(4));
        Assert.That(employee.DateOfBirth.Day, Is.EqualTo(23));
        Assert.That(employee.DateOfJoining.Year,
                    Is.EqualTo(2010));
        Assert.That(employee.DateOfJoining.Month, Is.EqualTo(7));
        Assert.That(employee.DateOfJoining.Day, Is.EqualTo(12));
        Assert.That(employee.IsAdmin, Is.True);
        Assert.That(employee.Password, Is.EqualTo("Password"));
        transaction.Commit();
      }
    }
  }
}
```

If you noticed, we have added a `[TestFixtureSetup]` attribute to the `Setup` method. This is a special attribute that tells NUnit that this method should be called once before the tests in this class are executed. Similarly, there is another attribute named `[TextFixtureTearDown]`. Method decorated with this attribute is called by NUnit after all the tests in that fixture are run.

We have a method named `Setup` in which we create an instance of `InMemoryDatabaseForXmlMappings` and get hold of the session object. We use this session to store the instance of the `Employee` object that we have created. Ignore the call to method `BeginTransaction` for now. After saving the `employee` instance, session is cleared in order to remove any traces of `employee` instance from previous database operation. We then use the same session object to load the employee record that we just saved and verify that properties on the loaded instance have same values as we had set previously.

I tend not to add more than 4-5 unit tests in one class. So the unit tests that we refer to in this chapter may not all be in the same class as this one. But there is one thing in common between all the unit test classes. The `Setup` method and its code are exactly same in every unit test. You can move this into a common base class if needed. Also note that, henceforth, I will only show you unit test in question but no `Setup` method or any other details. This is to keep the text of the chapter brief.

If you run this test now, it would fail for obvious reasons. We have not added any mappings yet. Let's go ahead and start writing mappings for the properties we are testing above.

The mappings

In the previous section, we have seen that XML mappings are written in a file with an extension `.hbm.xml`. In case of the `Employee` class, this would be `Employee.hbm.xml`. Following is how primitive properties of the `Employee` class would be mapped:

```xml
<?xml version="1.0" encoding="utf-8" ?>
<hibernate-mapping xmlns="urn:nhibernate-mapping-2.2"
assembly="Domain" namespace="Domain">
  <class name="Employee">
    <id name="Id" generator="hilo" />
    <property name="EmployeeNumber" />
    <property name="Firstname" />
    <property name="Lastname" />
    <property name="EmailAddress" />
    <property name="DateOfBirth" />
    <property name="DateOfJoining" />
    <property name="IsAdmin" />
    <property name="Password" />
  </class>
</hibernate-mapping>
```

Let's try to understand the purpose of different XML elements in the preceding code:

- `hibernate-mapping`: This element is root element of the mapping file and holds all the mapping information in its child elements. Other than its standard XML `namespace` attribute, this element has two other important attributes. First one is `assembly` which is used to declare name of the assembly in which the class `Employee` is declared. Second attribute is `namespace` which is used to declare the complete namespace the class is declared in. In our case both happen to be `Domain`.

- `class`: This element is used to declare the name of the class for which we are writing this mapping. Attribute `name` is clearly used to declare the name of the class.

- `id`: This element is used to specify details of the `identifier` property of this entity. Attribute name specifies the property on class that holds the identifier value. Attribute generator tells how NHibernate should generate the identifier value. We had briefly discussed this in the *Mapping the prerequisites* section at the beginning of this chapter. The value passed in this attribute is short name of one of the several identifier generation algorithms that come bundled with NHibernate.

- `property`: This element is used to map properties on class that are of primitive type. Attribute `name` specifies which property of class is being mapped.

If we run our test now, it should pass happily.

What we have seen above is the absolute minimum that NHibernate needs declared in order to make mappings work. But there are more attributes available for each of the elements we discussed previously. These attributes let us control mappings to a great level of detail. NHibernate assumes safe defaults when these attributes are not declared. Let's take a look at some of the important and most useful optional attributes of each of these elements.

Hibernate-mapping

A detailed hibernate-mapping declaration for the preceding example would look as the following:

```
<hibernate-mapping xmlns="urn:nhibernate-mapping-2.2"
  schema="EB"
  default-cascade="delete-all-orphan"
  assembly="Domain"
  namespace="Domain"
  default-access="property"
  default-lazy="true">
```

Let's look at what these additional attributes give us:

- `schema`: Often times, we use database schemas to divide our tables into logical groups. You must tell NHibernate if that is the case. Usually, you tell NHibernate of this at class level but if you have kept all your tables in the same schema then you will not want to repeat this information at every class level. NHibernate lets you declare this globally at hibernate-mapping level. If not declared, NHibernate assumes a default value of dbo in case of MS SQL Server.

- `default-cascade`: This lets you specify the default cascade style for your entire application. If not specified, `none` is assumed.

> Cascade defines how saves, deletes, and updates to tables, which are related with each other via foreign keys, work. When a record in the parent table is deleted then you can configure to have record in the child tables to be either deleted automatically or left there as orphan and so on. Similarly, when a parent entity is saved then contained associated entities are also saved automatically by NHibernate if cascade is set to do so.

- default-access: We have mapped properties on the Employee class in the mappings we just saw. But NHibernate is not limited to mapping properties only. It can map fields as well. With this attribute, you can tell NHibernate that you want to map fields by default and not properties. Again, if not specified, NHibernate assumes property.

- default-lazy: This attribute turns on lazy loading for the entire application if set to true. We have briefly talked about lazy loading at the beginning of this chapter. We will cover it in detail in one of the upcoming chapters. NHibernate assumes a default of true for this setting.

 The global scope of these attributes will come in effect only when you keep all mappings in one XML file under one hibernate-mapping node. I personally do not like this style and tend to keep mappings of related classes in one XML file, in which case, I would need to add these attributes once per file.

Class

A detailed mapping declaration for the class element from example would look as follows:

```
<class name="Employee"
   table="employees"
   mutable="true"
   schema="EB"
   lazy="true">
```

Let's examine the additional attributes to understand what additional features they offer:

- table: This attribute declares the name of the table the class should be mapped to. If not declared, NHibernate uses a concept called naming strategy to determine the name of the table to which entity is being mapped. A naming strategy is implemented by realizing the interface NHibernate.Cfg. INamingStrategy. There are two implementations of this, available out-of-the-box. First one, DefaultNamingStrategy uses the name of the entity as is for the table name. As the name suggests, this is the default naming strategy that NHibernate will use if the table name is not specified explicitly during mapping. Second implementation is ImprovedNamingStrategy which uses underscore separate Pascal case segments from the name of the entity to form the name of the table. For example, an entity named SeasonTicketLoan would be mapped to a database table named season_ticket_loan.

- `mutable`: This attribute specifies whether instances of this class should be mutable or not. By default, NHibernate assumes a value of `true` but you can make the instances immutable by setting this value to `false`.

- `schema`: This is the same as the `schema` attribute we discussed previously but the scope is limited to the class being mapped.

- `lazy`: This is similar to the `default-lazy` attribute discussed previously with scope limited to the class being mapped.

Property

Property mapping with important optional attributes specified would look as follows:

```
<property
    name="EmployeeNumber"
    column="employment_number"
    type="System.String"
    length="10"
    not-null="true"
    unique="true"
    lazy="false"
    mutable="true"/>
```

Again, let's examine the meaning of the additional attributes:

- `column`: It is used to specify the name of the mapped database table column. If not defined, NHibernate uses the naming strategy to determine the column name. This is the same naming strategy that we touched upon during discussion of the `table` attribute on class mapping previously.

- `type`: Type of the mapped database column. NHibernate has a carefully designed system that uses reflection to check the type of property being mapped and determine the most appropriate database type for the mapped table column. If for any reason you are not happy with the type that NHibernate decides for a particular column, you can override that and specify your own type using this attribute. NHibernate accepts some primitive .NET types as well as offers some more types that can be used here. In the appendix, you can find table that describes which .NET/NHibernate types is mapped to which database type.

- `length`: NHibernate can generate database scripts based on your mappings. We will look at this feature of NHibernate in one of the chapters. NHibernate uses information you specify in the mappings to come up with a database schema that accurately maps to your domain model. To that end, length attribute can be used on properties that map to database types supporting length for example, `char`. This attribute is optional and takes a default of `255` if not specified.

- `not-null`: This attribute is used in situation similar to the previous one and declare the mapped table column to be `NOT NULL`.

- `unique`: This is one more attribute in the same category. This attribute marks the mapped table column as `UNIQUE`.

- `lazy`: This is similar to the `lazy` attribute on class with the difference that scope is limited to the property being mapped. This is really useful only for CLOB and BLOB type of properties.

- `mutable`: This is same as the `mutable` attribute on the `class` element with the only difference being the scope is limited to current property.

I have intentionally skipped some of the important optional attributes here. These attributes control how NHibernate stores/ retrieves data for the property. I intend to talk about these in detail in *Chapter 5, Let's Store Some Data into the Database,* where we will look at storing and retrieving data.

So far we have just scratched the surface of NHibernate mappings. There is so much more to it that a chapter of a book is not enough to explain this topic in detail. In this section, I wanted to give you a glimpse of NHibernate mappings. Now that you have got some idea of what NHibernate mappings are, how to declare them, and how they work, I would like to present some details around some advanced mapping scenarios, mainly around mapping associations, component, and inheritance mapping strategies.

Identifier generation

We have seen that generator was specified while mapping the identifier. The `generator` attribute is used to declare the algorithm to be used to generate an identifier value. Value used in the `generator` attribute is either the short name of algorithm that NHibernate provides out-of-the-box or the assembly qualified name of the NHibernate class that implements the said algorithm. NHibernate has implemented several such algorithms which should fit any identifier generation requirement. But if you are not happy with these then you can build your own algorithm by implementing interface `NHibernate.Id.IIdentifierGenerator`.

Let's take a look at important identifier generation algorithms that NHibernate offers out-of-the-box.

Identity

This algorithm works on the back of identity columns supported by SQL Server and MySQL. NH will save the entity without assigning any identifier value and database would generate the identifier values before actual database record is saved. NHibernate then retrieves the identifier generated by database and makes it available to application code that saved the entity.

Sequence

Similar to identity, this algorithm works in conjunction with sequences supported by Oracle, PostgreSQL, and SQL Server 2014.

Hilo

This implementation uses **hi/lo** algorithm to generate identifiers. Algorithm uses a high value retrieved from database and combines it with range of low values to generate a unique identifier. High value is retrieved from column next_hi of table hibernate_unique_key by default. But you can override this to use a different table. This algorithm also supports specifying a where parameter which can be used to retrieve high value for different entities from different rows of the hibernate_unique_key table. In *Chapter 5*, *Let's Store Some Data into the Database*, we will go over hilo algorithm in more detail.

Seqhilo

This implementation is similar to hilo. Only difference is that it uses a named database sequence as source of hi values. This strategy obviously only works for the databases that support sequences.

GUID

If the identifier property of a class is of `System.Guid` type then you can use the **Globally Unique Identifier (GUID)** generator to generate identifier values. This algorithm generates a new `System.Guid` for every record being inserted in the database.

Guid.comb

This is an improved generator implementation for identifiers of type `System.Guid`. In most relational databases, primary keys (identifiers in NHibernate world) are clustered and automatically indexed. `System.Guid` values are not index friendly. Hence, Jimmy Nilsson proposed a different mechanism to generate new `System.Guid` values that are index friendly and result in better performance. The **Guid.comb** generator implements algorithm proposed by Jimmy. You can read more about this algorithm at `http://www.informit.com/articles/article.asp?p=25862`.

Native

A **native** generator does not have its own algorithm. It picks up one of identity, sequence or hilo, depending on the capabilities of the underlying database.

Assigned

Similar to native, **assigned** does not have any algorithm to generate the identifier values. It is used to let NHibernate know that an application will assign the identifier values before entities are saved in the database.

We have only covered most important and widely used algorithms here. Note that there are more available out of the box. Among the ones presented here, hilo is most famous and results in most efficient database operations. We will see this in detail in *Chapter 5, Let's Store Some Data into Database*. For now, let's move on to the next topic.

Mapping associations

Association between two classes is a very simple concept to understand. If you want to have association between `ClassA` and `ClassB`, then you can add a property of type `ClassB` on `ClassA`. This is the most basic form of association.

Associations come in four different forms as described next:

- **One-to-many**: One end of the association has single instance of the entity while the other end has multiple instances. In code, this is represented by a property of the Collection type. For example, IList<T>, [], ICollection<T> ,IEnumerable<T>. and so on

- **Many-to-one**: Opposite of one-to-many.

- **One-to-one**: Both ends of associations have one single instance of entities.

- **Many-to-many**: Both ends of associations have multiple instances of entities.

We have example of all associations except many-to-many in our domain. Let me refer to part of the Employee class and the Benefit class as follows:

```
public class Employee : EntityBase
{
   public virtual ICollection<Benefit> Benefits { get; set; }
   public virtual Address ResidentialAddress { get; set; }
}

public class Benefit : EntityBase
{
   public virtual Employee Employee { get; set; }
}

public class Address : EntityBase
{
   public virtual Employee Employee { get; set; }
}
```

The Benefits property on the Employee class is an example of one-to-many association. On one side of this association we have got one instance of the Employee class and on the other side we have got a list of instances of the Benefit class.

On the Benefit class, we have an association from benefit to employee. This is the other end of one-to-many association we just discussed. This clearly is many-to-one association. We can have multiple instances of the Benefit class belonging to the same Employee instance. The ResidentialAddress property on the Employee class, on the other hand, is an example of one-to-one association. Every employee has only one address. Similarly, association from Address back to Employee is also one-to-one for the same reason.

We do not have any example of many-to-many in our domain so I am going to extend the scope of our problem and add the following new business requirement to it:

Organization operates different communities for employees. Employees are encouraged to be members of different communities. These communities not only help in building a social circle but also give employees an opportunity to meet like-minded people and build on their skills by sharing experience. Employees can become members of more than one community at a time.

To satisfy the preceding requirement, we would need to add a new class to our domain to represent an employee community. There can be multiple members of a community and an employee can be a member of multiple communities. Following is the relevant part of the code:

```
namespace Domain
{
  public class Community : EntityBase
  {
    public virtual string Name { get; set; }
    public virtual string Description { get; set; }
    public virtual ICollection<Employee> Members { get; set; }
  }
}

namespace Domain
{
  public class Employee : EntityBase
  {
    public virtual ICollection<Community> Communities { get; set; }
  }
}
```

So, we have a collection of the Community class on Employee representing the communities that the employee is member of. At the same time, we have a collection of the Employee class on Community holding all employees who are member of that community.

Associations and database tables

Before we actually look into mapping different types of associations, it would be worthwhile to spend some time understanding how a relational database supports associations. We know that every entity in the domain model gets mapped to a database table. So in order to support association between two classes, the database must be able to relate two database tables somehow. Relational databases achieve this via a **foreign key** relationship between two tables. If I could use association between the `Employee` and `Benefit` class as an example, then following database diagram explains how these two entities are related to each other in the database:

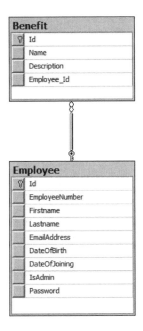

As you can see, column `Employee_Id` on the `Benefit` table is designated as a foreign key to the `Employee` table. The value held in this column is primary key/identifier of a record in the `Employee` table. You can repeat the same primary key in as many `Benefit` records as you want. This implies that for one record in the `Employee` table, you can store many records in the `Benefit` table. This is basis of a one-to-many relationship.

Fundamentally, databases only support one-to-many relationships and one-to-one relationship using shared primary keys. All other relationships we discussed previously are merely a different arrangement of one-to-many relationship to achieve different results. For example, by putting a logical constraint that "you would never insert more than one record in the `Benefit` table for a record in the `Employee` table" you achieve a one-to-one relationship. Similarly, you can combine two one-to-many relationships through an intermediate table to achieve a many-to-many relationship.

Next, we will look at how the associations between the classes are mapped to database relations. As with previous mapping exercises, we will use unit tests to confirm that our mappings achieve what we want it to achieve.

One-to-many association

The `Benefits` collection on the `Employee` class is the one-to-many association that we are going to map here. We will use the following unit test to drive the implementation of mapping. In this test, we add an instance of the `Leave`, `SeasonTicketLoan`, and `SkillsEnhancementAllowance` classes to the `Benefits` collection on the `Employee` class and store the employee instance in database. We then retrieve the instance and confirm that all the benefit instances are present:

```
[Test]
public void MapsBenefits()
{
  object id = 0;
  using (var transaction = session.BeginTransaction())
  {
    id = session.Save(new Employee
    {
      EmployeeNumber = "123456789",
      Benefits = new HashSet<Benefit>
      {
        new SkillsEnhancementAllowance
        {
          Entitlement = 1000,
          RemainingEntitlement = 250
        },
        new SeasonTicketLoan
        {
          Amount = 1416,
          MonthlyInstalment = 118,
          StartDate = new DateTime(2014, 4, 25),
          EndDate = new DateTime(2015, 3, 25)
        },
```

```
        new Leave
        {
          AvailableEntitlement = 30,
          RemainingEntitlement = 15,
          Type = LeaveType.Paid
        }
      }
  });
  transaction.Commit();
}

session.Clear();

using (var transaction = session.BeginTransaction())
{
  var employee = session.Get<Employee>(id);

  Assert.That(employee.Benefits.Count, Is.EqualTo(3));
  transaction.Commit();
}
}
```

This test is not very different from the previous test we saw. After retrieving the saved employee instance from the database, we are confirming that the Benefits collection on it has three items, which is what we had added. Let's add mappings to make this test pass. Mappings for this association would be added to the existing mapping file for the Employee class, which is Employee.hbm.xml. Following is how one-to-many association mapping is declared:

```
<set name="Benefits" cascade="all-delete-orphan">
  <key column="Employee_Id" />
  <one-to-many class="Benefit"/>
</set>
```

One-to-many mapping is also called collection mapping in NHibernate parlance. This is because property being mapped usually represents a collection of items. The only mandatory attribute that needs to be declared on set element is name of the property which is being mapped. This happens to be Benefits in this case.

There are two nested elements inside the set node. First one is key, which is used to declare the name of the foreign key column on the other end of the association. If you recall from the preceding diagram, foreign key from Benefit to the Employee class is named Employee_Id.

Second node inside the set is `one-to-many`. This is where we tell more about the many sides of this association. The only mandatory detail that is needed is `name` of the class on the other end.

You may have noticed that I have also added a `cascade` attribute on the mapping above. This is more of a personal preference and you can easily do away with this, but then remember that the default value that NHibernate assumes would be `none`.

I believe "pictures speak a thousand words". In the following image, I have tried to explain how mapping relates to database tables and domain classes:

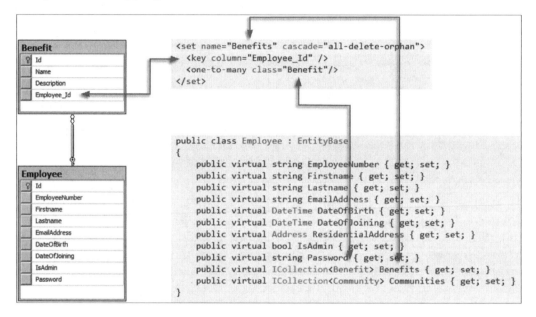

Types of collections

We have used set element to declare collection mapping. Set tells NHibernate that a property being mapped is a collection. Additionally, set also puts restrictions that the collection is unordered, unindexed, and does not allow duplicates. You can declare the collection to be ordered, indexed, and so on, using the following XML elements:

- Bag
- List
- Map
- Array

While they all map the collection properties to database, there are subtle differences in their runtime behavior and .NET types that they support. Following table gives key comparison of these mappings:

	Set	Bag	List	Map	Array
Duplicates	Duplicates not allowed in the collection	Duplicates allowed in the collection	Duplicates allowed in the collection	Duplicates not allowed in collection	Duplicates allowed in collection
Ordering	Not ordered	Not ordered	Ordered	Ordered	Ordered
Access	Collection items cannot be accessed by index	Collection items can be accessed by index	Collection items can be accessed by index	Collection items can be accessed by index	Collection items can be accessed by index
Supported .NET types	`IEnumerable<T>,` `ICollection<T>,` `Iesi.Collection.Generic.ISet<T>`	`IEnumerable<T>,` `ICollection<T>,` `IList<T>`	`IEnumerable<T>,` `ICollection<T>,` `IList<T>`	`IDictionary<TKey, TValue>`	`IEnumerable<T>,` `ICollection<T>,` `T[]`

Knowledge of the above key differences, coupled with knowledge of some other features offered by each of the collection mappings is useful in determining which collection mapping does the job best. I do not intend to cover those details here, as purpose is to only introduce you to collection mappings. As we go into more details in the coming chapters, we will revisit collection mappings and look into some of these features.

> All association mappings have quite a detailed level configuration available. I have preferred to show you only the minimum required to make the associations work. Some of the optional configurations will be covered at appropriate times throughout the book. Rest are used in rare and specific situations and are left for readers to explore on their own.

Many-to-one association

The other end of one-to-many association is many-to-one association. When both one-to-many and many-to-one associations are present between two entities, it is called bidirectional association. This is because you can navigate from one end to the other end in both directions. `Benefit` to the `Employee` association in our domain model is an example of many-to-one association. This is also a bidirectional association if you notice. Reason to highlight bidirectional nature of association is that NHibernate handles them in a different way. We are going to cover this aspect in *Chapter 5, Let's Store Some Data into the Database,* but it is worth highlighting now what bidirectional mapping is.

To test this mapping, we will extend the unit test from the earlier collection mapping example and add the following lines after the line where we asserted that benefit count is 3:

```
var seasonTicketLoan = employee.Benefits.OfType<SeasonTicketLoan>().
                       FirstOrDefault();
Assert.That(seasonTicketLoan, Is.Not.Null);
if (seasonTicketLoan != null) {
  Assert.That(seasonTicketLoan.Employee.EmployeeNumber,
                          Is.EqualTo("123456789"));
}


var skillsEnhancementAllowance = employee.Benefits
                                 .OfType<SkillsEnhancementAllowan
                                 ce>().FirstOrDefault();
Assert.That(skillsEnhancementAllowance, Is.Not.Null);
if (skillsEnhancementAllowance != null)
{
  Assert.That(skillsEnhancementAllowance.Employee.EmployeeNumber,
                                 Is.EqualTo("123456789"));
}


var leave = employee.Benefits.OfType<Leave>().FirstOrDefault();
Assert.That(leave, Is.Not.Null);
if (leave != null)
{
  Assert.That(leave.Employee.EmployeeNumber,
                 Is.EqualTo("123456789"));
}
```

At first look, this code may look complex but it is not actually. We have loaded employee instance from the database. On this instance, we confirmed that list of benefit has 3 benefit instances present. We query this list using LINQ and retrieve benefit instance of each type. On each of the benefit instance, we confirm that the `Employee` instance is present and it is the same employee instance that we had saved to database.

The mapping for this association is relatively easy as compared to collection mapping. Following is how you would declare this mapping inside of the `Benefit` class's mapping file, `benefit.hbm.xml`:

```
<many-to-one name="Employee"class="Employee"column="Employee_Id"/>
```

The node `many-to-one` signifies that this is a many end of a one-to-many association. There are only two mandatory attributes that this mapping takes. First one, `name` identifies the property on the mapped class that is at the singular end of the association. Second, `class` identifies the type of the singular end.

If the preceding text was any difficult to understand, then see if the following picture does any justice:

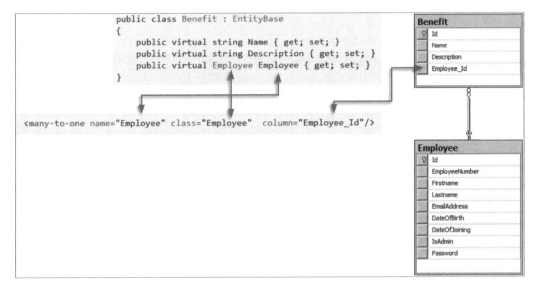

One-to-one association

In one-to-one association, both ends of association hold a single item. There are two variations of one-to-one association in relational databases. First is a variation of one-to-many association in that it uses a foreign key from one table to another. Difference from one-to-many association is that this foreign key has unique constraint applied to it so that only one record can be present on many side. Second variation uses a shared primary key approach in which associated tables share the primary key value. We are only going to look at unique foreign key approach here. Shared primary key approach is left as an exercise for the readers.

We will use the Employee to Address association to guide us. To elaborate the database relationship that we just discussed, let me show you database diagram for the Employee and Address table and how they are associated using the foreign key Employee_Id from the Address table to the Employee table.Refer to the following image:

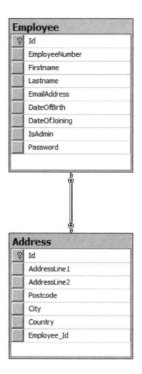

We will use the following unit test in order to verify mappings for the preceding association:

```
[Test]
public void MapsResidentialAddress()
{
  object id = 0;
  using (var transaction = Session.BeginTransaction())
  {
    var residentialAddress = new Address
    {
      AddressLine1 = "Address line 1",
      AddressLine2 = "Address line 2",
      Postcode = "postcode",
      City = "city",
```

```
      Country = "country"
    };

    var employee = new Employee
    {
      EmployeeNumber = "123456789",
      ResidentialAddress = residentialAddress
    };
    residentialAddress.Employee = employee;

    id = Session.Save(employee);
    transaction.Commit();
  }

  Session.Clear();

  using (var transaction = Session.BeginTransaction())
  {
    var employee = Session.Get<Employee>(id);
    Assert.That(employee.ResidentialAddress.AddressLine1,
            Is.EqualTo("Address line 1"));
    Assert.That(employee.ResidentialAddress.AddressLine2,
            Is.EqualTo("Address line 2"));
    Assert.That(employee.ResidentialAddress.Postcode,
            Is.EqualTo("postcode"));
    Assert.That(employee.ResidentialAddress.City,
            Is.EqualTo("city"));
    Assert.That(employee.ResidentialAddress.Country,
          Is.EqualTo("country"));
Assert.That(employee.ResidentialAddress.Employee.EmployeeNumber,Is
.EqualTo("123456789"));
    transaction.Commit();
  }
}
```

You might have noticed that I have explicitly set the `ResidentialAddress` property on the `Employee` class and the `Employee` property on the `Address` class. This is a bidirectional association and NHibernate usually makes sure that both ends are persisted correctly even if one end is set in code. But this is not always true in case of one-to-one association. We would cover details like these in *Chapter 5, Let's Store Some Data into the Database,* when we talk about persisting entities. I just wanted to highlight that the unit test for this scenario is written slightly differently.

So we have got a one-to-one association from `Employee` to `Address` and another one from `Address` back to `Employee`. Association from `Employee` to `Address` is mapped as follows:

```
<one-to-one name = "ResidentialAddress" class = "Address" property-ref
= "Employee" cascade = "all" />
```

By now, you may have guessed what node `one-to-one` and attributes `name`, `class`, and `cascade` are for. The only additional attribute `property-ref` is used to declare the name of the property on the other end of the association which refers back to this entity. In our example, that would be property named `Employee` on `Address` class.

Association from `Address` to `Employee` is actually many-to-one association constrained to single item. It is mapped using many-to-one XML node we have seen earlier with an additional attribute specifying the unique constraint.

```
<many-to-one name="Employee" class="Employee" column="Employee_Id"
unique="true" />
```

Following diagram should help you relate how this mapping associates domain model and database tables:

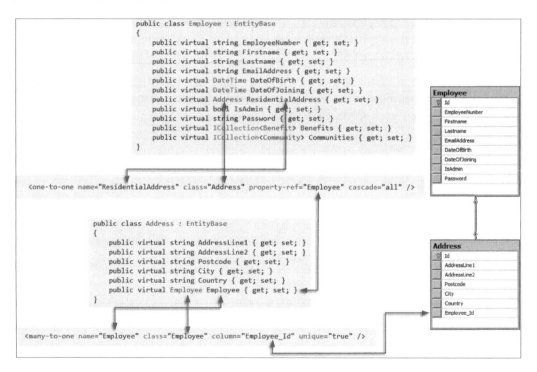

Many-to-many association

In database, many-to-many associations are just an arrangement of two one-to-many associations connected via an intermediate table. Employee communities' example from our domain could translate to a table schema which looks as follows:

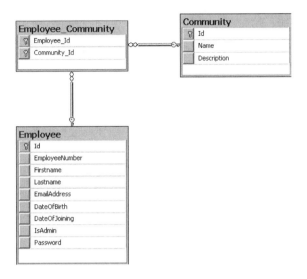

As you can see, we have got a connecting table named `Employee_Community`. There are two one-to-many relationships at play here, one going from `Employee` to `Employee_Community` and the other going from `Community` to `Employee_Community`. The end result is that if we navigate from `Employee` through to `Community`, we may end up with multiple communities and same if we navigate the other way round. Thus we get many-to-many relationship.

Following unit test verifies the behavior we want when employee to community association is mapped:

```
[Test]
public void MapsCommunities()
{
  object id = 0;
  using (var transaction = session.BeginTransaction())
  {
    id = session.Save(new Employee
    {
      EmployeeNumber = "123456789",
```

```
      Communities = new HashSet<Community>
      {
        new Community
        {
          Name = "Community 1"
        },
        new Community
        {
          Name = "Community 2"
        }
      }
    });
    transaction.Commit();
  }

  session.Clear();

  using (var transaction = session.BeginTransaction())
  {
    var employee = session.Get<Employee>(id);
    Assert.That(employee.Communities.Count, Is.EqualTo(2));
Assert.That(employee.Communities.First().Members.First().
EmployeeNumber, Is.EqualTo("123456789"));
    transaction.Commit();
  }
}
```

Here we are storing an instance of the `Employee` class with two instances of the `Community` class. We then retrieve the saved instance of `Employee` and verify that it has two instances of `Community` present on it. We also verify that community has employee instance in its `Members` collection. There are probably more things we can verify here but for the purpose of testing associations, I think this is enough.

Mapping for this association needs to be added on both `Employee` and `Community` end. This is because the association is bidirectional. Following is the mapping added to `employee.hbm.xml`:

```
<set name="Communities" table="Employee_Community" cascade="all-
delete-orphan">
  <key>
    <column name="Employee_Id" />
  </key>
  <many-to-many class="Community">
```

```
        <column name="Community_Id" />
    </many-to-many>
</set>
```

Next is the other part of the mapping added to `community.hbm.xml`:

```
<set name="Members" table="Employee_Community" cascade="all-delete-
orphan" inverse="true">
    <key>
        <column name="Community_Id"/>
    </key>
    <many-to-many class="Employee">
        <column name="Employee_Id" />
    </many-to-many>
</set>
```

The preceding mappings are quite similar to the collection mappings we saw earlier. There is no surprise there as we are really dealing with two collection mappings. Let's just note the key differences in this mapping from the collection mapping.

First difference is the additional `table` attribute on the set node. This attribute tells NHibernate what the name of the connecting table is.

Second difference is the node `many-to-many` inside the set node. In collection mapping, we had `one-to-many` here. Two mandatory pieces of information on the `many-to-many` node are `class` and `column`. `class` tells the name of the class on the other end of association. In employee mappings this is `Community` and in community this is `Employee`. `column` is used to declare the name of the foreign key column on the connecting table that relates to the other end of the association. For employee side, this is column `Community_Id` on the connecting table. For community side, this is column `Employee_Id` on the connecting table.

Again, the subsequent images might help. The following first image shows `Employee` to `Community` association mapping:

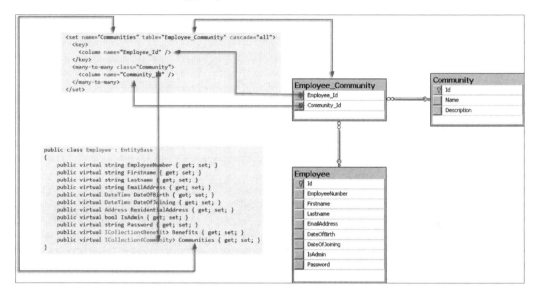

Next, the second image shows `Community` to `Employee` association mapping:

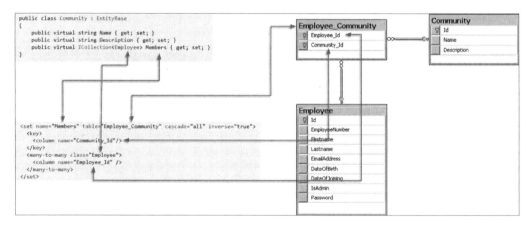

Similar to collection mapping, set is used as an example here and you can use map, bag, list, array, and so on.

We have the `inverse` attribute added to the mappings on `Community` side. This attribute controls who owns the association. I intend to cover this in detail in *Chapter 5, Let's Store Some Data into the Database,* so do not be bothered by inverse at this stage.

We have reached the end of association mapping for this chapter. Whatever we learned here should form a good foundation of knowledge. Associations are a vast and important area. We will keep revisiting association mappings throughout the book and learn more about them in the process. For the time being, let's move on to next topic.

Mapping inheritance

You will often have classes in your domain model that inherit from other classes. In our domain model, we have all classes representing a benefit inherited from the `Benefit` class. Following is a slimmed down version of the class diagram from our domain model representing this inheritance relationship:

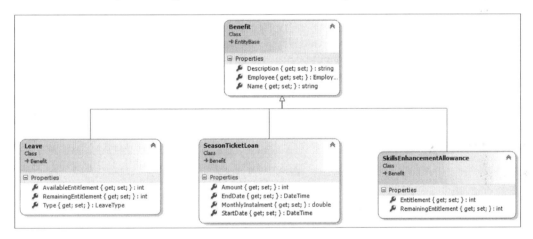

It is possible to map these classes to database tables as you would map any other class. But there are situations when you would want NHibernate to do more for you out of the box. One such situation involves **polymorphic associations**.

Polymorphic associations are associations where one of the ends is declared to be of base class type, but at runtime it holds instance of one of the derived types. For instance, the association from `Employee` to `Benefit` class in our domain model is an example of polymorphic association:

```
public class Employee : EntityBase
{
   public virtual ICollection<Benefit> Benefits { get; set; }
}
```

Here, though the collection property `Benefits` declared on the `Employee` class is of base class type, we know that, at run time, a particular instance of the `Benefit` class in this collection could be of any derived type. If we are building this collection in code, we can code it such that instances of right type are added to the collection. But what about NHibernate? Can NHibernate add the instances of right types when loading `Benefits` from database?

Fortunately, the answer to the question is yes. NHibernate is capable of dealing with polymorphic associations if we map the family of such classes using one of the inheritance mapping strategies offered by NH.

You can map any inherited classes using one of the inheritance mapping strategy but this may not be needed. For example, all our domain classes inherit from the class `EntityBase` but there is no need to map them as such. Main reason for doing so is that these classes are never used in the context of polymorphic associations and hence there is no need for NHibernate to be aware of the fact that they are inherited from some other class. Also, we introduced this inheritance because we noticed that the `Id` property was repeated on all the classes. In reality, all domain classes inheriting from `EntityBase` do not represent family of classes in true sense.

In order for NHibernate to handle polymorphic associations, the family of inheriting classes must be mapped using one of the many inheritance mapping strategies that NHibernate offers. NHibernate supports the following three basic strategies:

- Table per class hierarchy
- Table per subclass
- Table per concrete class

Besides the preceding three, NHibernate supports a slight variation of "table per concrete class". This is called implicit polymorphism. We will not cover this in the chapter and readers are encouraged to explore this on their own. NHibernate also lets you mix some of these strategies if you really have to. We will shortly jump into the details of each of the preceding strategies and see how our benefit classes would be mapped using these. Before that, let's take a look at the unit test that we are going to use to verify mappings.

Unit tests to verify the inheritance mappings

In order to test that our mappings are correct, we should be able to save an instance of one of the classes inheriting from the Benefit class and be able to retrieve it successfully. Following is one such test that we will be using:

```
[Test]
public void MapsSkillsEnhancementAllowance()
{
  object id = 0;
  using (var transaction = session.BeginTransaction())
  {
    id = session.Save(new SkillsEnhancementAllowance
    {
      Name = "Skill Enhacement Allowance",
      Description = "Allowance for employees so that their skill
      enhancement trainings are paid for",
      Entitlement = 1000,
      RemainingEntitlement = 250
    });
    transaction.Commit();
  }

  session.Clear();

  using (var transaction = session.BeginTransaction())
  {
    var benefit = session.Get<Benefit>(id);

    var skillsEnhancementAllowance = benefit as
              SkillsEnhancementAllowance;
    Assert.That(skillsEnhancementAllowance, Is.Not.Null);

    if (skillsEnhancementAllowance != null)
```

```
      {
        Assert.That(skillsEhancementAllowance.Name, Is.EqualTo("Skill
        Enhacement Allowance"));
        Assert.That(skillsEhancementAllowance.Description,
        Is.EqualTo("Allowance for employees so that their skill
        enhancement trainings are paid for"));
        Assert.That(skillsEhancementAllowance.Entitlement,
        Is.EqualTo(1000));
        Assert.That(skillsEhancementAllowance.RemainingEntitlement,
        Is.EqualTo(250));
      }
      transaction.Commit();
    }
  }
```

As you can see, we are storing an instance of the SkillsEhancementAllowance class. We then tell NHibernate to retrieve us an instance of the Benefit class using id that we received when we saved the instance of the SkillsEnahcementAllowance class. On this retrieved instance of the Benefit class, we verify three things:

- The retrieved instance is actually of type SkillsEnhancementAllowance class

- All properties of the Benefit class are retrieved correctly

- All properties of the SkillsEnhancementAllowance class are retrieved correctly

Interesting thing to note here is that we told NHibernate to load the Benefit class, which is a base class, but NHibernate intelligently loaded the correct derived class instance. This is polymorphic behavior offered by NHibernate. I actually have three of such tests, one each for every class deriving from the Benefit class. But for brevity, I have only presented one here. Others are very similar to this one and you can take a look at them from the source code of the book.

Let's make these tests pass by writing some inheritance mappings.

Table per class hierarchy

When I first used NHibernate, I had a hard time remembering what each of the strategies meant. One of the sources of confusion came from my relating the word "class hierarchy" to the wrong thing. I will not go into details of what assumption I made as that would be irrelevant for this discussion, but I would like to tell you that the word "class hierarchy" refers to a family of classes that inherit from one ultimate base class. In our example, the classes Benefit, Leave, SkillsEnhancementAllowance, SeasonTicketLoan together form a class hierarchy.

If you have more than one level of inheritance, the hierarchy would cover all the classes at all the levels of inheritance. Now you may have guessed what "table per class hierarchy" offers. This strategy maps all the classes in a hierarchy to a single table in database. Following is how we can map the `Benefit` class hierarchy using this strategy:

```xml
<?xml version="1.0" encoding="utf-8" ?>
<hibernate-mapping xmlns="urn:nhibernate-mapping-2.2"
assembly="Domain" namespace="Domain">
  <class name="Benefit">
    <id name="Id" generator="hilo" />
    <discriminator column="BenefitType" type="String" />
    <property name="Name" />
    <property name="Description" />
    <many-to-one name="Employee" class="Employee" />

    <subclass name="SkillsEnhancementAllowance" discriminator-
value="SEA">
        <property name="RemainingEntitlement" />
        <property name="Entitlement" />
    </subclass>

    <subclass name="SeasonTicketLoan" discriminator-value="STL">
        <property name="Amount" />
        <property name="MonthlyInstalment" />
        <property name="StartDate" />
        <property name="EndDate" />
    </subclass>

    <subclass name="Leave" discriminator-value="LVE">
        <property name="Type" />
        <property name="AvailableEntitlement" />
        <property name="RemainingEntitlement" />
    </subclass>
  </class>
</hibernate-mapping>
```

Though I declared all mappings in one XML file under a single class node, you can put each subclass mapping in its own XML file. NHibernate would use its own logic to weave together the mappings from multiple files. This applies to all inheritance mapping strategies.

This mapping would enable us to store data from all the `Benefit` classes into a table that looks as follows:

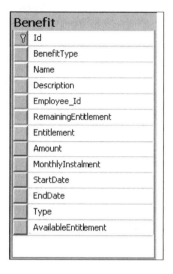

As you can see, this table has columns for all the properties of all four classes being mapped. Let's take a close look at the mappings.

Mapping of the base class is normal like any other class. Even mapping of derived class's attributes is also not unusual. There are two new things here as follows:

Element `discriminator` is used to declare a column on the database table that would be used as a discriminator. A discriminator, as the name suggests, discriminates between different rows of the table. In other words, the value of the column tells which class in the hierarchy this row belongs to. NHibernate uses this column to hydrate correct class when retrieving rows from the table. On the `discriminator` element, we have declared two attributes which are actually optional. Attribute `column` is used to declare the name of the discriminator column. Attribute `type` declares the type of the discriminator column. If not declared, NHibernate assumes default values for these attributes, which are `class` and `string` respectively.

Element `subclass` serves two purposes. One, it acts as the root element under which attributes of the derived class are mapped in the usual manner. Second, it lets you specify name of the derived class and what value in discriminator column is used to identify database record as belonging to that class.

Following are few important things to note around this strategy:

- This strategy maps to database table that is not normalized.

- An additional column called `discriminator` is required. This column does not store any business critical information but is used by NHibernate purely for the purpose of determining which class should be instantiated when a particular record from table is retrieved.

- It is not possible to mark properties of derived classes as not-null. This is because when a record belonging to one class in inserted into the table, columns mapping to other classes have to be left null.

Table per subclass

Most problems in "table per class hierarchy" are solved by the "table per subclass" strategy. In this strategy, every class gets mapped to its own table with a caveat that we would look into soon. Let's first look at how the mapping for this strategy looks, as shown next:

```xml
<?xml version="1.0" encoding="utf-8" ?>
<hibernate-mapping xmlns="urn:nhibernate-mapping-2.2"
assembly="Domain" namespace="Domain">
  <class name="Benefit">
    <id name="Id" generator="hilo" />
    <property name="Name" />
    <property name="Description" />
    <many-to-one name="Employee" class="Employee"/>

    <joined-subclass name="SkillsEnhancementAllowance">
      <key column="Id" />
      <property name="RemainingEntitlement" />
      <property name="Entitlement" />
    </joined-subclass>

    <joined-subclass name="SeasonTicketLoan">
      <key column="Id"/>
      <property name="Amount" />
      <property name="MonthlyInstalment" />
      <property name="StartDate" />
      <property name="EndDate" />
    </joined-subclass>
```

```
        <joined-subclass name="Leave">
          <key column="Id"/>
          <property name="Type" />
          <property name="AvailableEntitlement" />
          <property name="RemainingEntitlement" />
        </joined-subclass>
      </class>
  </hibernate-mapping>
```

As you can see, there is no discriminator column here. NHibernate is able to distinguish the database records belonging to different derived classes without resorting to a discriminator column. NHibernate uses joins on correct tables in order to fetch the complete database record. That is another reason the mapping is called `joined-subclass`. This mapping would map to the following table schema:

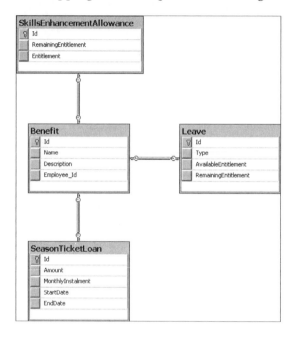

Here we have got one table for every class in the hierarchy. One thing to notice here is that every table has an `Id` column which is also the primary key on the respective tables. This primary key is shared between table for base class and table for derived class. Key points to note in this strategy are:

- Since every class gets mapped to its own table, you can make columns on derived class not-null, unlike "table per class hierarchy".

- NH uses joins while retrieving records from these tables. This has a slight performance overhead.

Table per concrete class

You can keep things simple and map all the four Benefit classes to their own tables without any inheritance mapping semantics. But flip side of such an approach is that you would not be able to use polymorphic associations. If you still want to map each class to its own table and be able to use polymorphic association, then "table per concrete class" is your friend. Following is how "table per concrete class mapping for our family of Benefit classes would look:

```xml
<?xml version="1.0" encoding="utf-8" ?>
<hibernate-mapping xmlns="urn:nhibernate-mapping-2.2"
assembly="Domain" namespace="Domain">
  <class name="Benefit">
    <id name="Id" generator="hilo" />
    <property name="Name" />
    <property name="Description" />
    <many-to-one name="Employee" class="Employee" />

    <union-subclass name="SkillsEnhancementAllowance">
      <property name="RemainingEntitlement" />
      <property name="Entitlement" />
    </union-subclass>

    <union-subclass name="SeasonTicketLoan">
      <property name="Amount" />
      <property name="MonthlyInstalment" />
      <property name="StartDate" />
      <property name="EndDate" />
    </union-subclass>

    <union-subclass name="Leave">
      <property name="Type" />
      <property name="AvailableEntitlement" />
      <property name="RemainingEntitlement" />
    </union-subclass>
  </class>
</hibernate-mapping>
```

As the element `union-subclass` suggests, this mapping strategy runs SQL union on all the four tables in order to retrieve a full database record. The mapped database tables for this strategy would look as shown in the following image. You can see in the following diagram that NHibernate has automatically remapped properties from the base classes onto tables corresponding to derived classes:

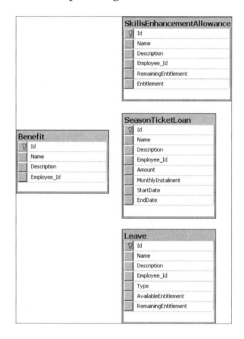

Every class is mapped to an independent table. There is no relation between the tables. Properties from the base classes are remapped on each table for the derived class. So the tables are not in a perfectly normalized form. Use of unions may signal some drop in performance. A serious concern with this strategy is that polymorphic associations do not work reliably. They may work in some situations but not always. Another limitation of this strategy is that you cannot use identity as identifier generation strategy. This is because each table has now its own identifier column. If we use identity then we would get duplicate identifier values across the tables. If you try to load the `Benefit` instances using an identifier value, NHibernate would be confused as there would be multiple records matching the given identifier value. Looking at this from a different angle, it is a good thing because identity is not a recommended identifier generation strategy anyway.

The Benefit table has columns that map to the Benefit entity. These same columns are also present on the tables for the derived entities. This is redundant. We can stop having the Benefit table by making use of an attribute called abstract that can be applied to class element. A value of true means that the class can be treated as abstract from NHibernate point of view. NHibernate then generates all SQL as if there is no Benefit table present in the database.

Note that the "table per concrete class" strategy can be implemented using implicit polymorphism. This is similar to the approach we discussed at the beginning of this section, where we said that every derived class can be mapped to a database table independent of each other. In this approach you cannot use polymorphic associations so I would use this strategy only if I was unable to use any other strategy.

Choosing the right inheritance mapping strategy

Which inheritance strategy should you use? This is not an easy question to answer. More than one factor is at play and you should look at each of these factors before you decide.

If you are working with a legacy database and you cannot make changes to the existing database schema then you must choose the strategy that would let you map your domain model to the schema. Here you do not have many options but stick to one that would get the job done. Sometimes, for reasons beyond your control, you might even need to mix different strategies in order to get mappings to work. The beauty of NHibernate is that it lets you mix the strategies without you having to worry about how NHibernate figures out storing and retrieving of data from tables.

If you are working on a green field project where you are free to define your own database schema, then you can look at other factors such as preference to have a normalized vs non-normalized database schema, expected performance, requirement to set table columns as NOT NULL, and so on. While "table per class hierarchy" gives the best performance, it maps to database schema that is not normalized. You also lose the ability to mark a column from the derived class as not null. "Table per subclass" lets you mark columns as not null and also maps to tables that are normalized but its use of joins to fetch records impacts the performance slightly. I personally prefer "table per subclass" as the performance overhead is not that significant in my opinion. I like working with normalized tables. In the end, "table per concrete class" is something I would tend to avoid unless I have no other option.

Mapping components

So far we have been using the term entity to refer to classes that NHibernate is able to persist to database. But when it comes to NHibernate, there is more to that term. An entity is something that has its own identifier and can be distinguished from another instance of same type by using the identifier value. An important feature of entity is that NHibernate is able to track the entity. This means that NHibernate knows whether the entity is only present in memory but is not persisted to database, or is persisted to database but the instance in the memory is updated, and so on (sometimes this is also called dirty tracking). Another important feature of entities is that they are saved in their own database table. The way NHibernate handles the entities gives them an identity of their own. This enables the entities to be fetched from database, navigate from one entity to other entity, and so on, using entity identifiers.

Not every class in the domain model needs to be an entity. For instance, the `Address` class from our domain model does not need to have its own identifier, and properties of this class can be persisted in `Employee` table itself. In such case, the `Address` class can be mapped as a component. But mapping a class as a component puts some restrictions on it, as listed next:

- A component does not have identifier property so it cannot be loaded from the database by using an identifier. The only way to load a component is by navigating from the entity that references the component.

- Association semantics do not work in the same way for components as they work for entities.

Mapping components is very simple. Mappings for `component` are declared inside the mappings of the class that references the component. You can declare the `component` mapping using XML node `component` as the following code snippet shows. Properties on the `component` class are mapped as properties on any other class:

```xml
<?xml version="1.0" encoding="utf-8" ?>
<hibernate-mapping xmlns="urn:nhibernate-mapping-2.2"
assembly="Domain" namespace="Domain.Component">
  <class name="Employee">
    <id name="Id" generator="hilo" />
    <property name="EmployeeNumber" length="10" />
    <property name="Firstname" />
    <property name="Lastname" />
    <property name="EmailAddress" />
    <property name="DateOfBirth" />
    <property name="DateOfJoining" />
    <property name="IsAdmin" />
    <property name="Password" />
```

```
    <component name="ResidentialAddress" class="Address">
      <property name="AddressLine1"/>
      <property name="AddressLine2" />
      <property name="Postcode" />
      <property name="City" />
      <property name="Country" />
    </component>
  </class>
</hibernate-mapping>
```

In the previous code sample, additional mappings of other properties on the Employee class are depicted to show you how component fits in the overall picture. Component mapping needs the name and class attributes to be specified. In the name attribute, declare the name of the property on the entity which is referring to the component class. In the class attribute, specify the type of the component class. Properties of the component class are mapped like any other properties.

The unit test we used previously to test mappings for the Address class cannot be used as is when Address is mapped as component. This is mainly because now the Address class does not have reference back to Employee and hence test needs to be written considering this in mind. I have omitted the refactored test here but you can find it in the source code of the book.

NHibernate's support for components is quite elaborate. What we have covered is the most common configuration of components. As beginners to NHibernate, the preceding should suffice you to move along. But if you are interested in learning different aspects of component support in NHibernate, then you may wish to head over to the official documentation at http://nhibernate.info/doc/nh/en/index. html#mapping-declaration-component.

With this we can conclude our discussion of XML mappings. We have covered most important aspects of XML mappings but there is a lot more to be learned. We will continue learning something new about mappings in every chapter of this book. For the moment, let's jump into the second mechanism of mapping offered by NH.

Mapping by code

By now, you should have got a very good idea of what purpose the mappings serve. This knowledge will make understanding this section and the next very easy. At the beginning of the chapter, we discussed what is mapping by code and why it is built. So without much ado, let me get straight into the "mapping by code" feature of NH.

In mapping by code, mappings for each class can be declared in a separate and own class. It is also possible to declare the mappings in a single place by using the `ModelMapper` class. We would prefer to declare mappings for each entity in its own class. This class must inherit from another class provided by NHibernate called `NHibernate.Mapping.ByCode.ClassMapping<T>`. Whatever mappings you want to declare should be declared in the constructor of the class. Following code snippet shows how this looks for the `Employee` class:

```
using NHibernate.Mapping.ByCode;
using NHibernate.Mapping.ByCode.Conformist;
using Domain;

namespace Persistence.Mappings.ByCode
{
  public class EmployeeMappings : ClassMapping<Employee>
  {
    public EmployeeMappings()
    {
      //Declare mappings here
    }
  }
}
```

We declared a class called `EmployeeMappings` which inherits from `ClassMapping<Employee>`. The generic parameter `Employee` tells NHibernate that this class will hold the mappings for the `Employee` class. We then added a default constructor where in all our mappings would be added. That was simple, wasn't it? Next, we are going to look at how to declare different mappings that we learned in the XML mapping section. I will cover these mappings in more or less the same sequence as we covered earlier.

The API for mapping by code uses the same name as the nodes in XML mappings, making it very easy to construct and understand mappings. Like XML mappings, you are required to provide only the absolute minimum configuration and NHibernate would assume safe defaults for optional configuration. We have discussed important optional configurations already so I will not repeat them here. Let's get started then.

Identifier

Following is how to map identifier with minimal configuration:

```
Id(e => e.Id, mapper => mapper.Generator(Generators.HighLow));
```

Let me take a moment to explain what constitutes the preceding code. `Id` method is used to declare identifier mapping. The first parameter to this method is lambda expression to the property that acts as identifier of the class being mapped. The second parameter is delegate that takes `NHibernate.Mapping.ByCode.IIdMapper` as its parameter. `NHibernate.Mapping.ByCode.IIdMapper` has several methods defined on it that let you define optional configuration for the identifier. We have used one of these methods to specify that we want to use hilo generator for our identifier. You can see identifier mapping with some additional configuration specified in the following example:

```
Id(e => e.Id,
    mapper =>
    {
        mapper.Generator(Generators.HighLow);
        mapper.Column("Id");
        mapper.Length(10);
        mapper.UnsavedValue(0);
    });
```

Following image should give you an idea of how XML mappings compare to mapping by code:

```
<id name="Id" generator="hilo" />     Id(e => e.Id, mapper =>mapper.Generator(Generators.HighLow));
```

Property

Property mapping is quite simple. The only mandatory parameter it needs is lambda expression of the property being mapped. Following is how the `EmployeeNumber` property of the `Employee` class would be mapped.

```
Property(e => e.EmployeeNumber);
```

We probably do not need a side-by-side comparison of this mapping with XML. Following is same mapping with all optional parameters specified:

```
Property(e => e.EmployeeNumber,
    mapper =>
    {
        mapper.Column("employment_number");
        mapper.Type(NHibernateUtil.String);
        mapper.Length(10);
        mapper.NotNullable(true);
        mapper.Lazy(true);
        mapper.Unique(true);
    });
```

Association

As you know association mappings come in four different flavors. Let's look at them one by one.

One-to-many

One-to-many or collection mapping is declared using `Set`, `Bag`, `List`, `Map`, and so on. Syntactically they are all same so I would only use set as an example here. The collection mapping from `Employee` to `Benefit` that we wrote in the previous section can be written in code as follows:

```
Set(e => e.Benefits,
  mapper =>
  {
    mapper.Key(k => k.Column("Employee_Id"));
    mapper.Cascade(Cascade.All);
  },
  relation => relation.OneToMany(
  mapping => mapping.Class(typeof(Benefit))));
```

As you can see, the `Set` API takes more than two parameters. The first one is usual lambda expression to property being mapped, which happens to be `Benefits` in this case. Second one is a delegate accepting `NHibernate.Mapping.ByCode.ISet PropertiesMapper<Employee,Benefit>`. You can use the instance of `ISetProp ertiesMapper<Employee,Benefit>` passed to this delegate to specify additional mapping configuration. Third parameter is another delegate accepting an instance of `NHibernate.Mapping.ByCode.ICollectionElementRelation<Benefit>` as its parameter. This instance can be used to specify details around one-to-many association between `Employee` and `Benefit`. This mapping is slightly complex than `id` and property mapping. Following picture comparing code mapping with XML mapping should help with understanding of this better:

```
                                      Set(e => e.Benefits,
                                         mapper => {
<set name="Benefits" cascade="all-delete-orphan">
  <key column="Employee_Id" />                    mapper.Cascade(Cascade.DeleteOrphans);
  <one-to-many class="Benefit"/>                  mapper.Key(k => k.Column("Employee_Id"));
</set>
                                         },
                                         relation => relation.OneToMany(mapping => mapping.Class(typeof(Benefit))));
```

Many-to-one

Many-to-one specifies the other end of one-to-many association. Only one parameter is mandatory on this mapping and following is how you declare this mapping in code:

```
ManyToOne(b => b.Employee, mapping =>
    mapping.Class(typeof(Employee)));
```

The example uses two parameters though only the first one is really required. Showing both parameters makes it easy in the comparison with XML mapping done as follows. First parameter is lambda to the property being mapped and second is delegate that lets you configure additional parameters for this mapping. This delegate accepts a parameter of type NHibernate.Mapping. ByCode.IManyToOneMapper which lets you declare more options for many-to-one association. Following is a side by side comparison of this mapping with many-to-one XML mapping:

`<many-to-one name="Employee"`
`            class="Employee"`
`            column="Employee_Id"/>`
	`ManyToOne(b => b.Employee,`
	`    mapper =>`
	`    {`
	`        mapper.Class(typeof (Employee));`
	`        mapper.Column("Employee_Id");`
	`    });`

One-to-one

As we learned during XML mapping of one-to-one association, one-to-one association is really only one-to-many with a constraint that "many side" can only hold one item at max. Employee to Address one-to-one association would be declared using code mapping as shown next.

The Employee side can be represented as follows:

```
OneToOne(e => e.ResidentialAddress,
    mapper =>
    {
        mapper.Cascade(Cascade.Persist);
        mapper.PropertyReference(a => a.Employee);
    });
```

The `Address` side can be represented as shown next:

```
ManyToOne(a => a.Employee,
  mapper =>
  {
    mapper.Class(typeof (Employee));
    mapper.Column("Employee_Id");
    mapper.Unique(true);
  });
```

Nothing unusual here. But mappings accept lambda to property being mapped as first parameter and second is the delegate that specified additional mapping configuration. The delegate accepts a parameter of type `NHibernate.Mapping.ByCode.IOneToOneMapper<Address>` which you can use to declare additional mapping options for many-to-one association. Following is a side by side comparison of the preceding code with XML mapping:

```
<one-to-one name="ResidentialAddress" class="Address"        OneToOne(e => e.ResidentialAddress, mapper =>
           property-ref="Employee"                           {
           cascade="all" />                                       mapper.PropertyReference(a => a.Employee);
                                                                  mapper.Cascade(Cascade.All);
                                                              });
```

Many-to-many

Similar to one-to-many, many-to-many is also declared using `Set`, `Bag`, `List`, `Map`, and so on. Let's take a look at set syntax for `Employee` to `Community` association:

```
Set(e => e.Communities,
  mapper =>
  {
    mapper.Key(k => k.Column("Employee_Id"));
    mapper.Table("Employee_Community");
    mapper.Cascade(Cascade.All);
  },
  relation => relation.ManyToMany(mtm =>
  {
    mtm.Class(typeof(Community));
    mtm.Column("Community_Id");
  }));
```

Again, this is not much different from one-to-many. The usual parameters are passed to the `Set` method. Last delegate parameter calls method `ManyToMany` and specifies the name of the foreign key column on the connecting table. Following is how this compares side by side to its XML equivalent:

```
<set name="Communities"
    table="Employee_Community"
    cascade="all">
  <key>
    <column name="Employee_Id" />
  </key>
  <many-to-many
    class="Community">
    <column name="Community_Id" />
  </many-to-many>
</set>
```

```
Set(e => e.Communities,
    mapper =>
    {
        mapper.Table("Employee_Community");
        mapper.Cascade(Cascade.All);
        mapper.Key(k => k.Column("Employee_Id"));
    },
    relation => relation.ManyToMany(mtm =>
    {
        mtm.Class(typeof(Community));
        mtm.Column("Community_Id");
    }));
```

Component

API to map components takes two parameters. First is lambda to property referring to component class. In our case, this is the `ResidentialAddress` property on the `Employee` class. Second parameter is a delegate taking `IComponentMapper<T>` as its parameter. Here type `T` is the type of component class, which in our case is `Address`. `IComponentMapper<T>`has methods that let you map properties on the component class. Following is how you would map the `Address` component:

```
Component(e => e.ResidentialAddress,
         mapper =>
             {
                 mapper.Property(a => a.AddressLine1);
                 mapper.Property(a => a.AddressLine2);
                 mapper.Property(a => a.City);
                 mapper.Property(a => a.Postcode);
                 mapper.Property(a => a.Country);
             });
```

Inheritance

Mapping inheritance by code is quite simple. Mapping of base class is like mapping any other class where you inherit from `ClassMapping<T>`. Mapping of the derived classes is slightly different depending on which inheritance strategy you want. Unlike XML mapping where you wrote mappings for all classes in one XML file, here you would declare the mappings for each class in its own mapping class. Following is a code snippet for mapping the base class `Benefit`:

```
public class BenefitMappings : ClassMapping<Benefit>
{
  public BenefitMappings()
  {
    Id(b => b.Id, idmapper =>
    idmapper.Generator(Generators.HighLow));
    Property(b => b.Name);
    Property(b => b.Description);
    ManyToOne(b => b.Employee, mapping =>
    mapping.Class(typeof(Employee)));
  }
}
```

As you can see, this is like usual mapping for any other class. Let's see how derived classes are mapped in different strategies.

Table per class hierarchy

When mapping for "table per class hierarchy" by code, you need to ensure the following two things:

- Mapping classes inherit from `SubclassMapping<T>` where `T` is the class being mapped

- Value of discriminator column is declared by calling the `DiscriminatorValue()` method

Following is our benefits family of classes mapped using this strategy:

```
public class LeaveMappings : SubclassMapping<Leave>
{
  public LeaveMappings()
  {
    DiscriminatorValue("LVE");
    Property(l => l.Type);
    Property(l => l.AvailableEntitlement);
    Property(l => l.RemainingEntitlement);
```

```
    }
}
public class SeasonTicketLoanMappings :
SubclassMapping<SeasonTicketLoan>
{
  public SeasonTicketLoanMappings()
  {
    DiscriminatorValue("STL");
    Property(s => s.Amount);
    Property(s => s.MonthlyInstalment);
    Property(s => s.StartDate);
    Property(s => s.EndDate);
  }
}
public class SkillsEnhancementAllowanceMappings :
SubclassMapping<SkillsEnhancementAllowance>
{
  public SkillsEnhancementAllowanceMappings()
  {
    DiscriminatorValue("SEA");
    Property(s => s.Entitlement);
    Property(s => s.RemainingEntitlement);
  }
}
```

Table per subclass

In "table per subclass", each class gets mapped to a table in database. As mentioned earlier, base class is mapped in exactly the same way as "table per class hierarchy". The derived classes are mapped slightly differently. Their mapping class derives from `JoinedSubclassMapping<Benefit>` and also declares mapping of the shared primary key column. Following are mappings for all the three `Benefit` classes:

```
public class LeaveMappings : JoinedSubclassMapping<Leave>
{
  public LeaveMappings()
  {
    Key(k => k.Column("Id"));
    Property(l => l.Type);
    Property(l => l.AvailableEntitlement);
    Property(l => l.RemainingEntitlement);
  }
}
```

```
public class SeasonTicketLoanMappings : JoinedSubclassMapping<SeasonT
icketLoan>
{
  public SeasonTicketLoanMappings()
  {
    Key(k => k.Column("Id"));
    Property(s => s.Amount);
    Property(s => s.MonthlyInstalment);
    Property(s => s.StartDate);
    Property(s => s.EndDate);
  }
}

public class SkillsEnhancementAllowanceMappings :
JoinedSubclassMapping<SkillsEnhancementAllowance>
{
  public SkillsEnhancementAllowanceMappings()
  {
    Key(k => k.Column("Id"));
    Property(s => s.Entitlement);
    Property(s => s.RemainingEntitlement);
  }
}
```

Note the declaration of primary key mapping using the method Key. This method accepts a delegate to which NHibernate.Mapping.ByCode.IKeyMapper<SkillsEnh ancementAllowance> type is passed as parameter. IKeyMapper<SkillsEnhancemen tAllowance> is used to specify mapping of key column. There are several mapping configurations you can specify here but we have only specified the mandatory one, which is name of the key column.

Table per concrete class

There is only one thing you need to remember while mapping classes using the "table per concrete class" strategy. The class that declares the mappings for derived classes inherits from the UnionSubclassMapping<T> class. We have already covered how to map the base class. Following is how this mapping looks for our benefit classes:

```
public class LeaveMappings : UnionSubclassMapping<Leave>
{
  public LeaveMappings()
  {
    Property(l => l.Type);
    Property(l => l.AvailableEntitlement);
    Property(l => l.RemainingEntitlement);
```

```
        }
    }

    public class SeasonTicketLoanMappings :
    UnionSubclassMapping<SeasonTicketLoan>
    {
        public SeasonTicketLoanMappings()
        {
            Property(s => s.Amount);
            Property(s => s.MonthlyInstalment);
            Property(s => s.StartDate);
            Property(s => s.EndDate);
        }
    }

    public class SkillsEnhancementAllowanceMappings :
    UnionSubclassMapping<SkillsEnhancementAllowance>
    {
        public SkillsEnhancementAllowanceMappings()
        {
            Property(s => s.Entitlement);
            Property(s => s.RemainingEntitlement);
        }
    }
```

Note that the only different thing we are doing here is that mapping classes inherit from `UnionSubclassMapping<T>` instead of usual `ClassMapping<T>`. Other than this, everything else is done in the usual way.

This concludes our discussion on mapping by code. Let's take a step back and look at complete mappings by code for our domain model.

Complete mappings by code for the employee benefits domain

So far we have seen snippets of mapping by code sprinkled across multiple sections. While that is useful in understanding one concept at a time, a complete picture is necessary to see how things fit together. Take time to go through the following code to get an idea of end-to-end mapping by code for our domain model.

The following is the code for the `Employee` domain:

```
public EmployeeMappings()
{
  Id(e => e.Id, mapper => mapper.Generator(Generators.HighLow));
  Property(e => e.EmployeeNumber);
  Property(e => e.Firstname);
  Property(e => e.Lastname);
  Property(e => e.EmailAddress);
  Property(e => e.DateOfBirth);
  Property(e => e.DateOfJoining);
  Property(e => e.IsAdmin);
  Property(e => e.Password);

  OneToOne(e => e.ResidentialAddress, mapper =>
  {
    mapper.Cascade(Cascade.Persist);
    mapper.PropertyReference(a => a.Employee);
  });

  Set(e => e.Benefits, mapper =>
  {
    mapper.Key(k => k.Column("Employee_Id"));
    mapper.Cascade(Cascade.All);
  },
  relation => relation.OneToMany(mapping =>
  mapping.Class(typeof(Benefit))));

  Set(e => e.Communities,
  mapper =>
  {
    mapper.Key(k => k.Column("Employee_Id"));
    mapper.Table("Employee_Community");
    mapper.Cascade(Cascade.All);
  },
  relation => relation.ManyToMany(mtm =>
  {
    mtm.Class(typeof(Community));
    mtm.Column("Community_Id");
  }));
}
```

The following is the code for the `Address` domain:

```
public class AddressMappings : ClassMapping<Address>
{
  public AddressMappings()
  {
    Id(a => a.Id, mapper => mapper.Generator(Generators.HighLow));
    Property(a => a.AddressLine1);
    Property(a => a.AddressLine2);
    Property(a => a.Postcode);
    Property(a => a.City);
    Property(a => a.Country);
    ManyToOne(a => a.Employee, mapper =>
    {
      mapper.Class(typeof (Employee));
      mapper.Column("Employee_Id");
      mapper.Unique(true);
    });
  }
}
```

The following is the code for the `Community` domain:

```
public class CommunityMappings : ClassMapping<Community>
{
  public CommunityMappings()
  {
    Id(c => c.Id, idmapper =>
    idmapper.Generator(Generators.HighLow));
    Property(c => c.Name);
    Property(c => c.Description);
    Set(c => c.Members,
    mapper =>
    {
      mapper.Key(k => k.Column("Community_Id"));
      mapper.Table("Employee_Community");
      mapper.Cascade(Cascade.All);
      mapper.Inverse(true);
    },
    relation => relation.ManyToMany(mapper =>
    {
      mapper.Class(typeof (Employee));
      mapper.Column("Employee_Id");
    }));
  }
}
```

The following is the code for the `Benefit` domain:

```
public class BenefitMappings : ClassMapping<Benefit>
{
  public BenefitMappings()
  {
    Id(b => b.Id, idmapper =>
    idmapper.Generator(Generators.HighLow));
    Property(b => b.Name);
    Property(b => b.Description);
    ManyToOne(b => b.Employee, mapping =>
    mapping.Class(typeof(Employee)));
  }
}
```

The following is the code for the `Leave` domain:

```
public class LeaveMappings : JoinedSubclassMapping<Leave>
{
  public LeaveMappings()
  {
    Key(k => k.Column("Id"));
    Property(l => l.Type);
    Property(l => l.AvailableEntitlement);
    Property(l => l.RemainingEntitlement);
  }
}
```

The following is the code for the `SkillsEnhancementAllowance` domain:

```
public class SkillsEnhancementAllowanceMappings :
JoinedSubclassMapping<SkillsEnhancementAllowance>
{
  public SkillsEnhancementAllowanceMappings()
  {
    Key(k => k.Column("Id"));
    Property(s => s.Entitlement);
    Property(s => s.RemainingEntitlement);
  }
}
```

The following is the code for the `SeasonTicketLoan` domain:

```
public class SeasonTicketLoanMappings :
JoinedSubclassMapping<SeasonTicketLoan>
{
```

```
public SeasonTicketLoanMappings()
{
  Key(k => k.Column("Id"));
  Property(s => s.Amount);
  Property(s => s.MonthlyInstalment);
  Property(s => s.StartDate);
  Property(s => s.EndDate);
}
}
```

Fluent mapping a.k.a. Fluent NHibernate

If you have liked mapping by code and are excited about being able to declare mappings programmatically, then I am sure you would fall in love with fluent mappings offered by **Fluent NHibernate (FNH)**. As far as I can tell, fluent mapping is the most widely used technique of mapping in NHibernate world and we will see why everyone likes it so much.

FNH scans your code based on mappings, processes them, and comes up with appropriate XML mappings. All this process is transparent to you as developer. But it is useful to remember that all FNH is doing is transforming code-based mappings into XML mappings.

Before we start writing fluent mappings for our classes, let me tell you that FNH, for some reasons, chose to name their APIs differently than their XML or mapping by code counterparts. For example, property mapping in FNH is named **Map**. This could be a cause of confusion if you are new to FNH but I'm sure your love for FNH would outweigh the confusion and you would soon get used it. Let's get started then.

We will take a slightly different approach to learning fluent mappings. Instead of going through how to map different types of attributes individually, I am going to show you complete mappings for classes in our domain model. We will then look at individual fluent mappings declared for each class. Let's start with `Employee`:

```
using Domain;
using FluentNHibernate.Mapping;

namespace Persistence.Mappings.Fluent
{
  public class EmployeeMappings : ClassMap<Employee>
  {
    public EmployeeMappings()
    {
```

```
        Id(e => e.Id).GeneratedBy.HiLo("1000");
        Map(e => e.EmployeeNumber);
        Map(e => e.Firstname);
        Map(e => e.Lastname);
        Map(e => e.EmailAddress);
        Map(e => e.DateOfBirth);
        Map(e => e.DateOfJoining);
        Map(e => e.IsAdmin);
        Map(e => e.Password);


        HasOne(e =>
        e.ResidentialAddress).Cascade.All().PropertyRef(a =>
        a.Employee);
        HasMany(e => e.Benefits).Cascade.AllDeleteOrphan();
        HasManyToMany(e => e.Communities)
                        .Table("Employee_Community")
                        .ParentKeyColumn("Employee")
                        .ChildKeyColumn("Community")
                        .Cascade.AllDeleteOrphan();
    }


  }
}
```

Let's see what is going on here:

- The class that holds mappings inherits from `FluentNHibernate.Mapping.ClassMap<T>` where `T` is the class being mapped.

- Mappings are declared in the default constructor of this class using helper methods available from base class.

- `Id` method is used to map the identifier. This takes lambda to identifier property on the class. Method chaining is used to provide additional method on top of the Id method. These additional methods can be used to declare optional mapping configuration. In our example, we have used the `GeneratedBy.HiLo("1000")` method to configure a hilo identifier generator for our mapping. In Visual Studio, if you put a dot next to `GeneratedBy`, IntelliSense will list all the available identifier generators for you.

- `Map` method is used to map properties on the class. The only mandatory parameter this takes is the lambda to property being mapped.

- `HasOne` method maps a one-to-one association. The parameter passed to it is lambda to the property being mapped. Chained methods are available to configure optional mappings. We have used `Cascade.All()` to declare cascade settings and `PropertyRef()` to specify value for the `property-ref` attribute of XML one-to-one mapping. Note how `PropertyRef` takes a lambda to a property on the other end of the association and makes our lives easier.

- `HasMany` method is used to map one-to-many relationship from the `Employee` to `Benefit` class. As you can see, the only mandatory parameter is lambda to the `Benefits` collection property on the `Employee` class. FNH chooses appropriate XML element for you out of `Set`, `Map`, `Bag`, `List`, and so on.

- `HasManyToMany` declares a many-to-many mapping. Are you not surprised by the simplicity? First parameter, lambda to property being mapped, is usual. You only have to specify the name of the connecting table via chained method `Table()` method and foreign keys from connecting table to both tables on many end via `ParentKeyColumn()` and `ChildKeyColumn()` methods.

Let's look at mapping of the `Community` class next to see how the other side of many-to-many is mapped. Following is complete fluent mapping for the `Community` class:

```
public class CommunityMappings : ClassMap<Community>
{
  public CommunityMappings()
  {
    Id(c => c.Id).GeneratedBy.HiLo("1000");
    Map(c => c.Name);
    Map(c => c.Description);
    HasManyToMany(c => c.Members)
    .Table("Employee_Community")
    .ParentKeyColumn("Community_Id")
    .ChildKeyColumn("Employee_Id")
    .Cascade.AllDeleteOrphan();
  }
}
```

There is nothing new in here from mappings of the `Employee` class except a minor detail. `ParentKeyColumn` is the passed name of foreign key column to the `Community` table and `ChildKeyColumn` is the passed name of the foreign key column to the `Employee` table. This was the other way round in `EmployeeMappings` for obvious reasons.

Mappings of the `Address` class are not vastly different as well, again except for mapping of many-to-one `Employee` association. Let's take a look:

```
public class AddressMappings : ClassMap<Address>
{
  public AddressMappings()
  {
    Id(a => a.Id).GeneratedBy.HiLo("1000");
    Map(a => a.AddressLine1);
    Map(a => a.AddressLine2);
    Map(a => a.City);
    Map(a => a.Postcode);
    Map(a => a.Country);
    References(a => a.Employee);
  }
}
```

Again, most of the things are same. Many-to-one association to the `Employee` class is mapped using the method `References`. If you ignore the unusual choice of name to represent many-to-one association, the mapping is quite succinct.

We have covered most of the mappings in our domain model, except for inheritance mappings which we would cover next.

Inheritance mappings

FNH supports all three ways of mapping classes inheriting from other entity. The only limitation is that you cannot mix different inheritance mapping strategies. Other than that, FNH offers quite a succinct and intuitive API for mapping inheritance.

Table per class hierarchy

By now, you know what "table per class hierarchy" means, hence I would directly show you the mapping code for this in FNH:

```
public class BenefitMappings : ClassMap<Benefit>
{
  public BenefitMappings()
  {
    Id(b => b.Id).GeneratedBy.HiLo("1000");
    Map(b => b.Name);
    Map(b => b.Description);
    References(b => b.Employee);
  }
}
```

```
public class LeaveMappings : SubclassMap<Leave>
{
  public LeaveMappings()
  {
    DiscriminatorValue("LVE");
    Map(l => l.AvailableEntitlement);
    Map(l => l.RemainingEntitlement);
    Map(l => l.Type);
  }
}


public class SeasonTicketLoanMappings : SubclassMap<SeasonTicketLoan>
{
  public SeasonTicketLoanMappings()
  {
    DiscriminatorValue("STL");
    Map(s => s.Amount);
    Map(s => s.MonthlyInstalment);
    Map(s => s.StartDate);
    Map(s => s.EndDate);
  }
}


public class SkillsEnhancementAllowanceMappings :
SubclassMap<SkillsEnhancementAllowance>
{
  public SkillsEnhancementAllowanceMappings()
  {
    DiscriminatorValue("SEA");
    Map(s => s.Entitlement);
    Map(s => s.RemainingEntitlement);
  }
}
```

There are two new things in the previous mappings:

- Mapping classes for the derived entities inherit from `SubclassMap<T>` instead of `ClassMap<T>`. That is how you tell FNH that you are mapping inheritance.

- Mappings of derived classes calls method `DiscriminatorValue()`. This serves two purposes. First, it tells FNH that this mapping should be a table per class hierarchy mapping, and second it tells what discriminator value NHibernate should use while mapping the class.

If you are thinking that this was simple then I can only advise you to keep reading.

Table per concrete class

In order to map a family of classes using the "table per concrete class" strategy, you need to do two things different from the "table per class hierarchy" strategy.

Remove the declaration of discriminator column from mappings of derived classes.

In the mapping of base class, tell FNH that this family of classes should be mapped using the "table per concrete class" strategy. The following code sample shows you how to do that.

If you remove the declaration of the discriminator column from mappings of derived classes then all you are left with is mapping of properties on the class itself. You have seen this code already in the "table per class hierarchy" strategy. To keep the text of the chapter brief, I will not present the mapping code for derived class. Following is how the Benefit class will be mapped:

```
public class BenefitMappings : ClassMap<Benefit>
{
  public BenefitMappings()
  {
    Id(b => b.Id).GeneratedBy.HiLo("1000");
    Map(b => b.Name);
    Map(b => b.Description);
    References(b => b.Employee);
    UseUnionSubclassForInheritanceMapping();
  }
}
```

Note the call to UseUnionSubclassForInheritanceMapping(). That is the only thing you need in order to tell FNH that this is a "table per concrete class" mapping.

If you are thinking that this was even simpler, then I can only tell you to keep reading.

Table per subclass

This is the most simple of the inheritance mappings in FNH. If you do not declare discriminator column and do not tell FNH to use the `union-subclass` mapping (or the "table per concrete class" strategy), then FNH by default maps as "table per subclass". So if I could omit the mapping of properties on our `Benefit` classes, then following is how a "table per subclass" mapping would look:

```
public class BenefitMappings : ClassMap<Benefit>
{
}


public class LeaveMappings : SubclassMap<Leave>
{
}


public class SeasonTicketLoanMappings : SubclassMap<SeasonTicketLoan>
{
}


public class SkillsEnhancementAllowanceMappings :
SubclassMap<SkillsEnhancementAllowance>
{
}
```

I don't think it can get any simpler than this.

Component mapping

Mapping components in FNH is similar to one in mapping by code. FNH has a method named `Component`, which like mapping by code takes two parameters. First one is lambda expression to property being mapped. Second is a delegate accepting parameter of type `ComponentPart<T>` where T is of component class type. For our domain model, it would be `ComponentPart<Address>`. Following is FNH's component mapping for the `ResidentailAddress` property on the `Employee` class:

```
Component(e => e.ResidentialAddress,
            mapper =>
            {
            mapper.Map(a => a.AddressLine1);
            mapper.Map(a => a.AddressLine2);
            mapper.Map(a => a.City);
            mapper.Map(a => a.Postcode);
            mapper.Map(a => a.Country);
            });
```

This code is exactly same as it's mapping by code counterpart.

We have finished fluent mappings unbelievably faster. That is the nature of it. As with XML mappings, we have only scratched the surface of fluent mappings. For now, I have to pause and reflect on all three mechanisms we have learned.

Choosing the right mapping method

Knowing more than one way of declaring NHibernate mapping may sound good but it may also be confusing. It is important to have knowledge of different methods of mapping but it is equally important to be able to choose the right method that best fits the bill, given a particular job. So how do you go about choosing the right mapping method?

If I am working on a green-field project, then my default stand is to use FNH. This is mainly because there is no legacy database or legacy domain model that I need to work with. So basically, I get all the freedom to define the best domain model that suits my business requirements and then use NHibernate and FNH to drive the design of database from there. This works quite nicely though FNH lacks few mapping features. FNH is most effective when used with auto-mapping feature on. In this mode, I do not have to declare any mapping and FNH would intelligently decide the best mapping for me looking at the domain model. I have worked in teams where there are rules around designing databases. So auto-mapping may not work there. In that case, I would either use FNH conventions to tweak the mappings that FNH generates automatically or resort to FNH's explicitly declared mapping. No matter which route I take, I always find myself most productive with FNH.

But there are times when FNH may not be the ideal solution. One situation that readily comes to my mind is when you are dealing with a legacy domain model and you need to map private/protected fields/properties. While FNH has ways of mapping private/protected fields/properties, it is not the most elegant. I can go down a non-elegant route if I have handful of such properties but for a large number of these, I would probably stick to XML.

XML has the biggest advantage that it supports every mapping feature that NHibernate has. But it is usually difficult to know from the beginning of the project whether you would need those features or not. Still, it is useful to understand XML mappings as I have stated earlier. Knowledge of XML mappings has benefited me immensely in situations when I had mapping defects in my projects. Knowledge of XML mappings has also benefited me in understanding more clearly how NHibernate mappings work.

Lastly, mapping by code – It is wise of NHibernate team to implement a code alternative to XML. If I was not able to use FNH for any reason, I would use mapping by code after considering two things. One, mapping by code cannot map private/ protected fields/properties. Second, mapping by code is freshly baked and may fall short of a finished product, so I would be wary of deploying it to production.

There you go! I have not answered the question for you but I have given you enough parameters to consider when choosing the right mapping method.

Summary

We have come to the end of an exhaustive chapter. NHibernate mapping is a vast topic. Especially if you are new to NHibernate or any ORM, you would find it challenging to remember and use all mappings effectively. What I have tried in this chapter is to present you with absolute minimum of NHibernate mappings that you need to know in order to hit the ground running. I hope that this chapter took the hardest part of the challenge away for you. You should now have a fair idea of how to map a simple domain model to an appropriate database schema. You may not feel very confident about NHibernate just yet and that is all but natural. This chapter and the next one are meant to introduce you to theoretical building blocks that are necessary before we get into interesting parts of NHibernate. In the next chapter, we would look at how to configure NHibernate which is another essential building block of NHibernate. As with mapping, NHibernate configuration is versatile and comes with lot of defaults that make our lives easier but knowing all the knobs makes you ready for those moments when you are just not able to get to the root of that annoying bug in your data access layer. Once you master the mappings and configuration, you are ready to conquer the world of data access using NHibernate.

When you download source code of this chapter, then you will find that the code for unit tests is not exactly the same as the one presented here. That is mainly because I had to refactor the unit tests as we progressed through the chapter in order to accommodate for the new concepts we were learning. I also used some advanced NUnit features so that some unit tests could be run multiple times for different mapping methods.

4

NHibernate Warm-up

After mappings, configuration is another important concept we should learn before we start using NHibernate for storing/retrieving data from database. In this chapter, we would unfold the knowledge of NHibernate configuration.

We will begin with NHibernate configuration that we had briefly looked at in *Chapter 2, Let's Build a Simple Application*, when we wrote our first unit test. I had asked you to ignore that piece of code then. Well, we will look in detail now what exactly that code did for us. After this elaboration has enlightened us of NHibernate configuration, we will look at different ways in which NHibernate can be configured. That will be followed by important and commonly used configuration options that we, as a developer, should be aware of. Towards the end of the chapter, we will look at a feature offered by NHibernate that is capable of generating database creation/ update scripts by inspecting the mappings declared.

There are no unit tests that we would write for the code in this chapter. This is partly because we were using a bit of configuration already in *Chapter 2, Let's Build a Simple Application*, which is tested through the unit tests we wrote there. Besides that, NHibernate configuration is not our application logic and hence there is no point in writing and maintaining unit tests for it.

Warming up NHibernate succinctly

Following is a piece of code from the previous chapter that I had asked you to ignore then:

```
using System;
using NHibernate;
using NHibernate.Cfg;
using NHibernate.Dialect;
using NHibernate.Driver;
```

```
using NHibernate.Tool.hbm2ddl;
using Environment = NHibernate.Cfg.Environment;

namespace Tests.Unit
{
  public class InMemoryDatabaseForXmlMappings : IDisposable
  {
    protected Configuration config;
    protected ISessionFactory sessionFactory;
    public ISession Session;
    public InMemoryDatabaseForXmlMappings()
    {
      config = new Configuration()
      .SetProperty(Environment.ReleaseConnections, "on_close")
      .SetProperty(Environment.Dialect, typeof
      (SQLiteDialect).AssemblyQualifiedName)
      .SetProperty(Environment.ConnectionDriver, typeof
      (SQLite20Driver).AssemblyQualifiedName)
      .SetProperty(Environment.ConnectionString, "data
      source=:memory:")
      .AddFile("Mappings/Xml/Employee.hbm.xml");

      sessionFactory = config.BuildSessionFactory();

      Session = sessionFactory.OpenSession();

      new SchemaExport(config).Execute(
      useStdOut:true,
      execute:true,
      justDrop:false,
      connection:session.Connection,
      exportOutput:Console.Out);
    }


    public void Dispose()
    {
      Session.Dispose();
      sessionFactory.Dispose();

    }
  }
}
```

I had told you that the preceding code is giving us an in-memory database that we could use to run unit tests. We will dissect this code now. This code collectively summarizes what we are going to learn in this chapter. Ignoring the usual class declaration and implementation of IDisposable, let's jump straight into the constructor of the preceding class:

```
config = new Configuration()
```

The preceding line creates an instance of the Configuration class. All NHibernate settings are configured via this class.

```
.SetProperty(Environment.Dialect, typeof(SQLiteDialect).
AssemblyQualifiedName)
```

Here you call the SetProperty method on configuration object to set various properties of your configuration. In this particular line, we are setting a property called Dialect. Dialect tells NHibernate what database technology the underlying database belongs to; for example, MS SQL Server 2008 R2, Oracle 10g, and so on. In a later section of this chapter, we will look at Dialect in detail along with other important properties that can be set via configuration object. Other properties that are set in the previous example are database driver, connection string, and connection release mode. Database driver, as the name suggests, tells NHibernate which database driver library it should use to communicate with the database. Connection string is well known – it is address of the database. Connection release mode defines when the acquired ADO.NET connection should be released. We have declared it to be on_close which means release the connection after the session is closed. Again, all these properties are discussed in detail later in this chapter. Let's move on to the next line of code:

```
.AddFile("Mappings/Xml/Employee.hbm.xml");
```

This preceding line tells the configuration object that it should use mappings declared in Employee.hbm.xml. Again, there are several ways we can tell configuration to use different mappings. Here, we are seeing one that is most simple. We will soon learn other ways. At this point, minimal configuration required to interact with database is complete. In order to start interacting with database, we first need to build a session factory. Next line of code does exactly that:

```
sessionFactory = config.BuildSessionFactory();
```

sessionFactory lets us create an instance of the ISession object by invoking the OpenSession method as we can see in the next line of code:

```
Session = sessionFactory.OpenSession();
```

`Session` is one object that you would be using most widely while working with NH. This object seamlessly manages database interaction while you keep saving/ retrieving entities using various methods offered by it. In the next line of code, we use the configuration object and session object to build an instance of a special class named `SchemaExport`:

```
new SchemaExport(config).Execute(
  useStdOut:true,
  execute:true,
  justDrop:false,
  connection:session.Connection,
  exportOutput:Console.Out);
```

The `SchemaExport` class uses mappings and settings from configuration to generate database creation scripts in accordance with the declared mappings. It can optionally run these scripts against the database specified in configuration via connection string. We will look at this aspect in detail towards the end of this chapter.

This brings us to the end of succinctly warming up NH. Rest of the chapter elaborates in more detail what we just covered briefly. Besides examining configuration options available to developers, we will also learn about different ways of configuring NH. We will start with a dive into session architecture of NHibernate next.

The NHibernate session architecture

We looked at configuration, `sessionFactory`, and `session` among other things in the previous section. These three components encapsulate most of the functionality offered by NH. I do not mean this in literal sense. If you look at NHibernate source code, you will see that a lot of NHibernate features are implemented independently of these components. But these components are gateways into using these features.

Following diagram shows how these three relate to each other:

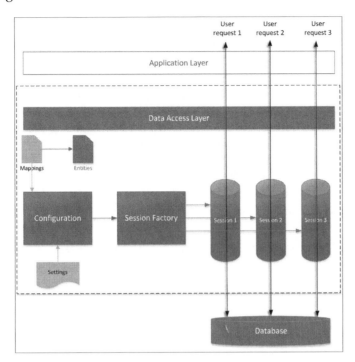

The preceding diagram represents components of a real life application. Layers above **Data Access Layer** are represented in an abstract way, combining everything into one layer. In **Data Access Layer**, you have got **Configuration** as one of the components. **Configuration** knows about mappings available in **Data Access Layer**. It also knows about lot of other details that are used either during warming up NHibernate or interacting with **Database**.

As we have seen earlier, calling the BuildSessionFactory method on the configuration object gives us a sessionFactory. Session factory, as the name suggests is factory of session objects. But more than that, **Session Factory** is an abstraction of the underlying database of your application. It knows everything about the underlying database and can open new sessions which can be used to perform operations against database. If your application needs to connect to more than one database then you should use more than one instance of session factory, one each for every database. Building a session factory is an involved operation and usually takes time. It is recommended that you create no more than one instance of session factory per database that your application connects to. Session factory once created, has no knowledge of configuration object. If you change any configuration options then the session factory has to be rebuilt, if changed configuration options are to be considered.

Session factory generates sessions on request. Any interaction with the database that you need to do needs to be done against session. Session is your gateway into databases. Session object comes loaded with multitude of APIs that you can use to store and retrieve data from database. *Chapter 5, Let's Store Some Data into the Database* and *Chapter 6, Let's Retrieve Some Data from the Database* will primarily deal with these aspects in detail so we will not talk much about them in this chapter. We have seen in the beginning of this chapter that you can call the OpenSession method on session factory to get a new instance of session object. That is just one of the ways that you can get hold of a session. Session factory has few overrides of the OpenSession method along with some other methods that you can use to get hold of session. This makes it possible to open session in a variety of different ways, for a variety of different situations. We would examine some of the important ways of obtaining the session object in this section.

This is not complete NHibernate architecture. The preceding diagram only depicts what we are going to learn in this chapter. As we dig deeper, we will keep on building this diagram to get a more complete picture of NHibernate architecture.

The code we walked through at the beginning of this chapter achieved configuration all through code. This is called programmatic configuration. NHibernate traditionally has offered configuration through XML as well. And if you are using FNH then it offers its own API for configuration of NHibernate fluently. We are not going to use XML configuration in this book but I do want to cover it briefly for the sake of completeness. Next, we will look at XML, loquacious and fluent configuration briefly before we go into details of important configuration options.

XML configuration

XML configuration, such as XML mapping is the first and original method of configuring NH. In this method, all configuration options are declared through XML elements inside either application configuration file or a separate file having extension .cfg.xml. A config section that is handled by NHibernate.Cfg. ConfigurationSectionHandler needs to be added to application configuration for NHibernate configuration to be processed successfully. All configuration options we discussed at the beginning of the chapter are declared using XML as follows:

```
<configuration>
  <configSections>
    <section name="hibernate-configuration"
    type="NHibernate.Cfg.ConfigurationSectionHandler,NHibernate"/>
  </configSections>
```

```xml
<hibernate-configuration xmlns="urn:nhibernate-configuration-
2.2">
  <session-factory>
    <property
name="dialect">NHibernate.Dialect.SQLiteDialect</property>
    <property name="connection.provider">
NHibernate.Connection.DriverConnectionProvider</property>
    <property
name="connection.driver_class">NHibernate.Driver.SQLite20Driver</
property>
    <property name="connection.connection_string">Data
Source=:memory: </property>
    <property name="show_sql">true</property>
    <mapping resource="Persistence.Mappings.Xml.Employee.hbm.xml"
assembly="Persistence"/>
    <mapping resource="Persistence.Mappings.Xml.Address.hbm.xml"
assembly="Persistence"/>
    <mapping resource="Persistence.Mappings.Xml.Benefit.subclass.
hbm.xml" assembly="Persistence"/>
    <mapping resource="Persistence.Mappings.Xml.Community.hbm.xml"
assembly="Persistence"/>
  </session-factory>
 </hibernate-configuration>
</configuration>
```

XML configuration is not very difficult to understand. For starters, you need to define a `config` section named `hibernate-configuration`. Next to that, you have got actual declaration of `hibernate-configuration` as top level XML element. Inside this element, you have got the `session-factory` element. It is inside this element that all options are configured. As you can see, there are mainly two types of options configured here. One is a set of properties configured using the `property` element. Second is mappings configured using the `mapping` element.

There is a `name` attribute on the `property` element which is used to declare name of the property. The value inside the element is value of the property.

Mappings need a `resource` and `assembly` declared. Assembly is obvious. Resource is a fully qualified name of the XML mapping file. Fully qualified name works like as namespace for classes. In our case, the XML mapping files are in the `Persistence` project in folder `Mappings/Xml`, hence the fully qualified name would be `Persistence.Mappings.Xml.<mapping file name>`.

After XML configuration is declared in application configuration file, NHibernate needs to be told about it. You do this by executing the following lines of code from a convenient place in your application:

```
var config = new Configuration();
config.Configure();
```

By now, you know that configuration object needs to be initialized only once. So make sure you execute the preceding code such that no multiple instances of configuration objects are created. This can be achieved by placing the preceding code in static constructor of a helper class or inside a singleton instance of a class.

As with XML mappings, XML configuration has lived its age in a way. With success of FNH and large number of enhancements being made to programmatic configuration recently, more and more people seem inclined towards using programmatic configuration or fluent configuration. I have covered XML configuration for the sake of completeness here but we will not be using it in rest of the book. We will mostly be using either programmatic or fluent configuration. Having said that, let me also tell you that you can combine XML based configuration with the programmatic configuration if you want. Part of configuration that needs to change from time to time can be kept in XML - while the part that does not change can be configured programmatically. If you want to use programmatic configuration completely then you can keep the changing parts under `appSettings` inside `web.config` in case of a web application. Similar option is available for desktop or WPF application.

Programmatic configuration

The code we walked through at the beginning of the chapter is an example of programmatic configuration. We have covered it in enough detail already so we will move straight to loquacious configuration.

Loquacious configuration

Loquacious configuration is the latest addition to the family of configuration options that NHibernate comes bundled with and it is the best option so far. Loquacious offers a code based and easy to infer API for configuring NHibernate. Parts of the API are also fluent which makes it less verbose to work with. Loquacious API is built by extending the programmatic configuration API and hence can be called a part of programmatic configuration. Without much ado, let's jump straight into the code:

```
public class LoquaciousConfiguration
{
  private readonly ISession session;
```

```
public LoquaciousConfiguration()
{
  var config = new Configuration();
  config.DataBaseIntegration(db =>
  {
    db.Dialect<SQLiteDialect>();
    db.Driver<SQLite20Driver>();
    db.ConnectionString = "data source=:memory:";
    db.ConnectionReleaseMode =
    ConnectionReleaseMode.OnClose;
    db.LogSqlInConsole = true;
    db.LogFormattedSql = true;
  })
  .AddMapping(GetMappings());

  var sessionFactory = config.BuildSessionFactory();
  session = sessionFactory.OpenSession();

  using (var tx = session.BeginTransaction())
  {
    new SchemaExport(config).Execute(
    new SchemaExport(config).Execute(
                                        useStdOut:true,
                                        execute:true,
                                        justDrop:false,
                                        connection:session.
Connection,
                                        exportOutput:Console.Out);
                                        tx.Commit();

  }
  session.Clear();
}

private HbmMapping GetMappings()
{
  var mapper = new ModelMapper();
  mapper.AddMapping<EmployeeMappings>();
  mapper.AddMapping<AddressMappings>();
  mapper.AddMapping<BenefitMappings>();
  mapper.AddMapping<LeaveMappings>();
  mapper.AddMapping<SkillsEnhancementAllowanceMappings>();
  mapper.AddMapping<SeasonTicketLoanMappings>();
  mapper.AddMapping<CommunityMappings>();
  return
  mapper.CompileMappingForAllExplicitlyAddedEntities();
```

```
    }

    public ISession Session
    {
      get { return session; }
    }
  }
}
```

Similar to programmatic configuration, we first create an instance of the
Configuration class. After that point, we use extension methods named
DatabaseIntegration to configure various properties including database dialect,
driver, connection string, and so on. You can notice that configuration of dialect
and driver has been made easy by making their types as generic parameters to each
methods. This works really nicely if you are using tools such as ReSharper. In the
same way, other properties such as connection.release_mode, show_sql, format_
sql, and so on, are wrapped inside easy to use and typed properties.

The part where we add mappings is almost same as programmatic configuration. We
have moved the ModelMapper code into a separate method GetMappings in order to
make the code more readable. Otherwise, it is exactly the same code we have used
earlier with programmatic configuration. Rest of the part to build session factory and
use of SchemaExport to build the database schema into SQLite in-memory database
is exactly same as the earlier examples.

Fluent configuration

If you are using FNH for declaring mappings, then loquacious configuration is not
an option. This is mainly because loquacious configuration would not be able to
recognize fluent mappings. Besides that, FNH offers its own fluent API to configure
session factory. The fluent API is more or less similar to loquacious API in terms
of functionality offered. But fluent API tries to be less verbose as compared to
loquacious. Let's do the same configuration we did using loquacious configuration,
but using fluent API this time:

```
var fluentConfig = Fluently.Configure()
.Database(SQLiteConfiguration.Standard.InMemory()
                          .ShowSql().FormatSql())
.Mappings(mapper =>
{
  mapper.FluentMappings.Add<EmployeeMappings>();
  mapper.FluentMappings
   .Add<CommunityMappings>();
  mapper.FluentMappings.Add<BenefitMappings>();
  mapper.FluentMappings.Add<LeaveMappings>();
```

```
    mapper.FluentMappings.Add<SkillsEnhancementAllowanceMappings>();
    mapper.FluentMappings.Add<SeasonTicketLoanMappings>();
    mapper.FluentMappings.Add<AddressMappings>();
});

var nhConfiguration = fluentConfig.BuildConfiguration();
var sessionFactory = nhConfiguration.BuildSessionFactory();
session = sessionFactory.OpenSession();
using (var tx = session.BeginTransaction())
{
    new SchemaExport(nhConfiguration)
    .Execute(useStdOut:true,
             execute:true,
             justDrop:false,
             connection:session.Connection,
             exportOutput:Console.Out);
    tx.Commit();
}
```

Let's take a look at important lines from the preceding code snippet:

- At the root of the fluent configuration API is a static class named `Fluently`. Calling a method named `Configure()` on this class gives us an instance of the `FluentConfiguration` class. This class exposes methods that you can use to configure NH.

- First method we call is `Database`. Here, you specify dialect using a set of helper classes that FNH has provided. In the preceding example, we have used helper class named `SQLiteConfiguration`. This class has a property named `Standard` for usual declaration of SQLite dialect. In the *Dialect* section ahead, we will look at other available helper classes in detail.

- Along with database configuration, we also enabled the `show_sql` and `format_sql` options by calling the `ShowSql` and `FormatSql` methods respective. Note how we can easily just chain the methods.

- We then called the `Mappings` method to add fluent mappings to configuration. Here, we added individual mappings explicitly. In the *Mappings* section ahead, we will look at this in detail with other options of adding mappings.

- At this point the fluent configuration object is ready to be used. If we need to access the underlying NHibernate configuration object then we can call the `BuildConfiguration` method on the fluent configuration object as we have done previously. We need the NHibernate configuration object to use with the `SchemaExport` class. If there is no need for the underlying NHibernate configuration, then you can call the `BuildSessionFactory` method directly on the fluent configuration object.

By calling `BuildConfiguration`, we get access to NHibernate configuration object after it is built, but if we need to access it before it is built then a method named `ExposeConfiguration` is available. This method is useful if you want to set some property on configuration that is not directly supported by Fluent API. Following short example shows how to use this method to set `command_timeout` value:

```
var fluentConfig = Fluently.Configure()
.Database(SQLiteConfiguration.Standard.InMemory())
.ExposeConfiguration(cfg =>
{
  cfg.SetProperty(Environment.CommandTimeout, "30");
});
```

That is it really about the preceding code. Rest of the code to deal with building session factory, opening session, and generating database creation scripts is no different than what we have seen earlier.

Configuration options

During code examples so far, we have seen various configuration options or properties such as dialect, driver, connection provider, and so on being set. In this section, we will try to know more about what these options mean, what are the different possible values that these options take, and what do we get out of these options. NHibernate has several such options available. In this section, we are going to look at some of the important and commonly used ones.

Connection release mode

One of the things we learned in the previous chapters about session is that it opens an ADO.NET connection to the database when it needs to connect to database for the first time. But when is this connection closed? That is what connection release mode defines. There are two connection release modes, described as follows:

- `OnClose`: This is a legacy of the first version of NHibernate where an ADO. NET connection acquired by a session was closed when the session was closed or disposed

- `AfterTransaction`: Connection is released when the NHibernate transaction associated with that connection is finished (either committed or rolled back)

In the coming chapters, we will talk more about NHibernate transactions where it would be clearer for you to understand where exactly the second connection release mode fits in the grand scheme of things. For now, remember that there are two supported connection release modes.

Connection release mode is configured on session factory. There are three configuration options available, two corresponding to the two modes discussed previously and a third and default option of `auto` that uses `AfterTransaction` as the connection release mode. It is recommended to use the default setting.

> There are two ways that session gets hold of an ADO.NET connection. A connection can be acquired via configured `IConnectionProvider`. This is transparent to our code and session object handles this internally for us. On the other hand, we can build our own ADO.NET connection and pass it to session object. Connection release mode is only relevant for the former types of connections.

Dialect

Dialect refers to the type of database, for example, SQL Server 2008, Oracle, MySQL, and so on. NHibernate needs to know which type of database your application interacts with. Declaring dialect serves two purposes. One, NHibernate knows which platform dependent features to enable or disable based on underlying database technology. Second, NHibernate is able to generate correct set of SQL statements for a given database technology. Though SQL is a language understood by most databases, there are subtle differences between implementations of SQL by each database. NHibernate offers you one way to interact with database no matter which database you are connecting to. NHibernate is able to do this because it knows how to generate correct SQL based on dialect information you provided during configuration. Every dialect that NHibernate supports is implemented as a class that inherits from `NHibenate.Dialect.Dialect`. For instance, dialect for SQL Server 2012 is implemented in the class `NHibernate.Dialect.Sql2012Dialect`.

Dialect is configured as one of the properties by calling the `SetProperty` method on configuration object as can be seen in the following code snippet:

```
var config=newConfiguration();
config.SetProperty(Environment.Dialect,
typeof(Sql2012Dialect).AssemblyQualifiedName)
```

FNH has made dialect declaration slightly easier by aggregating related database technologies under one helper class. This helper class has static properties on it for specific databases. For instance, all MS SQL Server versions are available under helper class `FluentNHibernate.Cfg.Db.MsSqlConfiguration`. This class has static properties to then choose versions 2000, 2005, 2008 R2, and so on. of MS SQL Server. To declare dialect, you can use method `Database()` that is available on the `FluentConfiguration` class. Following is how you can configure MS SQL Server 2012 database:

```
Fluently.Configure()
.Database(MsSqlConfiguration.MsSql2012)
.ConnectionString(c=>
     c.FromConnectionStringWithKey("EmployeeBenefits")))
```

For every supported database, NHibernate has a dialect defined. Following table lists the major supported dialects along with information about which database the dialect refers to, and any other important information you should know of:

Dialect class	FNH equivalent	Database technology
DB2Dialect	DB2Configuration. Standard	DB2
FirebirdDialect	FirebirdConfiguration	Firebird
InformixDialect		Informix database. Works only with OdbcDriver.
Ingres9Dialect	IngressConfiguration. Standard (Only supportsIngressDialect)	Ingres SQL. IngresDialect is available for older versions.
MsSql2012Dialect	MsSqlConfiguration. MsSql7 MsSqlConfiguration. MsSql2000 MsSqlConfiguration. MsSql2005 MsSqlConfiguration. MsSql2008 MsSqlConfiguration. MsSql2012	MS SQL Server 2012. Following dialects are available for other versions – MsSql2008Dialect, MsSql2005 Dialect, MsSql2000Dialect, MsSql7Dialect.

Dialect class	FNH equivalent	Database technology
MsSqlCeDialect	MsSqlCeConfiguration. Standard MsSqlCeConfiguration. MsSqlCe40	SQL CE.
MySQLDialect	MySQLConfiguration. Standard	MySQL
Oracle10gDialect	OracleConfiguration. Oracle8 OracleConfiguration. Oracle9 OracleConfiguration. Oracle10	Oracle 10g. Following dialects are available for other versions – Oracle9iDialect, Oracle8iDialect.
PostgreSQLDialect	PostgreSQLConfiguration. Standard PostgreSQLConfiguration. PostgreSQL81 PostgreSQLConfiguration. PostgreSQL82	PostgresSQL. Other available dialects are - PostgreSQL81Dialect, PostgreSQL82Dialect.
SQLiteDialect	SQLiteConfiguration. Standard SQLiteConfiguration. InMemory SQLiteConfiguration. UsingFile SQLiteConfiguration. UsingFileWithPassword	SQLite.
SybaseSQLAnywhere12 Dialect		Sybase SQL Anywhere 12. Following dialects are available for other versions - SybaseSQLAnywhere11 Dialect, SybaseSQLAnywhere10 Dialect, SybaseASE15Dialect, SybaseASA9Dialect.
MsSqlAzure2008 Dialect		SQL Azure.
OracleLite		Oracle Lite.

Driver

Every database technology is different and so are the libraries that allow you to connect to and interact with databases. A database driver is client library that lets you connect to database, send SQL commands, and receive results of executing the SQL commands on database server. While most databases have one preferred driver library available, there are cases where a particular database technology has more than one driver library in use. Moreover, some database technologies support more than one protocol of interacting with database server, for instance, SQL Server supports a native protocol along with OLE DB and ODBC protocols. So, you need to tell NHibernate which database driver you want to use in order to connect to database. Similar to dialect, NHibernate implements a class for each driver that it supports. A class implementing a driver support inherits from `NHibernate.Driver.DriverBase`.

Driver configuration is exactly the same as dialect configuration. SQL Server 2012 uses SQL client driver whose implementation is in class `SqlClientDriver`. Following is how the driver configuration will be done:

```
varconfig=newNHibernate.Cfg.Configuration()
.SetProperty(Environment.ConnectionDriver,
        typeof(SqlClientDriver).AssemblyQualifiedName)
```

If dialect is known then it is easier to make an assumption about the default driver that can be used. NHibernate does exactly that. For every supported dialect, NHibernate sets the default driver so that you do not have to worry about setting it up yourself. You only use the preceding code when you know that you want to use a specific driver. In case of any MS SQL Server version, NHibernate uses `SqlClientDriver`. Finding out default driver that FNH assumes for different database technologies is something I will leave to curious readers to explore.

Mappings

We covered mappings in *Chapter 3, Let's tell NHibernate about our database*, and we know why mappings exist. Mappings would be of no use if NHibernate does not know about mappings that exist in our application. Hence, mappings are an important configuration option. As with other options, you can configure mappings through XML, programmatically, or fluently. But even within each method, you have got multiple ways of configuring mappings.

If you remember from *Chapter 3, Let's Tell NHibernate About Our Database*, there are three types of mappings, namely XML mappings, mappings by code, and fluent mappings. XML configuration can only map XML mappings. Programmatic configuration is able to map both mapping by code and XML mapping. Fluent configuration is capable of mapping all three types of mappings. Moreover, there are multiple ways of configuring a particular mapping configuration. For instance, you can configure individual mapping files/classes one by one or you can ask configuration system to scan an assembly and configure all the mapping files/classes found in that assembly. In this chapter we are only going to look at a representative examples but do explore other options as well.

Programmatic configuration

With programmatic configuration, it is possible to configure both XML mapping files and mapping by code classes. In this section, we will quickly walk through how to do both.

XML mapping

NHibernate supports several different ways of configuring XML mapping files. You can declare the mapping in XML files have NHibernate load XML files directly or you could embed them as resources and load the mapping files from the assembly. You could even load the XML files yourselves into `XmlDocument` and pass it to NHibernate. We will look at how to configure individual XML files and mapping files embedded resources. To configure individual XML mapping files, you can call the `AddFile` method available on configuration object, as shown next:

```
config.AddFile("Mappings/Xml/Community.hbm.xml");
```

There are several versions of the `AddXXX` method available on configuration object. You can configure mappings by specifying directory in which XML files can be found, by the `FileInfo` object pointing to XML mapping file, by stream for XML mapping file, or even by URL on which XML mapping file can be found. It is out of scope for this book to discuss each of these methods so readers are encouraged to explore these on their own.

If you want to add all XML mapping files embedded as a resource into the assembly then you can use the `AddAssembly` method. In our case, all XML mapping files are in the `Persistence` assembly so you can call the `AddAssembly` method as follows:

```
config.AddAssembly("Persistence");
```

NHibernate will scan the `Persistence` assembly to look for embedded resources whose names end with `.hbm.xml` and load the mappings from those resources.

Mapping by code

Classes containing mappings by code need to be added to an instance of class `NHibernate.Mapping.ByCode.ModelMapper` before they can be passed to configuration object. `ModelMapper` compiles the mapping classes into `HbmMapping` which is a special type that holds the mapping information. Compiled `HbmMappings` are then added to configuration. Following piece of code shows how to compile mapping classes to `HbmMappings` and add them to configuration object:

```
varmodelMapper=newModelMapper();
modelMapper.AddMapping<EmployeeMappings>();
modelMapper.AddMapping<AddressMappings>();
modelMapper.AddMapping<BenefitMappings>();
modelMapper.AddMapping<LeaveMappings>();
modelMapper.AddMapping<SkillsEnhancementAllowanceMappings>();
modelMapper.AddMapping<SeasonTicketLoanMappings>();
modelMapper.AddMapping<CommunityMappings>();
config.AddMapping(modelMapper.
CompileMappingForAllExplicitlyAddedEntities());
```

If you want to add all mapping classes from an assembly then you will need to use the `AddMappings` method on the `ModelMapper` class, as shown in the following code snippet:

```
var modelMapper=new ModelMapper();
modelMapper.AddMappings(typeof(EmployeeMappings).Assembly.GetTypes());
config.AddMapping(modelMapper.
CompileMappingForAllExplicitlyAddedEntities());
```

Note the use of the `EmployeeMappings` class to get to the assembly containing all the mappings. Call to `GetTypes()` on `Assembly` would return all publically defined types inside that assembly. `ModelMapper` would then internally filter anything that is a "mapping by code" class (a class that inherits from `ClassMapping<T>`) and add it to configuration.

Fluent configuration

FNH is capable of configuring hbm mappings along with fluent mappings. But if you are using FNH then it is highly unlikely that you would be using mapping by code. So, we will skip configuration of hbm mappings and jump directly to fluent mappings.

The `FluentConfiguration` object of FNH has a method named
`Mappings` which is used for configuring mappings. This method accepts
`Action<MappingConfiguration>` as its parameter. `MappingConfiguration` objects
offers methods that can be used to configure individual fluent mapping classes or
scan an assembly to add all fluent mappings from the assembly. In the following code
snippet, all fluent mappings from our `Persistence` assembly are added individually:

```
var config = Fluently.Configure()
.Mappings(mapper=>
{
  mapper.FluentMappings.Add<EmployeeMappings>();
  mapper.FluentMappings.Add<CommunityMappings>();
  mapper.FluentMappings.Add<BenefitMappings>();
  mapper.FluentMappings.Add<LeaveMappings>();
  mapper.FluentMappings.Add<SkillsEnhancementAllowanceMappings>();
  mapper.FluentMappings.Add<SeasonTicketLoanMappings>();
  mapper.FluentMappings.Add<AddressMappings>();
})
```

Call to `Fluently.Configure()` gives us an instance of the `FluentConfiguration`
object. On this object, we have called the `Mapping` method to which a parameter
named `mapper` of type `MappingConfiguration` is passed. `MappingConfiguration`
has a property `FluentMappings` to which we can add classes containing fluent
mappings. For Hbm mappings, this class has another property named `HbmMappings`
to which you can add all your mappings by code.

If you want to add all mapping classes from an assembly, then the `FluentMappings`
property has another method named `AddFromAssemblyOf<T>` where `T` is type of any
one fluent mapping class.

```
var config = Fluently.Configure()
.Mappings(mapper=>
{
  mapper.FluentMappings.AddFromAssemblyOf<EmployeeMappings>();
});
```

Connection string

Think of the connection string as address of your database instance. NHibernate
needs to know connection string in order to connect to the database successfully.
Connection strings are written in different formats for different database technologies
but in a nutshell, it is just a string. Similar to dialect and driver, connection string
is configured as a property. We have already looked at how connection string is
configured so I will try to keep myself brief here by not repeating code examples.

If you have declared connection string in application configuration file of your application under the `connectionStrings` node, then you can also use the name of the connection string to configure NHibernate programmatically, as shown next:

```
var config = Fluently.Configure()
.Database(MsSqlConfiguration
.MsSql2012
.ConnectionString(c =>
c.FromConnectionStringWithKey("EmployeeBenefits")));
```

If you are not sure how to write connection string for your database, then check out www.connectionstrings.com. This website has collection of all possible connection string formats for all databases that exist.

Caching

NHibernate can cache the entities it loaded from database into memory or in a second level cache, such as ASP.NET cache. There are three types of caches available–first level cache, second level cache, and query cache.

First level cache is held within session object and managed by session for you. This is turned on by default and you cannot turn it off. All entities that a session loads can be kept in cache till the session is open. If application requests the same entity again, NHibernate returns it from first level cache.

Second level cache has a wider scope than one session. Entities added to second level cache can be accessed by any session. Use of second level cache needs a thorough thinking and design because of the complex nature of this caching strategy. Though caching enhances performance, use of second level cache should be considered a last resort after you have investigated every other area of your data access layer to improve performance. Moreover, it is only master or lookup data that should be cached because it changes less frequently.

If your application runs a query with same inputs multiple times then you can turn on query caching for that particular query. For the first time, results for the query will be fetched from database but subsequent executions of that query would return from cache. If any entity in the result set of that query changes, then that result set in invalidated and next time the query hits the database.

There is more to caching than this. NHibernate lets you declare different read/write strategies for entities that can be cached. This complicates the system at runtime but knowledge of this is very useful when you are trying to optimize the performance of data access layer using caching. We would cover caching in more detail in *Chapter 11, A Whirlwind Tour of Other NHibernate Features* where some of the occasionally used features are explained.

Session context

Every time you need to interact with a database, you need to get hold of a session object. Technically speaking, you can use a single session object for all your database interactions. However, that would lead to subtle defects since multiple threads would be accessing same session object which is not built to be thread safe. You might also have potential data inconsistency issues. Such usage of session is strongly discouraged. On the other hand, you can open a new session every time you need to interact with database. However, this would be too chatty and would have negative impact on performance. Moreover, you would not be able to use database transaction properly to maintain the integrity of data. What you need is something in the middle of these two options. NHibernate offers session context which can be used for precise control over when new sessions are opened and existing ones are closed. Depending on the runtime characteristics of your application, you can choose the right session context implementation. Following session contexts are available:

- `ThreadLocalSessionContext`
- `CallSessionContext`
- `ThreadStaticSessionContext`
- `WcfOperationSessionContext`
- `WebSessionContext`

We are not going to cover these in detail right now. In one of the upcoming chapters, we will see how the preceding session context implementations manage session for you and which one to use in which situation.

Batch size

As we will see in *Chapter 5, Let's Store Some Data into the Database*, NHibernate sends SQL statements to database server in batches to reduce the number of roundtrips to database. NHibernate will use its own heuristics to determine the right batch size. You can override that setting if needed, by setting the `batch_size` configuration option. Following is how batch size can be set using loquacious configuration:

```
var config = new Configuration();
config.DataBaseIntegration(db =>
{
  db.BatchSize = 20;
})
```

Command timeout

Command timeout setting is used to define time after which a SQL command execution should time out. Execution of a SQL command blocks an application thread. If SQL command execution takes a long time then the application thread keeps blocked thus starving other requests. This results in long wait queue of requests to be served leading to performance issues. An optimal value of command timeout helps alleviate such issues. Following code snippet shows how to override default command timeout setting using loquacious configuration:

```
var config = new Configuration();
config.DataBaseIntegration(db =>
{
  db.Timeout = 5;
})
```

Note that the timeout value is in seconds.

Show SQL

If you want to log to console those SQL statements that NHibernate sends to database, you can turn on the show_sql setting by setting its value to true. We have used this setting in *Chapter 3, Let's Tell NHibernate About Our Database*. I usually leave it on in the configuration used for unit tests. This makes it easy to investigate failing tests. While show_sql is helpful in seeing what SQL is actually generated behind the scenes, the formatting of the SQL is not great. If you want properly formatted SQL then another configuration option named format_sql can be used in conjunction. format_sql takes Boolean value and when set to true would format the generated SQL by inserting tab spaces and new lines to make it more readable. Following code snippet shows how to set both these properties using loquacious configuration:

```
var config = new Configuration();
config.DataBaseIntegration(db =>
{
  db.LogSqlInConsole = true;
  db.LogFormattedSql = true;
})
```

These options are simple mechanisms to see the SQL generated under the hood. If you want more detailed information about what is happening within NHibernate, then you could configure **log4net** which is a famous logging library for .NET. NHibernate has very good support for log4net and you can find an article describing configuration of log4net in the following *How to* article from official NHibernate website at `http://nhibernate.info/doc/howto/various/configure-log4net-for-use-with-nhibernate.html`.

We have covered most important and most commonly used configuration options. There are some more options available that can be useful in rare situations. Feel free to explore those on your own. Before we close this section, let's have a look at both programmatic and fluent configuration with all the previous options being configured.

Following is how programmatic configuration would look when all the previously discussed configuration options are specified. You should be familiar with most of this code by now:

```
var config = new NHibernate.Cfg.Configuration()
        .SetProperty(Environment.ReleaseConnections, "on_close")
        .SetProperty(Environment.Dialect, typeof(SQLiteDialect).
AssemblyQualifiedName)
        .SetProperty(Environment.ConnectionDriver,
typeof(SQLite20Driver).AssemblyQualifiedName)
        .SetProperty(Environment.ConnectionString, "data
source=:memory:")
        .SetProperty(Environment.ShowSql, "true")
        .SetProperty(Environment.UseQueryCache, "true")
        .SetProperty(Environment.CurrentSessionContextClass, typeof(T
hreadLocalSessionContext).AssemblyQualifiedName)
        .SetProperty(Environment.BatchSize, "20")
        .SetProperty(Environment.CommandTimeout,"30");
var modelMapper = new ModelMapper();
modelMapper.AddMappings(typeof(EmployeeMappings).Assembly.GetTypes());
config.AddMapping(modelMapper.
CompileMappingForAllExplicitlyAddedEntities());
var sessionFactory = config.BuildSessionFactory();
session = sessionFactory.OpenSession();
new SchemaExport(config).Execute(true,true,false,session.
Connection,Console.Out);
```

And following is how the same configuration would look when done fluently:

```
var config = Fluently.Configure()
            .Database(MsSqlConfiguration.MsSql2012
                    .ConnectionString(c=> c.FromConnectionStringWith
Key("EmployeeBenefits"))
                    .ShowSql()
            .AdoNetBatchSize(50))
            .CurrentSessionContext<ThreadLocalSessionContext>()
        .Mappings(mapper=>
                {
                    mapper.FluentMappings.AddFromAssemblyOf<EmployeeMa
ppings>();
                })
            .Cache(cacheBuilder=>
                {
                    cacheBuilder.UseQueryCache();
                    cacheBuilder.UseSecondLevelCache();
                    cacheBuilder.ProviderClass<HashtableCacheProvid
er>();
                })
            .ExposeConfiguration(cfg=>
                {
                    configuration = cfg;
                    cfg.SetProperty(Environment.CommandTimeout, "30");
                });
var sessionFactory = config.BuildSessionFactory();
session = sessionFactory.OpenSession();
new SchemaExport(configuration)
            .Execute(true,true,false,session.Connection,Console.Out);
```

Note that I have configured to use `HashTableCacheProvider` as cache provider. This is a default in-memory cache provider that NHibernate offers out of the box. This is not recommended for production use or for situations where you are putting huge amount of data in cache. The most common use of this cache provider is during unit tests. Also note, the use of `ThreadLocalSessionContext` a session context provider. This is again provided as an example but right session context must be chosen based on runtime characteristics of your application, for example, Web versus non-web, WCF, and so on.

Generating the database scripts from mappings

In the beginning, we looked at one use of the SchemaExport class where we used it to generate database creation scripts based on mappings declared. In this section, we would delve deeper into this to see what different options SchemaExport offers to generate database creation scripts. We are also going to look at another class named SchemaUpdate that can generate database update scripts by comparing changed mappings and existing database schema.

If you are working on a legacy project with an existing database then you would have little use of the SchemaExport class. Since you have already got a database in place, there is no need to generate a new database creation script. You may want to use SchemaUpdate to generate scripts to manage changes to domain model but exercise caution while doing so. Since the initial version of database is not created through SchemaExport, chances are that SchemaUpdate would not respect the semantics and rules that had gone into building the first version of the database. Thus the scripts you end up generating may not be compatible.

The database creation script

Earlier we used the Execute method on the SchemaExport class to generate and execute database creation script. The Execute method is quite involved and you do not have to use it for simple use cases. There is another method named Create available on the SchemaExport class which is simple to use. There are two overloads of the Create method but let's look at one that is generally more useful:

```
new SchemaExport(configuration).Create(Console.WriteLine, true);
```

Configuration object we created previously is passed into the constructor of the SchemaExport class. SchemaExport would inspect mappings that are added to the configuration object to generate database creation script. You can choose to run these scripts against the database instance configured by passing true as the second parameter. While you are doing this, make sure that a blank database with name passed in the configured connection string is present on the database server. This is not required for SQLite. Also make sure that the user connecting to database has permission to run create/modify tables.

If you are calling the preceding code from a console application then you can pass `Console.WriteLine` as the first parameter and that would print the script to console. This is useful when you just need to generate the database creation script to be deployed via other mechanisms. Make sure that you pass `false` as the second parameter if that is the case.

The `Create` method internally calls one of the many overloads of the `Execute` method. If you are happy with the control offered by the `Create` method then you do not need to go any further. But if you need more control over script generation process then feel free to explore other overloads of the `Create` and `Execute` method.

The database update scripts

Software changes all the time. New requirements come in or existing features change. Inevitably, you need to make changes to your domain model and subsequently to the database schema. The `SchemaUpdate` class of NHibernate makes the job of generating scripts to update database easier. All you need to do is make appropriate changes to your domain model, update the mappings, and then run the following line of code from a console application:

```
new SchemaUpdate(config).Execute(Console.WriteLine, true);
```

Make sure that the configuration object passed to the `SchemaUpdate` constructor is pointing to correct instance of database. `SchemaUpdate` would then look at the database schema and compare the updated mappings to find out what has changed. Based on this information, the `SchemaUpdate` class would generate update scripts that would be written to the console. The second parameter tells `SchemaUpdate` to also execute the scripts against the database that was specified in the configuration.

If we add a string property named `Designation` on the `Employee` class, add corresponding property mapping into the mapping class of `Employee`, and run the preceding code from a console app, then the following SQL statement would be printed to the console. Note how `SchemaUpdate` figured out that a new column needs to be added to the `Employee` table.

```
alter table Employee
       add Designation NVARCHAR(255)
```

A good thing about `SchemaUpdate` is that it is not destructive. If you have removed an entity or a property from an entity then `SchemaUpdate` would not drop the corresponding table or the column. This is by design.

NHibernate also has a class `SchemaValidator` which can be used to validate that our mappings conform to the database schema. It is a good way of programmatically ensuring that mappings are correct as per the database schema.

Automatically create/update the database schema

`SchemaExecute` and `SchemaUpdate` are good utility classes to have to generate/ execute database schema creation/update scripts. But if you want to hook into creation of session factory and execute the database schema creation/update scripts right after the session factory is built, then you could use set a configuration property named `hbm2ddl.auto`. This property takes one of the following four values:

- `create-drop`: This drops the existing database schema and recreates the new one using the mappings defined.
- `create`: This creates the database schema based on mappings defined using the `SchemaExport` utility class.
- `update`: This updates the database schema based on the changes made to mappings by making use of the `SchemaUpdate` utility class.
- `validate`: This validates that the database schema is compatible with the mappings defined. The utility class `SchemaValidate` is used internally for validation.

Loquacious configuration lets you set the `hbm2ddl.auto` property, as shown next:

```
var config = new Configuration();
config.DataBaseIntegration(db =>
{
    db.SchemaAction = SchemaAutoAction.Create;
})
```

`SchemaAutoAction` is a helper class that exposes different `hbm2ddl.auto` values, as shown in the following table:

SchemaAutoAction	Hbm2ddl.auto
`SchemaAutoAction.Recreate`	`create-drop`
`SchemaAutoAction.Create`	`create`
`SchemaAutoAction.Update`	`update`
`SchemaAutoAction.Validate`	`validate`

Since this feature internally uses the `SchemaExport`, `SchemaUpdate`, and `SchemaValidate` utility classes, all the pros and cons of these utility classes that we discussed previously still apply. You may want to practice caution while using this feature in production. I personally do not prefer to automatically run schema modification scripts in production unless they have gone through proper scrutiny. We can use these features to generate the appropriate database scripts and then use the tools like **RoundHouse** to hook into the continuous integration pipelines to run these scripts at the appropriate time during the deployment cycle. You can find more about RoundHouse from their GitHub project at `https://github.com/chucknorris/roundhouse`. We did not use this feature in any of our code samples. Reason for that is that `hbm2ddl.auto` would use a separate database connection to execute the database schema creation scripts. In all our samples, we are using in-memory SQLite database which lives only till the connection is open. The moment the connection used for executing database scripts is closed by NHibernate, the in-memory database will be dropped. What we wanted in our tests was that the connection we used in tests should be used for executing database schema creation scripts. Hence, we explicitly used `SchemaExport` to do the job.

Summary

We have covered all the basic building blocks of NHibernate. Understanding mappings and configuration is key to learning how to use NHibernate and how to efficiently perform data access. As I have been stating, both mappings and configuration are huge topics and we have covered the most important aspects so far. We would keep coming back to these topics as we get deeper into our NHibernate journey. From the next chapter onwards, we are going to cover details around storing data in the database, different ways of retrieving data from database, and tweaking mappings/configuration in order to optimize the performance of data access.

5
Let's Store Some Data into the Database

Almost every unit test that we looked at in *Chapter 3, Let's Tell NHibernate About Our Database* involved saving entities into database. Back then we had used very simple code to save entities into in-memory database. We had said that we would look at that particular piece of code in detail in one of the upcoming chapters. This is the chapter where we would learn more about what that piece of code did for us.

We will begin this chapter with three important concepts that we must understand before we start interacting with NHibernate API that lets us store data into database. The first concept is entity states. NHibernate uses entity states to determine what action needs to be taken when entity is presented to NHibernate API. Second concept is transactions. NHibernate offers an abstraction over database's native transaction in the form of its transaction API. Understanding transactions is very fundamental to understanding how NHibernate synchronizes entity changes to the database. The third concept is flush modes which determines when the changes we made to entity instances are sent to the database.

We will then explore the simple code we used in *Chapter 3, Let's Tell NHibernate About Our database* to store entities into in-memory database. We will look under the bonnet to understand the SQL generated by NHibernate for this code and try to understand every part in more detail. We will then look into some complex persistence examples where NHibernate does a lot of heavy lifting for us with features such as transitive persistence, cascade, and so on. We will then bring forward the NHibernate architecture diagram from previous chapter and update it with our learnings from this chapter, and try to get complete picture of our knowledge so far.

Let's get going then.

Entity states

From the time you create a new instance of an entity in memory till the time the instance is saved in the database, the entity instance goes through different states from NHibernate's point of view. It is important to understand these states because NHibernates's persistence behavior is largely dependent on this state of the entity. Depending on the state of the entity, you are allowed or not allowed to perform some operations on it. This state information is completely isolated from the entity instances and the entity itself is not aware of its own state. NHibernate manages the state of entities separately. To understand entity states, let's first look into some scenarios around saving/deleting entities.

When we create a new instance of an entity in the application, NHibernate is not aware of this instance. This instance is also not saved in the database yet and as such only exists in the application memory. Any changes you make to this entity instance would not be saved in the database yet.

In order to save this entity instance in the database, we can use one of the NHibernate APIs such as `Save`, `Update`, and such. We will discuss these APIs in detail in this chapter. When entity instance is passed to these APIs, NHibernate becomes aware of the entity and starts tracking it. Any changes you make to the entity after this point would be visible to NHibernate. At appropriate time, which is governed by multiple factors, this entity instance would be synchronized with database.

Often, we load entities that are present in database already. These entities are also tracked by NHibernate.

There are three states that NHibernate defines:

- **Transient**: An entity instance that is newly created and only exists inside the application memory and not in the database yet. NHibernate is not aware of existence of such entities and cannot track the changes being made to them.

- **Persistent**: An entity which exists in both database and in memory. Unlike transient entities, NHibernate knows about existence of such entities and is capable of tracking the changes being made to them. When an entity is loaded from database into memory, it is in persistent state by default. Also, when a transient entity is saved in database, it becomes persistent.

- **Detached**: These are entities that exist in the memory and database but NHibernate is not aware of their presence in the memory. Because of this, NHibernate is not able to track changes being made to them. There are two ways in which an entity can go into detached state. In this chapter we will look into both.

`ISession` interface of NHibernate provides methods that let you change the state of the entities. For instance, you can pass in a transient entity instance to the `Save` method of `ISession` to make that instance persistent. In the same way, invoking `ISession.Delete` on a persistent entity instance would make that instance detached. We will keep visiting these methods and preceding entity states throughout the chapter. For now, let's move on to the next concept.

Transactions and unit of work

Most business operations result in addition/removal of, updates to database records. A business operation is considered successful only when all constituent database operations are committed to database successfully, among other things. Failure of even a single database operation signals the failure of the whole business operation. In this situation, all other successful database operations need to be reverted back. Most relational databases offer ability to bundle multiple database operations as one unit called transaction. Relational databases offer a guarantee that either all operations inside a transaction succeed or they all fail, leaving the data in a consistent state. This behavior is also described using **ACID** properties which stand for **Atomic, Consistency, Isolation, and Durability**. These properties guarantee that database transactions are processed in a reliable manner. Let's briefly understand what behavior these properties define:

- **Atomicity**: All operations in a transaction are performed as one atomic unit. Either all of them succeed or all fail.

- **Consistency**: Database remains in a consistent state before the start of the transaction and after the end of the transaction, irrespective of whether transaction succeeds or fails.

- **Isolation**: During a transaction, no other database operation can access the data operated upon by the transaction. In reality, databases offer different levels of isolation to let applications define what level of access other database operations can have while the transaction is going on.

- **Durability**: Once the user has been notified of the success of the transaction then it cannot be undone. All the changes are persisted and are not lost even if the database system subsequently fails.

Unit of work is a design pattern which assists with reliably inserting, updating, and deleting records in database as one unit of work, in accordance with the business operations being carried out. NHibernate supports unit of work pattern through its own implementation of transaction. To make use of this, you first need to tell session object to begin a transaction by calling the `BeginTransaction` method on session object. Once a transaction is started, any database operation performed using the session object is recorded but is not actually sent to database. When you are finished with your business operation, you can call the `Commit` method on the transaction to tell NHibernate that you do not intend to carry out any more database operations as part of this business operation and NHibernate should send all the database operations to the database server as one unit. Following is a simplified version of how this code would look:

```
using (var session = config.OpenSession())
{
  using (var transaction = session.BeginTransaction())
  {
    try
    {
      //Database operations here
      transaction.Commit();
    }
    catch (Exception ex)
    {
      transaction.Rollback();
      throw;
    }

  }
}
```

Most important bits in the preceding piece of code are beginning the transaction and running database operations inside of a `try...catch` block. If there is any error while database operations are being carried out, an exception would be thrown which is caught in the `catch` block. Here, the transaction is rolled back, resulting in reverting any state changes that were applied to data in database and removing all database operations recorded in the session object. If database operation finished without errors then call to `Commit` at the end of the `try` block would make sure that all the database operations are sent to database as one unit. They all either update data in the database or throw an error and are rolled back.

Also keep in mind that if the ISession or ITransaction instance is disposed off without committing the transaction then the transaction would be rolled back. This behavior may lead to subtle bugs if you have mistakenly forgotten to commit a transaction.

Remember that NHibernate transaction ultimately results in a database transaction but it is not the same as a database transaction. SQL to start a database transaction is sent to database as soon as ITransaction.BeginTransaction is executed. The lifetime of database transaction is controlled by NHibernate transaction.

I said previously that database operations are only recorded by session object but are not actually sent to database till call to Commit happens. This is not entirely true. Commit internally calls the Flush method on session. The Flush method is responsible for generating and sending SQL commands to database. You can call Flush yourself from within a transaction and all your changes would be sent to database, though this is not a recommended practice.

Explicit and implicit transactions

Transactions, as we discussed previously, are called explicit transaction. This is because they are explicitly started by our code. Use of explicit transactions is a very strongly recommended practice, no matter what kind of database operations you are carrying out. If you do not make use of explicit NHibernate transactions then database server implicitly makes use of transactions for every database command that it executes. These transactions are referred to as implicit transactions. If a business operation results in multiple SQL commands then ideally these should all be executed as one unit as we just discussed. Explicit NHibernate transactions let us do that. With implicit transactions, every SQL command in the batch would be executed inside a different transaction. If one of the SQL commands fails then there is no way to recover the previously committed transactions. Such behavior makes it difficult to implement a reliable unit of work pattern. This not only leaves your data inconsistent in case of errors, but also adds to the execution time as there are more number of transactions started and committed. The overall effect of this is reduced performance and inconsistent data if anything goes wrong.

Entity states and transactions may not make much sense to you at this point. But as we learn more about using NHibernate persistence API to store our entities in database, these concepts would start becoming more relevant. Let's understand what flush mode is before we look at a simple use of NHibernate persistence API to save an entity.

Flush modes

When a transient entity instance is presented to NHibernate in order to persist to database, it is not saved in the database immediately. Rather, NHibernate keeps this instances into a special memory map called identity map maintained by the session object. Same happens when a persistent entity instance is modified. NHibernate keeps building the identity map as application code adds more and more transient entity instances to it or modifies persistent entities. At various times during the life cycle of session object, NHibernate would synchronize the entity instances present in the identity map with the database. This process is also called flushing. The `Flush` method on `ISession` implements this behavior. The times at which entities are flushed is determined by different flush modes. Flush modes have a bearing on how the application code should be written to ensure the entities are synchronized with the database. So it is important to understand different flush modes. NHibernate defines following four flush modes:

- `Never`: Changes are never flushed automatically by NHibernate. We must call `ISession.Flush` manually before closing the session. Failing to call `ISession.Flush` would result in loss of data.

- `Commit`: This flush mode is to be used in conjunction with a transaction. With flush mode set to `Commit`, the changes are flushed as soon as the transaction is committed and there is no need to call `ISession.Flush` manually.

- `Always`: When application code saves an entity, NHibernate can choose to perform the action later. But when application queries for data, the query has to be executed immediately to return the results to the application code. Whenever NHibernate hits the database to execute the query, it has an opportunity to synchronize all the new or modified entities to database. Flush mode `Auto` enables this behavior. There is no need to call `ISession.Flush` manually with flush mode set to `Always`.

- `Auto`: This mode can be considered as a more efficient version of `Always`. Similar to `Always`, session is flushed before executing queries, but unlike `Always`, not before executing every query. If session holds entities which when synchronized with database, may have an impact on the result of the query, then NHibernate would flush the session, otherwise it would not. This prevents the query execution from returning stale data. For instance, if session holds a modified version of the `Employee` instance and we are querying for `Employee`, then it is possible that the instance held within session may be part of the result of the query and entities in the session would be flushed.

Also, remember that modes `Always` and `Auto`, though intelligent, are doing more checks before every query execution to determine whether session should be flushed or not. This adds some overhead to the execution of the query. We cannot say that the overhead is significant as it may vary from application to application.

> When `ITransaction.Commit` is called, session is always flushed unless the flush mode is set to `Never`. From the above description of flush modes, it is easy to assume that commit of a transaction results in session being flushed only if flush mode is set to `Commit`. That is not true. Setting flush mode to `Commit` would stop the flush mode `Auto` or `Always` from coming into effect, but setting flush mode to `Auto` or `Always` would not stop `ITransaction.Commit` from flushing the session. In the previous unit of work implementation we went with the default value of flush mode which is `Auto`, which works. But we could also have gone with `Commit`.

Saving entities

As with previous chapter, we will begin by going through a piece of code we had used in *Chapter 3, Let's Tell NHibernate About Our Database*. If you can remember, we had used the following code to save an instance of the `Employee` class in the database:

```
object id = 0;
using (var transaction = Session.BeginTransaction())
{
  id = Session.Save(new Employee
  {
    EmployeeNumber = "5987123",
    Firstname = "Hillary",
    Lastname = "Gamble",
    EmailAddress = "hillary.gamble@corporate.com",
    DateOfBirth = new DateTime(1980, 4, 23),
    DateOfJoining = new DateTime(2010, 7, 12),
    IsAdmin = true,
    Password = "Password"
  });
  transaction.Commit();
}
```

We started with call to `Session.BeginTransaction` which signaled NHibernate to begin a fresh transaction for us. We then created a new instance of the `Employee` class, set required properties on it, and passed it into the `Save` method on session. The `Save` method on the `ISession` interface is one of the persistence APIs offered by NHibernate. The `Save` method is used to ask NHibernate to track an in-memory instance of an entity for addition into a database table. You should use the `Save` method when you know for sure that entity does not exist in database or in identity map of session.

> An identity map ensures that each entity instance is loaded into the memory only once. You can think of identity map as a hashtable where identifier value of the entity instance is used as key. You can read more about identity map pattern in Martin Fowler's article at `http://martinfowler.com/eaaCatalog/identityMap.html`. Session internally maintains an identity map or cache to store all the persistent entities that are added to session through the `Save` method or are loaded by session from the database via different querying methods. NHibernate makes significant use of identity map to avoid having to load the same entity instance more than once in the same session.

Also note that we created the `employee` instance right where we passed it into the `Save` method. But you can create it in a separate statement. This separate statement can even be placed outside of the `using` statement block.

The `Save` method returns a parameter of type `object`. This is the identifier for the entity being saved. The `identifier` property can be one of the many supported types and not just `int`. There is no way of knowing this at compile time, hence the `Save` method returns `object`. Note that the employee instance is still not saved in the database. The identifier value is generated by NHibernate using the identifier generation strategy we specified in the mappings for the `Employee` class.

We then call the `Commit` method on transaction. It is at this point that NHibernate generates appropriate set of SQL statements to insert new record in the `Employee` table and sends them to database for execution.

Some identifier generation strategies also play a role in determining when entities are actually stored in the database. Strategies such as identity and sequence, which depend on the database to generate identifier value, would result in the entity being stored in the database as soon as ISession.Save is called. NHibernate assigns the identifier value to a fresh entity when it is passed to the Save method. In case of strategies such as identity and sequence, identifier value can be obtained only after inserting the database record. This is why NHibernate would store the entity in database immediately after call to ISession.Save.

The Employee instance is persisted at this point. If we hold this instance in a local variable, close the session, and retain the local variable even after the session is closed, then the instance becomes detached. This is mainly because the instance is not associated with any session. If the instance is associated with some other session then entity would still be persistent relative to that session. Since detached entities are not associated with any session, changes made to them cannot be tracked by NHibernate. However, if the same entity is persistent relative to some other session then that session would track any changes made to the entity. Entity state can be changed to detached while keeping the session still open by passing the entity to the Evict() method on ISession. Calling the Evict() method would remove the entity from session, thus making it detached.

Following is the sequence of SQL statements generated by the preceding piece of code. Note that we are using hilo identifier generation strategy here.

```
select
  next_hi
from
  hibernate_unique_key

update
  hibernate_unique_key
set
  next_hi = @p0
where
  next_hi = @p1;
@p0 = 2 [Type: Int32 (0)], @p1 = 1 [Type: Int32 (0)]

INSERT
INTO
  Employee
    (EmployeeNumber, Firstname, Lastname, EmailAddress,
    DateOfBirth, DateOfJoining, IsAdmin, Password, Id)
```

```
VALUES
    (@p0, @p1, @p2, @p3, @p4, @p5, @p6, @p7, @p8);
@p0 = '5987123' [Type: String (0)],
@p1 = 'Hillary' [Type: String (0)],
@p2 = 'Gamble' [Type: String (0)],
@p3 = 'hillary.gamble@corporate.com' [Type: String (0)],
@p4 = '23/04/1980 00:00:00' [Type: DateTime (0)],
@p5 = '12/07/2010 00:00:00' [Type: DateTime (0)],
@p6 = True [Type: Boolean (0)],
@p7 = 'Password' [Type: String (0)],
@p8 = 32768 [Type: Int32 (0)]
```

Let's try to understand what SQL statements NHibernate has generated for us. Preceding statements can be divided into two parts. The first part is all about identifier generation. Since we have configured to use `hilo` as identifier generation strategy, NHibernate is making itself ready with all the data it needs in order to generate identifiers using hilo algorithm. What I mean by that is – hilo needs a set of two numbers to work with. One is `hi` which is sourced from a database table and other is `lo` which is calculated by NHibernate. NHibernate combines these two numbers using a formula to generate a unique number that can be used as identifier. The way this works is, for generating lo value NHibernate uses range defined by the `max_lo` parameter that can be specified during mapping of identifier column in question. If `max_lo` configured is 10 then NHibernate starts generating identifier numbers at `(max_lo * initial hi value) + 1`. Usually the initial hi value coming out of database is 1, so the first number becomes 11. Next time an INSERT operation needs an identifier, NHibernate increments the last value and returns 12. Every time an identifier value is returned, NHibernate also checks if it has gone over the range defined by `max_lo` value, which in our case is 10. So after returning 20, NHibernate knows that it has gone over the range and gets the next hi value from database, which is 2. It runs the same algorithm again to return numbers from 21 to 30 this time, and so on.

If you do not specify `max_lo` in mapping then NHibernate assumes a default of `Int16.MaxValue` which is 32767. This is what we see in the preceding example. NHibernate keeps generating unique identifier values without hitting the database till it runs out of the `max_lo` value range. Using appropriate `max_lo` and `hi` values, you can ensure that NHibernate generates unique identifier values without hitting the database too much. There are two times when NHibernate needs a trip to database when using this strategy:

- When a new session factory is built, NHibernate fetches the next hi value from the database and retains it. At the same time, NHibernate also updates the next hi value in database by incrementing the value that it just fetched. This is what we see in the previous example.

- When session factory runs out of the `max_lo` value range. At this point, NHibernate resets the `max_lo` value and fetches the next `hi` value from database again.

Being able to generate unique identifier without having to hit the database is biggest strength of hilo algorithm. Besides that, the identifiers values are integers which work well with indexing of the `Id` column, which is also primary key of the table. On the flip side, a low value of `max_lo` would mean that NHibernate would run out of `max_lo` range frequently, leading to more database hits than expected. On the other hand, a very high value of `max_lo` would lead to sparse identifier values if session factory is recreated before the `max_lo` range is exhausted. You should choose the ideal `max_lo` value after carefully studying the application's runtime behavior and the environment in which the application is running.

The next statement in the previous SQL is a simple insert into the `Employee` table. Note that the value used for the `Id` column is what NHibernate calculated using `hi` and `lo` values.

The example we looked at is quite simple. It involved a single transient entity without any associations to the other entities. Next, we will look into complex scenarios and see what NHibernate offers to deal with these scenarios.

Saving entities – complex scenarios

Persistence, as we saw in the previous example, is simple because NHibernate does not need to do much work like building multiple SQL `insert`/`update` statements and executing them in the right sequence at appropriate time. But persistence requirements of real world software are usually more complex than this. In real life, we may encounter one or more of the following situations:

- A transient entity with associations to one or more other transient entities needs to be persisted

- A transient entity with one or more associations to other persistent entities needs to be persisted

- One or more properties of a persistent entity are modified by application that needs to be synchronized to database

- One or more associations are added/removed from a persistent entity

- A persistent entity needs to be deleted

- Updates are made to detached entities

We have seen that session has the `Save` method that can be used to save a transient entity instance into database. Other than `Save`, session has the following methods available to deal with different situations:

- `Update`: This is used to persist the changes made to a detached entity.

- `Delete`: This is used to delete a persistent entity (as a side effect of this, the in-memory copy of the entity becomes transient).

- `SaveOrUpdate`: This is used to let NHibernate figure out whether the entity being passed is transient or persistent and action it accordingly.

- `Merge`: This is used to persist changes made to detached entity. This may sound confusing with `Update` but there is a subtle difference that we would look at in a moment.

- `Refresh`: This is used to synchronize the latest state of an entity from database into the memory. This method is typically used in scenarios where database has triggers which alter the state of an entity (or add more details) after it has been saved. By calling the `Refresh` method after call to the `Save` method, any changes made by the database trigger would be synchronized with the entity instance.

- `Persist`: This is similar to `Save` with some differences in how it works internally. `Persist` saves the entity instance into the database only if it is invoked inside of a transaction, whereas `Save` does not need to be invoked inside a transaction. `Persist` assigns the identifier value when the changes are actually flushed to the database as against `Save` which would assign the identifier value immediately.

`Refresh` and `Persist` are introduced here so that readers are aware that these methods are available. We will not go into details of these methods as they are used in very specific situations. For instance, the `Persist` method is used alongside long-running transactions where a business transaction spans beyond a single user interaction. Let's explore the other methods in more detail. We would start with `Delete` as other three have a bit of a similarity and should be looked at together. If you want to delete a persistent entity then you can pass it to the `Delete` method. When transaction is committed (or session is flushed), NHibernate would issue appropriate SQL statements to delete the entity from database and also remove it from the session. Following is how you would do it:

```
using (var tx = Session.BeginTransaction())
{
  var emp = Session.Get<Employee>(id);
  Session.Delete(emp);
  tx.Commit();
}
```

At this point, the entity becomes transient as it is still present in the application memory but is not present in any NHibernate session. `Delete` has some subtleties around it which we will cover in an upcoming section.

The `Update` method is useful when you have made changes to a detached entity and you want them to be synchronized to database. NHibernate automatically tracks any changes made to persistent entities. This capability is built into session and works as long as the entity is associated with a session. But detached entities are not associated with any session so any changes you make to such an entity are not tracked by NHibernate. Hence, it is not possible to detect and commit changes made to detached entities when transaction is committed. Instead, you need to explicitly tell NHibernate that you have updated this entity while it was disconnected from the session and the new session should treat it as such. Let's look at how it works:

```
var emp = //loaded from previous session which is now closed
using (var tx = Session.BeginTransaction())
{

    emp.Firstname = "Hillary";
    emp.Lastname = "Gamble";

    Session.Update(emp);

    tx.Commit();
}
```

Note that the `Update` method is provided to be used in a situation when you are sure that an entity which was previously loaded from database is no more present in the session cache. One way you can be in this situation is when session that loaded the entity is closed. Another way this can happen is when an entity is removed from session by calling the `Evict` method on session.

What if the detached `employee` instance is already present in the new session? In that case, calling the `Update` method would result in an exception. The `Merge()` method is provided to handle this situation. If you know that a particular detached entity is present in a session that you want to use to synchronize the detached entity, then you first pass the detached entity to the `Merge()` method. NHibernate would then update the entity instance in its identity map with the one passed into the `Merge()` method. Any changes detected during this update and any changes made to the entity after that point are all synchronized to database when transaction is committed.

A caveat you should keep in mind while working with the Merge method is that the Merge method returns the merged entity which may be an entirely different instance than the one that was passed into the Merge method. After passing an entity to the Merge method, your code should work with the instance returned by the other call to Merge than the original instance. Let's take a look at the following code snippet to understand this better:

```
[Test]
public void MergeReturnsNewEntityInstance()
{
  object id = 0;

  //This is out first employee instance
  var employee1 = new Employee
  {
    Firstname = "John",
    Lastname = "Smith"
  };

  //Lets first save it so that we have it in session
  using (var tx = Session.BeginTransaction())
  {
    id = Session.Save(employee1);

    tx.Commit();
  }

  //Let's create another instance of Employee with same id
  var employee2 = new Employee
  {
    Id = (int) id
  };

  //Let's merge this new entity with session
  var employee3 = Session.Merge(employee2);

  //Let's confirm that employee2 and employee3 are not the same
  Assert.That(Object.ReferenceEquals(employee2, employee3),
  Is.False);

  //Let's assert that employee1 and employee3 are same instances
  Assert.That(Object.ReferenceEquals(employee1, employee3),
  Is.True);

}
```

The code has comments that explain most part of the code. The important part is that `employee1` is the persistence instance which is present in the identity map of session. When detached instance `employee2` is passed to the `Merge` method, it returns the same `employee1` instance that is present in the identity map already. But `employee2` is not the same as `employee3`, the instance returned by the `Merge` method.

To some extent, these methods help to make real life persistence situations we just described, easier to deal with. But there still remains a level of complexity that developer has to handle manually. Imagine a situation when you need to save an `employee` instance with all three types of `benefit` instances associated, a residential address present, and employee being part of few communities. You would have to first persist each individual entity independently and then update the persistent `employee` entity with associations to other persistent entities set. Besides being complex, imagine the number of lines of code you would end up writing for every such situation.

Fortunately, NHibernate makes it very easy to deal with real life persistence situations similar to ones we discussed previously and many more. NHibernate achieves this through an intricate implementation of something called transitive persistence. On top of that, NHibernate, through its implementation of cascade styles, offers the users fine grained control over how different entities in an object graph are persisted.

Transitive persistence using cascade styles

NHibernate implements transitive persistence wherein updates made to a persistent entity are automatically synchronized to database on commit of the transaction. Let's look at a very simple example of how this works. In the following unit test, we save a transient `employee` instance, thus making it persistent. We then load the persistent instance from database inside a new transaction, update the `FirstName` and `LastName` property, and commit the transaction. Lastly, we clear the session and load the same entity instance from database and confirm that `FirstName` and `LastName` is updated correctly.

```
[Test]
public void UpdateEmployee()
{
  object id = 0;
  using (var tx = Session.BeginTransaction())
  {
    id = Session.Save(new Employee
    {
      Firstname = "John",
      Lastname = "Smith"
```

```
    });

    tx.Commit();
  }

  Session.Clear();

  using (var tx = Session.BeginTransaction())
  {
    var emp = Session.Get<Employee>(id);

    emp.Firstname = "Hillary";
    emp.Lastname = "Gamble";

    tx.Commit();
  }

  Session.Clear();

  using (var tx = Session.BeginTransaction())
  {
    var employee = Session.Get<Employee>(id);
    Assert.That(employee.Firstname, Is.EqualTo("Hillary"));
    Assert.That(employee.Lastname, Is.EqualTo("Gamble"));
    tx.Commit();
  }
}
```

We placed a call to `ISession.Clear()` in the preceding test. This is done in order to clear everything held in the identity map of the session so that we can have a fresh session. We need to do this because we are using the in-memory SQLite database which is destroyed the moment session is closed. A new instance of in-memory database would be created next time we open a new session. So all the data we saved in the previous instance would be lost. In order to keep that database instance around, we are clearing the session. There are other ways of fixing this issue. For instance, we could have used a file-based SQLite instance instead of in-memory one. Or we could have just evicted the entity instances that we do not want to have in the session for our tests to work. Both of these options are not as easy and straightforward to use than clearing the session. But at the same time, remember that `ISession.Clear` should be used with extreme care. It should be avoided in production code unless you know what you are doing. `ISession.Clear` not only clears the objects in the identity map but it also removes any objects queued for inserts/updates to database.

In the preceding code, we did not call any method on session object to tell NHibernate that we have updated few properties on the `employee` instance. When the preceding code is run, NHibernate would send the following SQL to database on commit of transaction:

```
UPDATE
    Employee
SET
    EmployeeNumber = @p0,
    Firstname = @p1,
    Lastname = @p2,
    EmailAddress = @p3,
    DateOfBirth = @p4,
    DateOfJoining = @p5,
    IsAdmin = @p6,
    Password = @p7
WHERE
    Id = @p8;
@p0 = NULL [Type: String (0)],
@p1 = 'Hillary' [Type: String (0)],
@p2 = 'Gamble' [Type: String (0)],
@p3 = NULL [Type: String (0)],
@p4 = '01/01/0001 00:00:00' [Type: DateTime (0)],
@p5 = '01/01/0001 00:00:00' [Type: DateTime (0)],
@p6 = False [Type: Boolean (0)],
@p7 = NULL [Type: String (0)],
@p8 = 11 [Type: Int32 (0)]
```

> The SQL generated to update the employee record updates all the columns of the `Employee` table though only the `FirstName` and `LastName` properties were updated. This is NHibernate's default behavior. A property called `dynamic-update` controls this behavior. This property is configured through mapping at entity level. When set to `true`, NHibernate only includes the changed properties in the generated `update` statement. There are some pros and cons of dynamic updates which are left for the readers to explore. Similar to dynamic updates, another feature, `dynamic insert` offers behavior on the same lines around inserts.

The way transitive persistence works internally is through a feature called **dirty checking**. When session is flushed (or transaction is committed), NHibernate checks for all entities present in its identity map to see if there is any entity which is newly added, deleted, or changed. For the changed entities, NHibernate checks the current state of the entity with the one that was loaded from the database and still held within identity map. All changed entities are marked as dirty and NHibernate generates appropriate SQL to synchronize the changes to the database.

The example we just saw only updated primitive properties on a single entity. What about updating an entity having associations to other entities? This is a most common persistence requirement and NHibernate has taken care of it through cascading the `save`/`update`/`delete` operations on parent entity to the associated child entities. Not only that, but NHibernate gives you total control over this cascading operation and lets you choose which actions of `save`, `update`, and `delete` on parent entity are cascaded down to the associated child entities. The `Cascade` option on association mapping is used to declare this. We have briefly looked at the `cascade` option in *Chapter 3, Let's Tell NHibernate About Our Database,* during discussion of mapping associations. Let's dig deeper into cascade now.

Cascade setting on association mapping lets you specify how NHibernate should cascade a particular action performed on parent object to its associated objects. For instance, if you have a transient instance of the `Employee` entity referencing an instance of the `Address` entity and the `Employee` entity is saved in the database, would you like the associated `Address` entity to be saved in database as well? A `cascade` setting of `none` would leave the associated entity as is but a cascade setting of `save-update` would save the `Address` entity in database. There are several cascade options defined but following are most commonly used options:

- `none`: Do not cascade any actions from parent entity to associated child entities. This is NHibernate's default when no cascade option is specified on association mapping.

- `save-update`: When an entity is passed to the `SaveOrUpdate` method, NHibernate navigates the associations from passed entity to other entities. If any of the associations are mapped with the `cascade` option of `save-update`, NHibernate would save or update the associated entity (internally, NHibernate would pass associated entity to the `SaveOrUpdate` method).

- `delete`: When an entity is deleted using the `Delete` method and any associations from this entity to other entities have the `cascade` option set to `delete`, then those associated entities are also deleted.

- delete-orphan: This setting is used to handle a special situation. When a child entity is dereferenced from its parent entity then all that NHibernate does by default is to set the foreign key on child entity's table to null, so that association between parent and child records in the database does not exist anymore. Child records like these are sometimes called orphan records as they do not have any meaning without being associated to their parent records. If you want NHibernate to additionally delete the orphan child record as well, then setting cascade to delete-orphan would do the job. Note though that this setting has nothing to do with the delete setting.

- all: This option cascades any operation performed on an entity to its associated child entities.

- all-delete-orphan: This is just a union of all and delete-orphan. With this cascade option specified, NHibernate would cascade any action from parent entity to child entity and in addition, it would also delete any orphan entities.

The other cascade options are persist, refresh, remove, and detach. Each of these correspond to a method on ISession with same name. As with most NHibernate features, a question may have come to your mind – how to decide which cascade style to use? There is no black and white answer. If there was one, NHibernate would not have given us these many options, isn't it? But there fortunately are some guidelines that you can follow:

- Always use all-delete-orphan as your default choice. This would cascade all operation down to every association so you do not have to think about associations once they are mapped correctly. This option would also ensure that there are no orphan records lying around the database. In the next section, we would explore this in more detail.

- In some legacy databases, you may not be allowed to delete existing database records. In such situations, save-update is your best friend.

- If your domain model involves self-referencing bidirectional associations (associations from an entity to itself), then you may want to choose none as cascade option on one of the associations. This would prevent NHibernate from navigating the whole object graph in memory leading to bad performance.

Cascading is such an important concept that just giving a brief description of each cascade style does not do enough justice to it. So next we would look at some examples of persistence situation where cascading along with transitive persistence do their magic, while we write very little code to synchronize to the database the changes made to entities.

Transitive persistence/cascading in action

In this section, we are going to look at a select few persistence situations to explore the transitive persistence and cascading in detail. We will not be able to explore each and every possible scenario, so we are going to be looking at the following few and understand in detail how these play out under the hood. Understanding these examples should give you enough knowledge to understand any code for any complex scenario:

- Saving a transient entity with association to one or more other transient entities
- Updating a persistent entity with one or more associations added/removed
- Deleting a persistent entity with one or more associations set

Let's get started then.

Saving a transient entity with association to other transient entities

We have seen examples of saving an entity graph involving all transient entities in *Chapter 3, Let's Tell NHibernate About Our Database,* while discussing association mappings. But let's look at the examples again and understand what happens under the hood. In the following example, we try to save a transient instance of employee having some transient benefit instances added to its `Benefits` collection:

```
object id = 0;
using (var transaction = Session.BeginTransaction())
{
  id = Session.Save(new Employee
  {
    Benefits = new HashSet<Benefit>
    {
      new SeasonTicketLoan
      {
        Amount = 1200,
        MonthlyInstalment = 100,
        StartDate = new DateTime(2014, 5, 12),
        EndDate = new DateTime(2015, 4, 12)
      }
```

```
    }
  });
  transaction.Commit();
}
```

When the preceding code is run, NHibernate first saves the `employee` entity. After that, NHibernate inspects the associations and checks the cascade setting on the association mapping to determine what needs to be done to the associated `benefit` entity. If we had set `cascade` to `none`, then NHibernate would ignore the transient `benefit` entity and commit the transaction. On the other hand, had the cascade been set to `save-update` or `all`, NHibernate would generate necessary insert statements to insert the benefit records in database. Following SQL statements would be sent to database by NHibernate in that situation:

```
INSERT
INTO
      Benefit
      (Name, Description, Employee_Id, Id)
VALUES
      (@p0, @p1, @p2, @p3);
      @p0 = NULL [Type: String (0)],
      @p1 = NULL [Type: String (0)],
      @p2 = NULL [Type: Int32 (0)],
      @p3 = 65536 [Type: Int32 (0)]

INSERT
INTO
      SeasonTicketLoan
      (Amount, MonthlyInstalment, StartDate, EndDate, Id)
VALUES
      (@p0, @p1, @p2, @p3, @p4);
@p0 = 1200 [Type: Int32 (0)],
@p1 = 100 [Type: Double (0)],
@p2 = '12/05/2014 00:00:00' [Type: DateTime (0)],
@p3 = '04/12/2015 00:00:00' [Type: DateTime (0)],
@p4 = 65536 [Type: Int32 (0)]

UPDATE
      Benefit                  <----
SET
      Employee_Id = @p0
WHERE
      Id = @p1;
@p0 = 32768 [Type: Int32 (0)],
@p1 = 65536 [Type: Int32 (0)]
```

If you notice, NHibernate has generated an extraneous update statement to set correct foreign key value in the `Employee_Id` column of the `Benefit` table. This looks a bit unwise on part of NHibernate but fortunately there is way to fix this. In one of the upcoming sections, we will look at why NHibernate generates this extraneous `update` statement and how to fix this.

Another thing to note here is that when the record is inserted into the `Benefit` table, `Employee_Id` is inserted as null. This is because we did not correctly set the `Employee` property on the `SeasonTicketLoan` instance, leaving it as null. In the next section, we will talk about why it is important to set both ends of a bidirectional association.

A word on bidirectional associations

An association between two database records is usually bidirectional. When two database tables are associated using a foreign key, then you are able to navigate from one to other in any direction via different SQL joins. The same is not true for the entities that map to these database tables. In C#, you can choose to restrict the navigation to go from one end of the association to the other but not the other way round. Or like in case of `Employee` to `Benefit` mapping in our domain model, you can choose to make them bidirectional by having a property of other type on each side.

Because bidirectional associations have navigations from both ends, additional responsibility of setting both ends has to be handled by someone. In some cases, NHibernate takes care of that. You set only one end of the association and NHibernate ensures that both ends of the association are set when entity is saved in the database. But this is not guaranteed to work all the time and there always are edge-cases where this would fail. So, it is recommended that we always set both ends of a bidirectional association. Another reason why we should always set both ends of a bidirectional relation is that we are creating a graph of .NET objects in the memory. We may use these objects in the context of NHibernate or we may use these just like plain .NET objects. If there is a valid bidirectional relation present between two objects, then it is always safer to set it than leave it for someone else to update that relation. You never know if some piece of code tries to navigate that relation even before NHibernate has a chance to update it properly. Following is how the preceding code listing would look when this is implemented:

```
object id = 0;
using (var transaction = Session.BeginTransaction())
{
    var seasonTicketLoan = new SeasonTicketLoan
    {
        Amount = 1200,
        MonthlyInstalment = 100,
        StartDate = new DateTime(2014, 5, 12),
        EndDate = new DateTime(2015, 4, 12)
    };
    var employee = new Employee
    {
```

```
      Benefits = new HashSet<Benefit>
      {
        seasonTicketLoan
      }
   };
   seasonTicketLoan.Employee = employee;

   id = Session.Save(employee);
   transaction.Commit();
}
```

Note that we instantiated the `Employee` and `SeasonTicketLoan` instances
independently. We then added the `SeasonTicketLoan` instance to the `Benefits`
collection on `Employee` and set the `Employee` property on the `SeasonTicketLoan`
instance to the `Employee` instance. This code does the job but is not perfectly
reusable. Every time a benefit is added to an employee, we need to remember to set
both ends of the association. It would be hard to trace subtle bugs that may arise out
of forgetting to do this. This can be avoided by defining a method on the `Employee`
class and making sure that only this method is used when a benefit needs to be
added to an employee, as shown next:

```
public virtual void AddBenefit(Benefit benefit)
{
   benefit.Employee = this;
   Benefits.Add(benefit);
}
```

This method makes sure that the `Employee` property at the benefit end is set
correctly every time and also adds the passed benefit instance to the `Benefits`
collection. Note that we are not checking if the `Benefits` collection is initialized or
not. You can either add a check for that and initialize the collection if not initialized
already or add the following default constructor to make sure that the `Benefits`
collection is always initialized:

```
public Employee()
{
   Benefits = new HashSet<Benefit>();
}
```

Same logic applies to bidirectional association between `Employee` and `Address`.
You can add a method similar to the previous one that lets you set the
`ResidentialAddress` property on the `Employee` class or just change the
property to look as follows:

```
private Address residentialAddress;
public virtual Address ResidentialAddress
{
```

```
get
{
  return residentialAddress;
}
set
{
  residentialAddress = value;
  if (value != null)
    residentialAddress.Employee = this;
}
}
```

Here, we have introduced a backing field for the property. From the setter of the property, we also set the `Employee` property on the backing field to `this` which is an `employee` instance. Now, you can set the `ResidentialAddress` property in the usual way and both ends of the association are guaranteed to be set.

Updating associations on a persistent entity

At the beginning of this section, we have seen the example of updating simple properties on a persistent entity, so I will not repeat that here. We have just looked at an example of adding entities to a collection on a transient entity. Adding entities to a collection on persistent entity is no different. The only thing you need to ensure is that both ends of the association are set if there is a bidirectional association. Removing items from a one-to-many association on a persistent entity works slightly differently and that is what we are going to discuss here.

Previously, when we discussed various cascade options, we learned that `all-delete-orphan` should be our default cascade style for one-to-many associations. Here, we would see with example what difference does that option bring in contrast to something such as `save-update` or `delete`. In the following code listing, a `benefit` instance of type `Leave` is removed from the `Benefits` collection on `employee`:

```
using (var tx = Session.BeginTransaction())
{
  var emp = Session.Get<Employee>(id);

  var leave = employee.Benefits.OfType<Leave>().FirstOrDefault();
  emp.RemoveBenefit(leave);

  tx.Commit();
}
```

We have a used convenience method named `RemoveBenefit` defined on the
`Employee` class in order to remove the `benefit` instance from collection. This is in
line with discussion around setting both ends of a bidirectional association. The same
logic applies when breaking a bidirectional association. In this case, just removing
the benefit from the `Benefits` collection of `Employee` is not enough. We also need
to set the `Employee` property on `Benefit` to `null`.

> In the next section, we will look at a setting called **inverse** which
> affects how NHibernate persists associations. Inverse also drives the
> need to make sure that removal action is carried out at the correct end
> of association. But as a general guiding principal, we would ensure
> that association is broken from both ends. And to make it fool-proof,
> we would use convenience methods such as `RemoveBenefit`.

Following is how the `RemoveBenefit` method looks:

```
public virtual void RemoveBenefit(Benefit benefit)
{
  benefit.Employee = null;
  Benefits.Remove(benefit);
}
```

If cascade setting on mapping of the `Benefits` collection is set to `save-update` or
`all`, then the preceding code would result in following SQL being generated:

```
UPDATE
  Benefit
SET
  Name = @p0,
  Description = @p1,
  Employee_Id = @p2
WHERE
  Id = @p3;
@p0 = NULL [Type: String (0)],
@p1 = NULL [Type: String (0)],
@p2 = NULL [Type: Int32 (0)],
@p3 = 65537 [Type: Int32 (0)]
```

Note that, though we asked NHibernate to remove leave instance, NHibernate only updated the value of foreign key column `Employee_Id` in the `Benefit` table to `NULL`. It effectively only deleted the association between `employee` and `benefit` but the `benefit` instance is still there in the database. Such behavior is desired if there are other records in database referring to this `benefit` record or for some reason you are not allowed to delete the so called orphan records not referenced anymore. But what if you want these orphan records to be deleted when no other database record references this record? That is when you use cascade setting `delete-orphan` which tells NHibernate that the moment it detects an orphan record resulting out of any database operation, it should delete it. Following code listing shows how you can set cascade value of `delete-orphan` using mapping by code:

```
Set(e => e.Benefits, mapper =>
{
  mapper.Key(k => k.Column("Employee_Id"));
  mapper.Cascade(Cascade.All.Include(Cascade.DeleteOrphans));
  mapper.Inverse(true);
},
relation => relation.OneToMany(mapping =>
mapping.Class(typeof(Benefit)))));
```

Note that we have set the cascade value to `All` first and then included `DeleteOrphan` on top. This is because cascade values work in a similar way to a set or union. You are telling NHibernate which set of operations you want to cascade by combining them as we did in the preceding example. After setting the cascade value to `all-delete -orphan`, following SQL is generated by NHibernate for the same piece of code:

```
DELETE
FROM
  Leave
WHERE
  Id = @p0;
@p0 = 65537 [Type: Int32 (0)]

DELETE
FROM
  Benefit
WHERE
  Id = @p0;
@p0 = 65537 [Type: Int32 (0)]
```

You can see that NHibernate has detected an orphan record and issued the commands to delete it. It also figures out that record from the `Leave` table needs to be deleted before it can delete the record in the `Benefit` table.

Deleting a persistent entity with one or more associations set

In more than one way, the API for deleting a persistent entity is similar to the API for saving an entity. Similar to `Save()`, session has a method named `Delete()` to which you pass the entity instance that you want to delete. The way NHibernate navigates through the associations and checks cascade settings while saving the entities, it does the same thing while deleting the entities. Following code listing deletes an `employee` instance:

```
using (var tx = Session.BeginTransaction())
{
  var emp = Session.Get<Employee>(id);
  Session.Delete(emp);
  tx.Commit();
}
```

If the preceding `employee` instance has all its associations set with a cascade value that would propagate the `delete` operation (`delete` or `all`), then NHibernate would navigate all the associations and issue delete commands in correct order to ensure that all the entities are deleted without any violation of dependency.

After the entity is deleted from the database, NHibernate also removes it from the session.

The code listings used previously is taken from the unit tests that I wrote for this section. To keep the text brief, I have only included the relevant lines of code from the different tests. Feel free to look at the full tests by downloading the source code of the chapter.

Bidirectional associations and ownership

In NHibernate parlance, bidirectional associations have a notion of ownership. Ownership defines how the foreign key that underpins the bidirectional association is updated when new items are added to an association in memory. You can declare any end of the association to be the owner. Your choice of ownership affects the SQL that is generated in order to synchronize the association correctly to database. Let's elaborate this with an example.

Following diagram depicts the bidirectional relationship between the `Employee` and `Benefit` class:

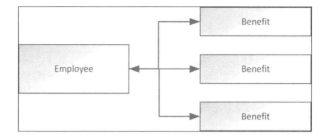

The Employee to **Benefit** association is a bidirectional association which can also be seen as parent-child relation. **Employee** acts as parent and has multiple child benefits associated to it. From purely technical point of view, this is a one-to-many association. In one-to-many association, if ownership is not defined, then "one" side is considered as owner by default. So in our example, `employee` is owner of the association. What that tells NHibernate is that employee is responsible for setting this association up in the database correctly. So, for every benefit record that gets inserted into the database, employee would make sure that foreign key column `Employee_Id` on the `Benefit` table is updated with its own `id`. This is clear from the SQL that is generated by the following piece of code:

```
using (var tx = Session.BeginTransaction())
{
   var employee = new Employee();
   employee.AddBenefit(new SeasonTicketLoan
   {
      Amount = 1200,
      MonthlyInstalment = 100,
      StartDate = new DateTime(2014, 5, 12),
      EndDate = new DateTime(2015, 4, 12)
   });
   id = Session.Save(employee);

   tx.Commit();
}
```

The preceding code sends the following SQL to the database (stripped down to essential part for brevity):

```
INSERT
INTO
    Benefit
    (Name, Description, Employee_Id, Id)
VALUES
    (@p0, @p1, @p2, @p3);
    @p0 = NULL [Type: String (0)],
    @p1 = NULL [Type: String (0)],
    @p2 = NULL [Type: Int32 (0)],
    @p3 = 65536 [Type: Int32 (0)]

INSERT
INTO
    SeasonTicketLoan
    (Amount, MonthlyInstalment, StartDate, EndDate, Id)
VALUES
    (@p0, @p1, @p2, @p3, @p4);
    @p0 = 1200 [Type: Int32 (0)],
    @p1 = 100 [Type: Double (0)],
    @p2 = '12/05/2014 00:00:00' [Type: DateTime (0)],
    @p3 = '04/12/2015 00:00:00' [Type: DateTime (0)],
    @p4 = 65536 [Type: Int32 (0)]

UPDATE
    Benefit          ⬅
SET
    Employee_Id = @p0
WHERE
    Id = @p1;
    @p0 = 32768 [Type: Int32 (0)],
    @p1 = 65536 [Type: Int32 (0)]
```

If you remember, we have seen this example earlier when we talked about setting both ends of bidirectional association. As we had noted back then, after inserting the `Employee` and `Benefit` record, an additional `update` statement is issued to update the `Employee_Id` column on the `Benefit` table. Think of it like this - because employee is responsible for making sure that foreign key column is updated correctly, employee would issue additional update statement for every benefit item in its `Benefits` collection. This additional update is actually unnecessary and at times may impact performance. If we turn the tables around and make the `Benefit` entity the owner of the association, then this extra `update` statement goes away. So how do you make `Benefit` the owner of association? This is where the `Inverse` property of one-to-many association mapping comes in. `Inverse` is a Boolean property that you can declare on the one-to-many mapping, as shown next:

```
Set(e => e.Benefits, mapper =>
{
   mapper.Key(k => k.Column("Employee_Id"));
   mapper.Cascade(Cascade.All.Include(Cascade.DeleteOrphans));
   mapper.Inverse(true);
},
relation => relation.OneToMany(mapping =>
mapping.Class(typeof(Benefit)))));
```

The preceding code listing is part of employee mapping. Note the code in bold where `Inverse` is set to `true`. This is telling NHibernate that other end of this association (`Benefit` in this case) is owner of the association and should be responsible for updating the foreign key in the database. After this change, if we run the preceding code again, we would notice that the extraneous `update` statement is no more generated.

So to summarize – in one-to-many association, if "one" side is declared as owner then you get an unnecessary update statement during insertion of new records. On the other hand, if "many" side is made the owner, the unnecessary `update` statement is not generated.

In the preceding code, we passed `employee` instance to the `session.Save()` method. You could have passed the `benefit` instance as well here and got the same outcome. NHibernate does not care in which order you added entities to session or which entity is passed into the `Save` method. NHibernate uses cascade settings and navigates as deep into the association tree of the entity as possible to determine which entities to `save` or `update`. In case of one-to-many associations, it is easier to pass in the "one" side entity. If you choose to pass "many" side entity into the `Save` method then you would have to pass every entity in the collection. Imagine how your code would look when you have large number of entities on "many" side.

Ownership in many-to-many associations

As we know, many-to-many association is just a combination of two one-to-many associations. So ownership concepts that apply to one-to-many association also apply to many-to-many association. There are two differences though that you need to be aware of. To understand these differences, let's use many-to-many association between `Employee` and `Community` in our domain as example.

- You have got collection mapping present on both the `Employee` and `Community` class mappings. So you can, in principle, set `Inverse` to `true` on both of these mappings. Setting `Inverse` to `true` on the `Communities` mapping of the `Employee` class tells NHibernate that the `Employee` class is not the owner of this association and hence not responsible for updating foreign key. Similar setting on the `Members` mapping of the `Community` class tells NHibernate that the `Community` class is not the owner of this association. Do you see where this is going? We end up telling NHibernate that none of the two sides own the association. The end result is that no records are inserted into the intermediate table holding the foreign keys.

Though NHibernate would report that all entities in the association are saved successfully, in reality, the association would not be saved. So, always ensure that you set `Inverse` only on one end of the association.

- When saving transient entities involving many-to-many association, association on the owner's end must be set. Failing to do that would result in no records being inserted into the intermediate table. In our case, if `Employee` is declared as the owner (mapping of the `Members` collection on the `Community` class has `Inverse` set to `true`) then the `Communities` collection on `Employee` must be initialized with the community instances that we want to persist. This can be confusing to beginners and experts alike, hence setting both ends of associations would save you from frustration when something goes wrong.

The preceding points really boil down to two simple guidelines. One - always set only one end as inverse. Two - always use convenience methods to add items to collection instead of directly accessing collections, so that both ends of the association are set correctly. Convenience methods for many-to-many collection should not be very different from those for one-to-many collection. I will leave it to readers as an exercise to come up with these methods.

`Inverse` is probably not the best name to describe the behavior it offers. Also, the way this property works in not intuitive. Instead of being able to say that "this end is owner", you need to configure to say "the other end is owner". The negative nature of the property makes it even difficult for the beginners to understand how inverse works. There is not much we can do about it. Take your time and let the idea sink into your brain and then inverse would be second nature to you.

Inverse and cascade

In beginning, I used to get confused by `cascade` and `inverse`. I always thought that they have some relation and one impacts the other. But in reality, they are totally independent and have nothing to do with each other. `Cascade` determines whether the current action (`save`, `update`, `delete` and so on.) should be propagated down the association or not. On the other hand, `inverse` determines who is responsible for setting correct value in the foreign key column. `Cascade` settings can be applied to any type of associations whereas `inverse` can be specified only on the singular end of one-to-many association.

Order of operations

When you save an instance of a complex entity such as `Employee` which may have associations to several other entities, NHibernate has to do a lot of work to figure out how to insert/update/delete particular database records. It is important to not only generate correct set of SQL statements to get the work done, but it is even more important to fire these SQL statements in right order. With complex database table structures with lot of foreign key associations, it may be daunting to figure out right order of running a set of SQL statements. NHibernate makes the job easy for us by using the following order to ensure that SQL statements always go in right order:

1. All entity insertions in the same order they were passed into the `Save` method of session.
2. All entity updates.
3. All collection deletions.
4. All collection element deletions, updates, and insertions.
5. All collection insertions.
6. All entity deletions in the same order they were passed into the `Delete` method of session.

You do not need to remember the preceding sequence in order to work with NHibernate. It is only provided here so that you know what happens under the hood.

Entity equality

In .NET, two objects are supposed to be equal when they both point to the same object in memory. This is also called reference equality. This is what the `Equals` method on `System.Object` implements. Reference equality works for normal .NET objects but is not adequate for persistent entities. Two persistent entities can be said to be equal if they point to the same database record. So if you have loaded two instances of same employee record then they are not equal on reference equality measures, but for NHibernate they are equal.

Why does equality matter?

Equality obviously matters if you want to compare two entities. But beyond the basics, equality matters because some basic collection operations depend on equality of objects. Calling the `Add` or `Remove` methods on `ICollection` in order to add or remove items to/from collection, internally depends on the equality check of the item being added. This is more important during removal of an item because some kind of equality check has to happen before the correct item to be removed is determined. For add, as long as the collection allows duplicates, no equality checks are required. For a collection represented using sets/maps which does not allow duplicates, every time a new item is added to the collection, equality check happens. Fortunately, NHibernate handles situations like these quite well if the entities involved are persistent entities loaded using the same session. But following are two situations where NHibernate cannot handle the equality and defers to .NET's implementation of equals (which defers to reference equality):

- First situation is when the entities being compared are loaded using two different sessions resulting in two different instances in memory. This also applies when you are adding or removing items from collections outside of a session context. In a nutshell, the equality checks made outside of the context of a NHibernate session are not handled by NHibernate and hence defer to reference equality checks.

- Second situation involves composite keys. We are yet to cover composite keys. A composite key is a primary key (or identity for NHibernate) which consists of more than one database column. Composite keys result in more than one property on entity acting as identifier. Even inside a session, NHibernate is not capable of determining equality of two instances of an entity that uses composite key. A non-composite identifier of some primitive types such as `int`, `guid` is what NHibernate can handle for equality checks.

Let's see with the following example how absence of proper equality checks may fail some operations. The code is written in the form of a unit test. We would then implement equality to make this test pass.

```
[Test]
public void SameEntityLoadedFromTwoDifferentSessionsMatches()
{
  var config = new DatabaseConfigurationForSqlServer();

  object id = 0;
  var employee1 = new Employee
  {
    EmployeeNumber = "123456789",
    DateOfBirth = new DateTime(1980, 2, 23),
```

```
        DateOfJoining = new DateTime(2012, 3, 15)
    };

    using (var session = config.OpenSession())
    {
      using (var transaction = session.BeginTransaction())
      {
        id = session.Save(employee1);
        transaction.Commit();
      }
    }

    Employee employee2 = null;
    using (var session = config.OpenSession())
    {
      using (var transaction = session.BeginTransaction())
      {
        employee2 = session.Get<Employee>(id);
        transaction.Commit();
      }
    }

    Assert.That(employee1.Equals(employee2));
}
```

In the preceding test, we have saved an instance of the Employee entity named employee1. This operation is carried out in a session and that session is then disposed. We then open a new session and load the same employee instance from database and assign it to a different local variable named employee2 this time. In the end, we compare the two instances using the Equals method. If you run the preceding test, it would fail saying employee1 and employee2 do not match. This happens because in absence of our custom equality checks, CLR defers to reference equality checks and being two different .NET objects, employee1 and emplpoyee2 fail on that count.

In the preceding test, we have used a class named DatabaseConfigurationForSqlServer. This class builds NHibernate configuration against a SQL Server 2012 instance. We have been using SQLite for tests and that is the preferred database to use for tests. But SQLite has a limitation when used in in-memory mode; it does not support multiple sessions connecting to same database instance. Multiple sessions connecting to same database instance are exactly the thing we wanted for this test and hence I had to use SQL Server.

Next, we will see how to implement the custom equality checks that compare two persistent entities and consider them to be equal if they both point to the same database record.

Implementing equality

Two entities can be said to be equal if they both correspond to the same database record. In order to implement such a notion of equality for entities, we would need to override the following two methods on all our entities:

```
public int GetHashCode()
public bool Equals(object obj)
```

These methods are defined as `virtual` methods on `System.Object`. Before we implement these methods, let's take a moment and think about what we want to implement here. First and foremost, we want to make sure that the `Id` properties of the two entity instances have same value. We can extend the same logic for implementation of the `GetHashCode()` method. We can return hashcode of the `Id` property from our implementation of the `GetHashCode` method. But what if the entity is transient and does not have any id set? Since transient entities do not correspond to any database records, we can resort to .NET's reference equality check. So, we would use reference equality if entity is transient, else we would compare the identifier values of the two entity instances. That would give us the following implementation of these two methods:

```
public override int GetHashCode()
{
  return Id.GetHashCode();
}


public override bool Equals(object obj)
{
  var thisIsTransient = Id == 0;
  var otherIsTransient = other.Id == 0;

  if (thisIsTransient && otherIsTransient)
    return ReferenceEquals(this, other);

  return Id == other.Id;
}
```

There are two problems with the preceding code:

- The object passed into the Equals method could be of any type. Even worse, it could be a null. We need to safeguard our code against such situations.

- GetHashCode always returns hash code of the Id property. When a transient entity is saved and it is assigned an ID, the hashcode returned by this method would change. That is a violation of the GetHashCode implementation contract. Hashcode once assigned to an object must not be changed.

To fix the first problem, we just need to typecast the object passed into the Equals method to correct type and also check that it is not null. The second problem is more challenging to fix. We would need to generate hashcode for entity when it is transient and cache it. For this, we can fall back to .NET's default implementation of the GetHashCode method. Once the hashcode is generated and cached, we can return the same hashcode even when the entity becomes persistent. And if entity is already persistent (an entity loaded from database), we would cache and return the hashcode of its identifier. Following code listing shows this implementation:

```
private int? hashCode;
public override int GetHashCode()
{
   if (hashCode.HasValue) return hashCode.Value;

   var transientEntity = Id == 0;
   if (transientEntity)
   {
      hashCode = base.GetHashCode();
      return hashCode.Value;
      }
   return Id.GetHashCode();
}
```

Note the use of nullable int type to cache the hashcode. Another thing to note is that the preceding code uses a value of 0 for the identifier property to say that the entity is transient. This works for identifier strategies such as identity/hilo but would not work for other strategies such as guid or guidcomb, which do not generate an integer type of identifier value. Also, we have ignored a setting called unsaved-value declared during the mapping of identifier properties to specify the identifier value for transient entities. If this setting is declared to be other than 0 then preceding code needs to change accordingly.

The above implementation still has a minor flaw. If the identifier of an entity changes then the GetHashCode contract is violated because the method now starts returning a different hashcode. While it is easy to cache the hashcode generated by calling Id.GetHashCode(), I would advise against it. I would rather suggest to try and not set identifier of a persistent entity to a different value. This is not ideal to do and can lead to subtle bugs.

In the code samples of this chapter, you will have seen that I have done additional refactoring of the above code. Because every entity needs implementation of equality, I moved these two methods into the EntityBase class. But then I could not anymore check the type of the object passed into the Equals method. To enable the type checking, I added a generic parameter on EntityBase to make it EntityBase<T>. A constraint is added to T that is must be a type that inherits from EntityBase<T> so that you can only pass domain entities as T. This way, we now know what is the type of the entity at runtime for which the Equals method is called.

Moreover, I have also overloaded the == and != operator. This comes in handy if you need to compare two instances of persistent entities in your code using these operators.

The modified code looks as follows:

```
namespace Domain
{
  public class EntityBase<T> where T : EntityBase<T>
  {
    private int? hashCode;
    public override int GetHashCode()
    {
      if (hashCode.HasValue) return hashCode.Value;

      var transientEntity = Id == 0;
      if (transientEntity)
      {
        hashCode = base.GetHashCode();
        return hashCode.Value;
      }
      return Id.GetHashCode();
    }

    public virtual int Id { get; set; }
```

```
public override bool Equals(object obj)
{
  var other = obj as T;
  if (other == null) return false;

  var thisIsTransient = Id == 0;
  var otherIsTransient = other.Id == 0;

  if (thisIsTransient && otherIsTransient)
  return ReferenceEquals(this, other);

  return Id == other.Id;
}
public static bool operator ==(EntityBase<T> lhs,
EntityBase<T> rhs)
{
  return Equals(lhs, rhs);
}
public static bool operator !=(EntityBase<T> lhs,
EntityBase<T> rhs)
{
  return !Equals(lhs, rhs);
}
  }
}
```

Preceding code is all we need to make sure that two instances of entities in the memory pointing to same record in the database are treated as equal by NHibernate and CLR both. As we will see in *Chapter 8, Using NHibernate in a Real-world Application*, a generally recommended approach while developing web application using NHibernate is to use one session per incoming request. In such situation, most object equality needs are satisfied by NHibernate itself. But, it is still a good practice to implement the preceding code to ensure that you are not leaving some edge cases to chance.

The architecture diagram

We are coming to the end of a very important set of features of NHibernate. Before we close this chapter, I wanted to bring back the NHibernate architecture diagram that I had shown you in the previous chapter and update it with the concepts we learned in this chapter.

The following diagram is not vastly different from the previous one but it does highlight important concepts around sessions and transactions. You can begin one or more transactions inside a session. When a transaction is committed, session is flushed. It is at this point that all the SQL statements required to synchronize the in-memory state of the entities to database, are sent to database server for execution.

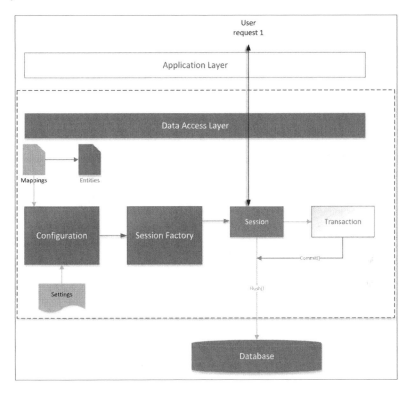

Summary

Being able to store new data or update existing data in the database is an important milestone in our NHibernate journey. In this chapter, we learned how to save transient entities and how to update persistent entities. We also learned how transitive persistence and cascading of operations takes a lot of complication away from your data access layer. We then looked at subtleties around different cascade styles and hopefully know more about when to use which cascade style. Bidirectional associations make working with code easy but they may add challenges to saving the data. It always helps to use convenience method that would transparently set both ends of bidirectional association. One of the most important take away from this chapter was to understand the use of transactions in NHibernate.

We are now ready to plunge into another important feature of NHibernate (or should I say set of features) that let us retrieve data from database using various different criteria. In our next chapter, we will dive deep into features of NHibernate which are specifically built to make querying of data from database a breeze.

6

Let's Retrieve Some Data
from the Database

So far we have covered the most important building blocks of NHibernate. This chapter will cover the last important building block – retrieving data. I find this topic most interesting for two reasons. One, of the total time you spend on working with NHibernate, you will spend about 90 percent time writing code to retrieve data and 10 percent on working with other parts of NHibernate. Second, you are spoilt for choices when it comes to retrieving data. I know that I have been saying the same for most features of NHibernate. But with data retrieval we really are offered number of different options. On top of that, NHibernate offers features such as lazy loading, polymorphic queries, implicit joins, fetching strategies, and so on, which makes data retrieval a very interesting concept to learn. I do not want to throw jargon at you and confuse you more. We are going to learn all these features in this chapter. Let me give you a brief overview of what we are going to learn.

We will begin with a short discussion of something I call querying workflow in which we will talk about how NHibernate queries work. We will then take a quick tour of different querying methods available in NHibernate. At this point, you should be able to write simple queries involving a single entity. Next, we will look at how to join multiple entities in a query. We will then spend some time talking about things such as ordering, pagination, and aggregation. Discussion of concepts such as lazy loading, polymorphic queries, and fetching strategies would follow at appropriate times. Before we actually dive into the details, let's take a moment to recall the code from the previous chapters that we have used to load entities from database:

```
using (var transaction = session.BeginTransaction())
{
  var benefit = Session.Get<Benefit>(id);
  Assert.That(benefit.Name, Is.EqualTo("Benefit 1"));
  transaction.Commit();
}
```

So far we have used the `ISession.Get<T>` method to load an entity from database using the identifier value. Towards the end of the chapter we will see how powerful this method is. But you cannot use it much because the queries you will end up writing most of the times would not be based on identifiers of the entities but some other business criteria. That is why NHibernate offers different querying mechanisms.

Querying the workflow

NHibernate supports different ways of retrieving data from database. The basic semantics of writing a NHibernate query is no different than that of a standard SQL query which consists of the following three main parts:

- You specify which tables are involved in query
- You specify an optional filter using WHERE statement
- You specify which columns you want to return using SELECT statement

There are other optional things you can add to a SQL query such as ordering, grouping, pagination, and so on, which is also supported by NHibernate. Queries written in NHibernate fundamentally differ from standard SQL queries on one aspect – **composability**. A query is represented by a query object. You can compose a query object by incrementally adding constructs such as joins with more tables, ordering, the `where` clauses, and so on. When you have finished building the query object, you call one of the terminal method on it, such as `List<T>` or `First<T>` which will tell NHibernate to go and build SQL from the query object, execute it, and return the results in specified type. Following image may make it easier to understand how this works:

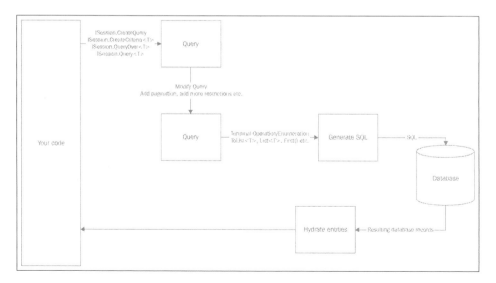

Note that the different ISession methods referred in the preceding workflow refer to different querying mechanisms available in NHibernate which we are going to look into next. No matter which querying method you use, the workflow remains more or less the same.

Different querying methods

NHibernate supports more than one way of retrieving entities from database. These different ways are built at different times with each new implementation adding something new that was not present in the earlier methods. While new ways of querying entities added new features, in most cases, some of the existing features were also lost. In this section, we will try to get a quick overview of these different methods and understand the key differences between them.

Native SQL

NHibernate supports writing queries in native SQL supported by your database. While this feature is available, do not use it generously. Two main reasons this feature is provided are:

- There is a need to utilize database specific features that are not exposed by other recommended querying methods, for example, query hints

- You have a legacy SQL/ADO.NET-based application that you intend to migrate over to use NHibernate, so it is easier to use native SQL queries from existing application as is

Following are some of the reasons for not recommending use of native SQL while working with NHibernate:

- Use of native SQL is not refactoring friendly. It is also prone to typing mistakes which at times may be very difficult to track and fix.

- Since you need to use the original database table and column names you used in the mappings, you need to remember them every time you write a SQL query. If you work in an organization which has strict rules about how database tables/columns should be named then you will not be able to use the names of the entities/properties as names of database tables/columns. This mind mapping of names from domain model to database and vice versa is cumbersome and soon becomes frustrating to work with.

- While simple SQL queries work like a charm, for complex queries you would need to remember caveats such as – always fetch ID of "many" side when retrieving "one" side in many-to-one association scenario, and so on. Failing to remember and adhere to these rules will just mean more and more errors coming out of NHibernate.

If you are using NHibernate, then you have made a choice about letting NHibernate generate SQL for you and it works best that way. When you leave the job of generating SQL to NHibernate, you not only take advantage of NHibernate's capability of generating best possible SQL for your use case but also abstract away the notion of SQL from your code and concentrate on POCOs and object-oriented code. Since I am not recommending using native SQL, I will not talk about it in great detail. I only intend to cover a simple example for the sake of completeness. Following code listing shows how you can query and load the `Employee` instance having first name as `John`, using native SQL:

```
var employeeQuery = Database.Session
.CreateSQLQuery("select * from Employee where Firstname = 'John'")
.AddEntity(typeof (Employee));

var employees = employeeQuery.List<Employee>();
```

`ISession` has a method `CreateSQLQuery` to which we can pass native SQL query. This method returns an instance of `ISQLQuery` interface which is your query object to work with. Usually the result of native SQL query is returned in an object array but you can ask NHibernate to return the result in an entity instead. This is done by calling the `AddEntity` method on the `ISQLQuery` interface and passing the type of the entity that we want returned. In the end, we call terminal method `List<T>` to get us the list of employee instances returned by the query.

Hibernate Query Language

Hibernate Query Language (HQL) syntax is very similar to standard SQL syntax with one fundamental difference. In standard SQL you refer to table names and in HQL you refer to entity names. NHibernate uses the mapping metadata to figure out tables being referred to in the query. HQL also comes with added capabilities such as understanding of inheritance, polymorphism, and associations. These capabilities make it very easy to work with entities involving complex inheritance or association patterns. In this section, we would look at some basic examples of HQL. Advanced querying concepts are dealt with separately in later sections.

HQL is written using string and passed into the `CreateQuery` method on `ISession`. This returns an instance of the `IQuery` interface which holds the HQL query object. Simplest HQL query is where you query instances of a particular entity without any filter. For instance, following HQL query would fetch all the `Employee` instances that are present in the database:

```
var employeeQuery = Database.Session
.CreateQuery("select e  from Employee as e");
```

> The `select e` part of the preceding query is optional. It is presented here for the sake of completeness. When you want to restrict what is returned by the query, then specifying `select` clause is useful.

To execute the preceding query, as with any other querying methods, you need to call one of the terminal methods on the query object. In case of HQL, you can either call `List<T>` or `Enumerable<T>` in order to execute the query. It should be clear from the name of these methods that one returns the list of type `T` and other returns an enumerable of type `T`. Make sure that the type parameter `T` can be casted to the entity being referred to in the SELECT statement of HQL query. Preceding query with terminal method called would look as follows:

```
var employees = Database.Session.CreateQuery(
"select e from Employee as e ").List<Employee>();
```

To filter the results, a WHERE clause similar to the one in standard SQL can be added. Following example shows how to query all the employees whose first name is John:

```
select e from Employee as e where e.Firstname = 'John'
```

> Calls to `ISession.CreateQuery` and terminal method `List<Employee>` are left out in almost all examples for brevity. Preceding example and any other HQL examples would need to be passed into the `CreateQuery` method of `ISession`.

HQL queries are case-insensitive but the parts where you refer to names of entities and properties on the entities are case sensitive. So you can write SELECT or select, but when you refer to `Employee`, you cannot use `employee`.

Parameter binding

The example with a `where` clause that we saw previously is more of a text book example. In real life, you would not prefer to hardcode the conditions in the `where` clause like we hardcoded the first name to be equal to `John`. In reality, this could be coming in as a parameter, in which case the HQL query needs to be built dynamically, as shown next:

```
var firstName = "John";
var employees = Database.Session.CreateQuery("select e from Employee
as e where e.Firstname = '" + firstName + "'").List<Employee>();
```

The variable `firstName` in the preceding example may contain values entered by the end user. We are passing those values in the query as it is, without making any checks. Such a practice leads to popular **SQL injection attack**. A remedy offered by most relational database technologies against SQL injection attacks is to use parameterized SQLs. In parameterized SQL, the variable data is sent separately as parameters and database server takes the responsibility of substituting the parameters correctly after making all the safety checks. HQL supports parameterized SQL through a feature called parameter binding. In parameter binding, you use parameters while writing HQL query and then provide the substitution values for those parameters separately. Parameter binding comes in two flavors – **named parameters** and **positional parameters**. I intend to cover only named parameters as these are safer and less prone to errors in case your HQL changes. Positional parameters may lead to subtle defects, if enough care is not taken while writing queries.

Let's write the previous query to retrieve employees having the first name `John`, but this time using parameter binding. Here is how the query would look:

```
var employeeQuery = Database.Session.CreateQuery(
"select e from Employee as e where e.Firstname = :firstName");
employeeQuery.SetParameter("firstName", "John");
var employees = employeeQuery.List<Employee>();
```

Parameters are introduced in an HQL query by naming them arbitrarily and beginning the name with a colon. We have declared `:firstName` as a parameter. We have then used the `SetParameter` method on the query to substitute the `firstName` parameter with value of `John`. Note that colon is not required when calling the `SetParameter` method. Rest of the code is exactly the same as the earlier code. Preceding HQL results in following SQL:

```
SELECT employee0_.id            AS Id0_,
       //…other columns…//
FROM   employee employee0_
WHERE  employee0_.firstname =@ p0;
@p0 = 'John' [TYPE: String (0)]
```

Note that the WHERE clause in the generated SQL uses parameter whose value is set to John separately.

One of the biggest advantages of HQL is that syntax-wise, it is very close to standard SQL. If you have experience of using SQL, then it is not very difficult to get started with HQL. HQL supports a range of standard SQL functions that are not available under other querying methods. Let's look into one example of such functions. Following HQL query retrieves employees who have joined in the last 12 months:

```
select e from Employee as e where e.DateOfJoining between :startdate
and :enddate
```

In the preceding example, we have used keyword between to limit the records to those having DateOfJoining between two particular dates. Explanation of all standard SQL functions supported by HQL is beyond the scope of this book. Readers may wish to visit the NHibernate's documentation on this topic at http://nhibernate.info/doc/nh/en/index.html#queryhql.

Besides the support for standard SQL functions, there are some additional constructs that are supported by HQL. HQL's internal implementation also makes it possible to reference from the queries the protected/private fields on the entities– another feature that is not supported by other querying methods.

Previous queries generated SQL that loads details of employee instances. But what about other entities that are associated with Employee. Can we use the employee instance returned by the previous query and navigate to the Benefits collection on it? We did not see any SQL being generated that hydrated the Benefits collection. If this is bothering you, then hold your thoughts for a few pages. We are going to open the bonnet and see what's happening in there.

Criteria API

HQL may sound bit out of time. Similar to XML mappings, HQL is not refactoring-friendly. Criteria query API addresses this problem to some extent. Let's take an example of a very simple query to get employees who are named john.

To work with criteria query API, you first need to get an instance of the NHibernate.ICriteria interface. The ICriteria interface is associated with a persistent entity and represents query against that particular entity. You call method CreateCriteria<T> on ISession to get an instance of ICriteria as follows:

```
var employeeQuery = database.Session.CreateCriteria<Employee>();
```

We used a generic `CreateCriteria<T>` method in the preceding example but there is a non-generic version `CreateCriteria` available as well. We would prefer to use generic version in this section but feel free to explore the non-generic version if you need to.

Now `employeeQuery` can be used to build our query to fetch instances of the `Employee` entity. This query instance is ready to be used. But without any filters to narrow down the results to what we need, this query can be dangerous. Let's see what I mean here. Terminal method `List<T>` would run this query and return the results by hydrating the list of `T` types. Let's run the following line of code and see what we get:

```
var employees = employeeQuery.List<Employee>();
```

This code would generate the following SQL:

```
SELECT this_.Id              as Id0_1_,
       /*Other columns removed for brevity*/
FROM   Employee this_
       left outer join Address address2_
                on this_.Id = address2_.Employee_Id
```

Preceding SQL has multiple issues but the one I want to highlight now is the fact that this SQL is fetching every record from the `Employee` table. There is no filter applied to narrow down the results of this query. Why? That is because we did not specify any filter in our criteria query. Let's see how to do that.

 Another thing to note here is that generated SQL contains a join to the `Address` table. We did not specify anything about `Address` in our query but NHibernate still went ahead and generated that join. I have left this as a self-study question for readers to figure out.

Filtering the criteria queries

Results of a criteria query can be filtered by applying *restrictions* to the query. In this case, we need a restriction on the `Firstname` property of the `Employee` class, that its value must be `john`. Criteria API offers factory methods to build various different restrictions. Restrictions are then applied to criteria query by passing them to the `Add()` method available on the `ICriteria` interface. Following code listing shows how to add a restriction:

```
employeeQuery.Add(Restrictions.Eq("Firstname", "john"));
```

Note that we have used factory class `NHibernate.Criterion.Restrictions` to build an equality restriction by calling factory method `Eq()`. First parameter passed to the `Eq()` method is the name of the property on which restriction needs to be applied and second parameter is the value with which the property value needs to be equated. Putting together everything we get the following code listing:

```
using (var transaction = database.Session.BeginTransaction())
{
  var employeeQuery = database.Session.CreateCriteria<Employee>();
  employeeQuery.Add(Restrictions.Eq("Firstname", "john"));
  var employees = employeeQuery.List<Employee>();

  transaction.Commit();
}
```

Criteria queries are built so that they can be chained together to save us few keystrokes. Preceding code can be rewritten as follows:

```
using (var transaction = database.Session.BeginTransaction())
{
  var employees = database.Session.CreateCriteria<Employee>()
  .Add(Restrictions.Eq("Firstname", "john"))
  .List<Employee>();

  transaction.Commit();
}
```

Following SQL is generated on execution of the preceding criteria query:

```
SELECT          this_.Id               AS Id0_1_,
                /*Other columns removed for brevity*/
FROM            Employee this_
LEFT OUTER JOIN Address address2_
ON              this_.Id=address2_.Employee_Id
WHERE           this_.Firstname = @p0;@p0 = 'john' [Type: String(0)]
```

Note that a proper WHERE clause is now applied and only records having john as first name are returned.

The `Restrictions` factory class defines several factory methods to cater to different kinds of restrictions. If we want to query all employees who have joined in the last year then you could use the `Restrictions.Between()` method, as shown next:

```
using (var transaction = database.Session.BeginTransaction())
{
  var employees = database.Session.CreateCriteria<Employee>()
```

```
      .Add(Restrictions.Between("DateOfJoining",
      DateTime.Now.AddYears(-1), DateTime.Now))
      .List<Employee>();
      transaction.Commit();
  }
```

The `Restrictions` factory class defines a number of methods to help with different types of filtering requirements. It would not be possible to cover every factory method in a section, hence this area is left for readers to explore on their own. However, readers might get a good head start by visiting the official documentation of this topic at http://nhibernate.info/doc/nh/en/index.html#querycriteria.

The QueryOver API

Criteria API is great in many aspects. It lets you build queries dynamically which can be useful in real life applications. It offers object oriented API to build queries which is better than HQL's string-based approach. But criteria API does not get rid of magic strings completely. Names of entities and properties are still hardcoded in criteria queries. QueryOver is built on top of criteria API and has managed to get rid of most of the magic strings from criteria API. In this section, we will rewrite the examples from criteria section and see how QueryOver enhances criteria queries.

Following is our first query that retrieves the `employee` instances with `John` as their first name:

```
      var employees = Database.Session.QueryOver<Employee>()
      .Where(x => x.Firstname == "John")
      .List<Employee>();
```

There are two main differences between the preceding query and criteria query. First, you call the `ISession.QueryOver<T>` method in order to build a QueryOver query. Second, you have got a `Where` method to specify the where clause of your query using lambdas so that you do not have to refer to properties using magic strings. For instance, another query we wrote in the criteria section was retrieving employees who joined in the last 12 months. The same query can be written using QueryOver as follows:

```
      var employees = Database.Session
      .QueryOver<Employee>()
      .Where(x => x.DateOfJoining > DateTime.Now.AddYears(-1) &&
      x.DateOfJoining < DateTime.Now)
      .List<Employee>();
```

QueryOver tries to offer a lambda-based syntax for almost everything. But for those times when you are unable to express a query entirely using lambda syntax, QueryOver also offers backwards compatibility with most `Restrictions` factory methods we looked at earlier. What is even better is that QueryOver enhances them with lambdas. So the previous query written using the `Restrictions` factory methods of QueryOver would look as follows:

```
employees = Database.Session.QueryOver<Employee>()
.WhereRestrictionOn(x => x.DateOfJoining)
.IsBetween(DateTime.Now.AddYears(-1)).And(DateTime.Now)
.List<Employee>();
```

QueryOver takes criteria queries a step further but still feels clumsy in some areas. Specifically, the syntax for joining two entities is not very intuitive as we would see in the joins section. Between QueryOver and criteria, I would recommend QueryOver to my readers anytime.

Next, we will look at the most recent addition to querying methods – LINQ. LINQ not only does away with any magic strings in the queries but is also very intuitive.

LINQ

Since LINQ was introduced in .NET, it has become de-facto standard for querying. LINQ extends querying capabilities of C# by providing SQL-like querying syntax and intuitive API based on lambda expressions. LINQ support in C# hinges around an interface named `IQueryable<T>`. The SQL-like query syntax and lambda expression-based syntax are both built around this interface. Type parameter `T` is the type of the entity against which you want to write queries.

NHibernate implements its own version of `IQueryable<T>` which is used to convert the LINQ queries that we write into appropriate SQL statements. `ISession` has an extension method `Query<T>` which returns NHibernate's implementation of `IQueryable<T>`. Once you have an instance of `IQueryable<T>`, you can write queries using regular LINQ syntax. The following code listing shows how the query to retrieve the `Employee` entities having `John` as first name:

```
var employees = from e in Database.Session.Query<Employee>()
        where e.Firstname == "John" select e;
```

You may have noticed that the preceding code is a SQL-like querying syntax of LINQ. An alternative lambda expression-based syntax looks as follows:

```
var employees = Database.Session.Query<Employee>()
.Where(e => e.Firstname == "John");
```

There are pros and cons of both the methods and there is no preferred way of using LINQ. Some features are easier done with lambdas while others are easier with query like syntax. For instance, as we would see in joins section, theta style joins are not easy to do with lambdas. Let's write another query that we have previously written using other querying methods. Following query retrieves all employees who have joined in the last 12 months. First one is query syntax followed by lambda syntax:

```
var employees = from e in Database.Session.Query<Employee>()
where e.DateOfJoining > DateTime.Now.AddYears(-1) &&
e.DateOfJoining < DateTime.Now
select e;

var employees = Database.Session.Query<Employee>()
.Where(e => e.DateOfJoining > DateTime.Now.AddYears(-1) &&

e.DateOfJoining < DateTime.Now);
```

A point worth noticing here is that the query syntax is very close to standard SQL syntax and lambda syntax is very close to QueryOver. Another thing to note here is that the preceding queries will not be executed unless terminal methods such as `ToList` or `ToArray` are invoked on them.

We have covered different querying methods very quickly. Examples that we looked at were very simple and involved a single entity. In real life scenarios, you will mostly need to join multiple entities to fetch the data you need. Sometimes you also need to restrict the number of records returned or even transform the data coming out of a query in some way. We will look at all of these scenarios and see how these are supported by different querying methods in the next few sections.

Before we close this section, it would be good to spend some time to look into pros and cons of different querying methods we have just covered. The idea is to make you feel more empowered than confused.

Which querying method should I use?

A flip side of multiple ways of doing something is the confusion it creates for beginners when it comes to choosing the right way. This is equally true for different querying mechanisms of NHibernate because there is no one way which has all the pros and no cons. So instead of telling you which is the best querying method, what I will do is give you the following two guidelines to follow and help determine which querying method you should use:

- Choose the querying method that does not involve any literal strings that refer to entities or database tables. This only leaves QueryOver and LINQ to choose from. I cannot reiterate this fact enough – "literal strings" = "lack of refactoring". More agile/iterative development you do, more inclined you will be towards refactoring code to make it better. You do not want to use HQL, criteria, or native SQL which can hold you back when it comes to refactoring your code.

- If you are aware of a particular querying method then stick to that. You do not want to learn too many things at one go. Lots of .NET developers know LINQ already so it is only natural to prefer LINQ over QueryOver. Besides that, syntax-wise, LINQ just seems more natural than QueryOver. If you do not know LINQ but are used to writing native SQL, then it would be easier for you to learn HQL.

Querying data is an interesting problem and native SQL offers capabilities that can lead to several solutions to a particular querying problem. Most important thing to keep in mind is that there is no one querying method that lets you tackle any situation. There will be times when LINQ cannot do something and you need to choose something else. So do not shy away from learning a new querying method if the need be.

We have covered basic querying syntax using different querying methods. We will now look into extending our basic queries and write complex queries involving joins, pagination, and also use features such as lazy loading on the way. Let's start with joins.

Joins

Join syntax of SQL allows you to connect two database tables which share a column value. On most occasions, the shared columns constitute foreign key relation between two tables but having such relationship is not mandatory. As long as the columns hold the value referring to the same record, you can run a meaningful join query. For instance, in our domain, the `Employee` table's `Id` column and the `Benefit` table's `Employee_Id` column hold the Id of particular employee record. We can join the two tables using value in those two columns.

Different types of joins

There are mainly two types of joins. An **inner join** and an **outer join**. The best way to understand the difference between the two is to use Venn diagram from set theory. If you think of employee as one set and benefit as another set, then intersection between the two can be represented by a Venn diagram as follows:

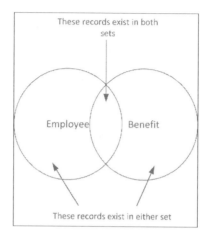

The overlapping area or intersection of the **Employee** and **Benefit** sets represents the records that are present in both sets. These are employee records having associated benefit records or vice versa. The non-overlapping area represents the records that are either present only in the **Employee** set or the **Benefit** set.

A SQL join lets you connect two tables and return records that are either present in both tables or present in one of the tables. If you want the records that are present in both the tables, then you should use inner join. If you want records that are present in either of the tables then you use an outer join. Following modified Venn diagram depicts which is the inner join and which is outer:

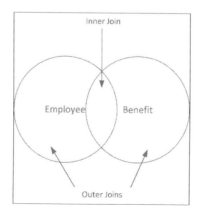

Outer joins have three subtypes – a **left outer join**, a **right outer join**, and a **full outer join**. A left outer join would return records that are present in the overlapping part of the preceding Venn diagram plus the records that are present in the left non-overlapping part. A right outer join returns records that are present in the right non-overlapping part and the overlapping part of the preceding Venn diagram. A full outer join is combination of right and left outer join. Syntactically, following is how you write these different joins:

```
SELECT *
FROM Employee E
INNER JOIN Address A ON E.Id = A.Employee_Id

SELECT *
FROM Employee E
LEFT OUTER JOIN Address A ON E.Id = A.Employee_Id

SELECT *
FROM Employee E
RIGHT OUTER JOIN Address A ON E.Id = A.Employee_Id

SELECT *
FROM Employee E
FULL OUTER JOIN Address A ON E.Id = A.Employee_Id
```

The equality construct after the preceding ON is how your associate records from two sets. This is mostly a foreign key relationship between the two tables. Most relational database technologies support both inner and outer joins but there may be a few which do not. If you are using such database, then NHibernate would throw an exception if you happen to use outer join while it is not supported.

Since NHibernate knows from the mapping metadata how two entities are related to each other, it takes away the complexity and makes joining two entities simple. This is also called implicit joins.

Implicit joins

NHibernate supports notion of implicit join. It means that if you have mapped two entities as having association between them, then NHibernate would implicitly join the mapped tables when one entity is navigated from the other in the query. This could be difficult to understand, so let's take an example. Suppose you want to load all employees who live in London. You would need an inner join between the Employee and Address tables to load those employees. Since we have mapped the association between the Employee and Address class, NHibernate knows to use inner join when the ResidentialAddress property on the Employee class is navigated in LINQ query, as shown next:

```
[Test]
public void QueryEmployeesWhoLiveInLondon()
{
  IList<Employee> employees = null;
  using (var transaction = Database.Session.BeginTransaction())
  {
    employees =
    Database.Session.Query<Employee>()
    .Where(e => e.ResidentialAddress.City == "London").ToList();
    transaction.Commit();
  }

  Assert.That(employees.Count, Is.EqualTo(3));
}
```

Take a look at the part in bold where we specify restriction on the City property just by navigating the ResidentialAddress property of Employee. Because of the mapped association between the two classes, NHibernate knows that a foreign key relationship exists between the tables that these entities are mapped to. NHibernate will use that knowledge to generate the following SQL involving an inner join between the Employee and Address tables:

```
SELECT  employee0_.id           AS Id0_,
        //...other columns...//
FROM    employee employee0_
        inner join address address1_
                ON employee0_.id = address1_.employee_id
WHERE   address1_.city =@ p0;
@p0 = 'London' [TYPE: String (0)]
```

Criteria and QueryOver support implicit joins but the syntax is slightly verbose. Following is how the preceding query can be written using QueryOver:

```
[Test]
public void QueryEmployeesWhoLiveInLondon()
```

```
{
    IList<Employee> employees;
    using (var transaction = Database.Session.BeginTransaction())
    {
        employees = Database.Session.QueryOver<Employee>()
        .JoinQueryOver(x => x.ResidentialAddress)
        .Where(r => r.City == "London").List<Employee>();
        transaction.Commit();
    }

    Assert.That(employees.Count, Is.EqualTo(3));
}
```

For LINQ version, the navigation of the ResidentialAddress property inside call to the Where method gave us the join we needed. But that does not work with QueryOver. In QueryOver, you need to explicitly tell NHibernate about your intention to perform a join by calling method named JoinQueryOver. It is in this method that you navigate to the ResidentialAddress property. Call to JoinQueryOver returns a new instance of IQueryOver<Address>, so any subsequent restrictions are applied on properties of the Address entity. Internally, there is a lot going on here. Let's take a look at this in detail to understand how exactly joins work for QueryOver.

QueryOver joins explained

The QueryOver examples we have seen so far have used the ISession. QueryOver<T> method. This method returns an instance of IQueryOver<T1, T2> where both T1 and T2 are of same type T. For instance, when we called ISession. QueryOver<Employee>, we got IQueryOver<Employee, Employee>.

T1 is the root entity which we are trying to retrieve from database. It is obvious that terminal methods such as List and Select can only use T1. T2 is used in the Where method to declare filters or restrictions on the entities being retrieved.

T1 cannot change after an IQueryOver<T1, T2> is instantiated. T2 changes every time you introduce a join clause by calling JoinQueryOver. The lambda expression passed into JoinQueryOver determines the new type of T2. In our case, we passed x => x.ResidentialAddress into JoinQueryOver which changed T2 from Employee to Address. An immediate effect of this is that you can now apply restrictions only on the properties of the Address entity (remember restrictions can only be applied on T2?).

Another point to note is that you can only make further joins on associations that are present on T2. Again, in our previous example, T2 was Employee to being with, so we could join on ResidentialAddress which is present on T2 (or Employee). After this join, T2 changes and hence further joins can only be applied on associations that are present on the new T2, Address. This is a problem. What if you want to run another join on the Benefits association present on root entity Employee? Well, there is a solution to that. But before I get into the solution, let me take a moment to talk about another problem you may hit with this.

The restrictions that you can apply in the Where method can only be applied on the properties of T2. So in our example, you can only apply restriction on properties of the Address entity. What if we want to retrieve employees having first name John and who live in London? Solution to both this and the previous problem is to use JoinAlias which is what we are going to look at next.

JoinAlias

Similar to JoinQueryOver, JoinAlias lets you join on an association present on T1 but it does not change T2. Rather it gives you a new type that you can use wherever you want in your query. Following query retrieves employees having first name John and who live in London:

```
Address addressAlias = null;
var employees = Database.Session.QueryOver<Employee>()
.JoinAlias(x => x.ResidentialAddress,() => addressAlias)
.Where(e => e.Firstname == "John" && addressAlias.City =="London")

.List<Employee>();
```

We are using JoinAlias here. JoinAlias takes in two parameters. First one is a lambda to the association to be joined. So far this is same as JoinQueryOver. Second one is Expression<Func<T>> type of parameter which returns a local variable of type T. In the preceding example, we chose T to be of type Address. If I had to explain in plain English what this code is doing, then it is like telling the following to QueryOver:

> *"Hey. QueryOver, I want you to join on the ResidentialAddress property which is present on your root type Employee. I also want you to use my local variable addressAlias to represent this join so that I can use my local variable further down the line in this query if I have to."*

Simple isn't it? And then as you can see, we have two restrictions applied in the Where method. One is on FirstName which is present on Employee and another on City for which we have used our local variable addressAlias.

You can call `JoinAlias` as many times as you want. The only downside of that is, your queries would start looking a bit ugly with too many local alias variables. This is where I prefer the power of LINQ which interprets an implicit join as you navigate the association inside the `Where` method. Following is how the same query written in LINQ would look:

```
var employees = Database.Session.Query<Employee>()
.Where(e => e.Firstname == "John" &&
e.ResidentialAddress.City == "London").ToList();
```

> I have chosen to skip explaining criteria query for an implicit join as I do not want to encourage you to use criteria queries if you can use LINQ or QueryOver. But if for any reason you must use criteria, feel free to explore it on your own.

Outer joins

In QueryOver, specifying left or right outer joins is not very different from specifying inner joins. Rather, the implicit join syntax can be slightly modified to tell NHibernate that it should consider an outer join in place of inner join. The QueryOver example we just saw can be changed as follows to result in a left outer join instead of inner join:

```
using (var transaction = Database.Session.BeginTransaction())
{
  employees = Database.Session.QueryOver<Employee>()
  .Left.JoinQueryOver(x => x.ResidentialAddress)
  .Where(r => r.City == "London").List<Employee>();
  transaction.Commit();
}
```

The preceding code is exact reproduction of the earlier code except for one minor modification in bold. Call to chained property `Left` before `JoinQueryOver` tells NHibernate that a left outer join should be considered here. Similarly, chained properties `Right` and `Full` are available to declare our intent to consider right outer join and full outer join respectively.

Support for outer joins in LINQ is limited and syntax is not intuitive. For starters, you cannot use lambda expressions for outer joins. Following is an example of left outer join between `Employee` and `Benefit` using a LINQ query:

```
from b in e.Benefits.DefaultIfEmpty()
select e).ToList();
```

Note the call to `DefaultIfEmpty()` in bold after join with `e.Benefits`. This is LINQ's implementation of left join. What this is telling NHibernate is that if benefit side is empty then consider a default record – which is what a left join does. A caveat to remember with this syntax is that it only works for the joins with the properties that can be navigated from the root entity. In the preceding query, root entity is `Employee` and the joined entity is `Benefit` which can be navigated from `Employee` via the `Benefits` collection on it.

Theta style joins

The joins we have seen so far are called ANSI joins. There is another class of joins called theta style joins. Theta style joins are similar to Cartesian product of two tables with a `where` clause limiting the records that end up in the result. The previous query to return employees living in `London` can be rewritten using theta style join as follows:

```
SELECT  employee0_.id           AS Id0_,
        //… other columns …//
FROM    employee employee0_,
        address address1_
WHERE   address1_.employee_id = employee0_.id
        AND address1_.city =@ p0;
@p0 = 'London' [TYPE: String (0)]
```

Theta joins are useful when you need to join two entities without having any mapped association between them (or two database tables not related through a foreign key). It is strange to have two entities which are related but do not have that relation reflected in database or in mappings. But you may encounter such situation while working with legacy databases, so it is useful to know how to do theta joins. Lack of association between the entities means that we cannot use implicit joins. Unfortunately, not all querying methods of NHibernate support theta joins. Only HQL and LINQ queries support theta joins. Following is an example of theta join using LINQ that would result in the previous SQL being sent to database:

```
var employees = from e in Database.Session.Query<Employee>()
                join a in Database.Session.Query<Address>()
on e equals a.Employee
                where a.City == "London"
                select e;
```

Here, instead of navigating the `ResidentialAddress` property on the `Employee` class, we are getting a new independent `IQueryable<Address>` instance in order to perform a join. This results in a theta style join being issued.

Lazy loading

In the beginning of the chapter we saw that when the `Employee` entity was loaded, NHibernate did not load the associated collection entities such as `Benefits` and `Communities`. That is default behavior of NHibernate. At first it may sound strange, but think what would happen if NHibernate tried loading `Benefits` and `Communities` along with the `Employee` entity. Each `Community` instance in the `Communities` collection has collection of the `Employee` instances associated with it. NHibernate will need to load all those `Employee` instances. Each of those `Employee` instances will have further `Community` instances to load. This cycle will only stop when the entire database is loaded into memory. To avoid situations like this, NHibernate only loads the entity that you asked for with all its primitive properties (or properties which are mapped to columns on the table of the entity) populated. Associated collection entities are loaded only when they are accessed. This feature is called lazy loading. NHibernate marks all the mapped entities as lazily loaded unless we override the default in the mapping configuration at each entity level. In mapping by code, we can include a call to method `Lazy` which takes a Boolean value to indicate whether the entity should be marked lazy or not.

> You can even have primitive properties of entity configured to be loaded only when they are accessed similar to collections. They are called lazy properties. I omitted the detail to simplify the discussion. We would look at lazy properties in the section ahead.

Internal mechanism of lazy loading for collection associations (one-to-many and many-to-many) are slightly different from that of single-ended association (many-to-one). Similarly, mechanism for lazy loading of properties is again different from that of associations. In this section, we would take a look at lazy loading in detail, understand how it works, and get acquainted with best practices around lazy loading.

Lazy collections

There is nothing you need to do to enable lazy behavior on collections. All collection mappings are lazy by default. With lazy loading enabled, when an entity is loaded, NHibernate sets all the collection properties on this entity to a special collection type implemented by NHibernate. This special collection type is capable of loading entities in the collection when the collection is accessed (on demand). Let's take an example and see how this works.

In the following test, we are loading the Employee entity having first name as John:

```
[Test]
public void QueryEmployeeByName()
{
  IList<Employee> employees = null;
  using (var transaction = Database.Session.BeginTransaction())
  {
    employees = Database.Session.CreateCriteria<Employee>()
                        .Add(Restrictions.Eq("Firstname", "John"))
                        .List<Employee>();

    transaction.Commit();

  }
  Assert.That(employees.Count, Is.EqualTo(1));
}
```

If you look at the SQL generated for the preceding code then you would notice that NHibernate has not generated any SQL to load the Benefits and Communities collection. As shown in the following image, on inspection of the loaded employees collection, we can see that the Benefits and Communities collection on these entities is set to a special type NHibernate.Collection.Generic. PersistentGenericSet<T>:

`PersistentGenericSet<T>` is a special type that NHibernate implements. This is commonly referred to as collection wrapper. Let's take a close look at definition of this type.

```
public class PersistentGenericSet<T> : AbstractPersistentCollection,
ISet<T>,
```

`PersistentGenericSet<T>` is NHibernate's persistence-aware implementation of `ISet<T>`. Whenever you access the collection property in your code, `PersistentGenericSet<T>` will issue required SQL statements to load the items in the collection. There are several implementations of collection wrappers in NHibernate. Depending on the type of the collection, NHibernate chooses the right collection wrapper. In our case, since the `Communities` collection property on the `Employee` class is of type `ICollection<T>` and `ISet<T>` inherits from `ICollection<T>`, NHibernate chooses to use `PersistentGenericSet<T>`. For other collection types, other implementations are available. As a user of NHibernate, you do not need to know what those types are. NHibernate manages this transparently for you.

Disabling laziness

Using lazy collections is recommended but if there is a need to disable laziness on a collection then you can do so in mapping declaration. Following code listing shows how to disable laziness on the `Benefits` collection of the `Employee` entity:

```
Set(e => e.Benefits,mapper =>
{
  //… other mappings…//
  mapper.Lazy(CollectionLazy.NoLazy);
  },
relation => relation.OneToMany(mapping =>
mapping.Class(typeof(Benefit)))));
```

Preceding code is from mapping of the `Employee` entity. Mapping of other properties is skipped to keep the text brief. Remember that disabling laziness via mappings stops the lazy loading for that collection globally. As stated at the beginning of the section, lack of lazy loading can lead to entire table data being loaded into memory. In the worse case scenario, even entire database can be loaded into the memory. So make sure you understand nature of the data before you turn off lazy loading globally. NHibernate lets you disable lazy loading of collections for a particular query. This is called **eager fetching**. If there is a need to load a collection eagerly only for a particular data retrieval operation, then you can use eager fetching for that query without disabling lazy loading globally. We will look at eager fetching in the next section.

Another option to disable laziness on collections is to disable laziness on the collection entity itself. But that would have a bigger impact as the entity is then always eager fetched and not just when fetched as part of a particular collection.

Different lazy behaviors

Did you notice that we used an enumeration named `CollectionLazy` to disable lazy loading in the previous code listing? If lazy loading has only two states – enabled and disabled – then why not use a Boolean to enables or disable it? That is because lazy loading has not two but three different settings to choose from. You have already looked at `CollectionLazy.NoLazy` which is used to disable lazy loading. Rest of the two settings are as follows:

- `Collection.Lazy`: Enables lazy loading. This is default value when none is specified.

- `Collection.Extra`: This option adds extra smartness to lazy loading in some cases. If the collection is an indexed collection, then marking it as extra lazy will let you load individual items in the collection as you access them, as opposed to all items being loaded when collection is accessed. For non-indexed collections, extra laziness will generate more optimized SQL statements when aggregate functions such as `Count()` are called on the collection. For instance, if code that is accessing the collection calls the `Count()` method on the collection, then NHibernate would issue SQL statement that returns the count of the items in collection instead of loading the collection and then counting the number of items in memory.

Single-ended lazy associations

Single-ended associations are the other end of collection type of association. In mapping, these are represented by many-to-one element. Similar to lazy collections, lazy behavior for these type of associations is enabled by default. But unlike lazy collections, lazy behavior setting takes different values indicated as follows:

- `NoLazy`: Disable lazy behavior.

- `Proxy`: Enable lazy behavior. Why such a strange name? This goes back to what happens during lazy loading of single-ended associations. If you remember, in case of lazy collections, NHibernate used special wrapper collection types which load the collection when accessed. It is possible to implement such wrapper collection types because the actual collection types you are allowed to use in your code are known to NHibernate.

In case of single-ended associations, the type that is to be loaded lazily is not a .NET framework type but a type defined by developers as part of their domain model. NHibernate does not know of these types and hence cannot provide an implementation that can be substituted for these types dynamically at runtime. Instead, NHibernate uses proxies that it builds dynamically. Every entity that is mapped has a corresponding proxy class generated by NHibernate dynamically at the start of the application unless lazy loading is disabled during mapping. This proxy class is implemented by inheriting from the entity being mapped. Like collection wrapper, proxy classes are capable of lazily loading themselves. NHibernate uses these classes for lazy loading of single-ended associations and hence the value `Proxy`.

- `NoProxy`: From lazy behavior point of view, this is exactly same as the previous `Proxy` value. Using value of `Proxy` may give you trouble if the entity being lazily loaded is at the root of an inheritance hierarchy. `NoProxy` solves this problem still maintaining the lazy behavior.

Let's look into an example to see how lazy loading for single-ended associations works. We will use the association from `Benefit` to `Employee` to explore this topic. Following image from *Chapter 3, Let's Tell NHibernate About Our Database*, summarizes this association briefly:

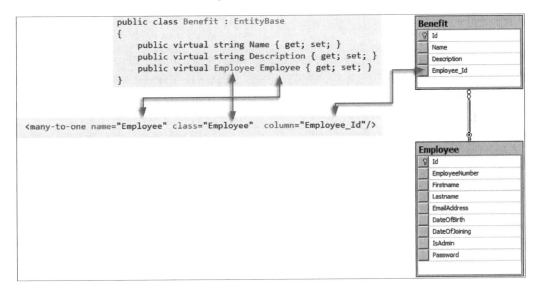

Following code listing from the mapping of the Benefit entity shows how to explicitly enable lazy behavior on the Employee property of the Benefit class:

```
ManyToOne(a => a.Employee, mapper =>
{

    mapper.Column("Employee_Id");
    mapper.Class(typeof (Employee));
    mapper.Lazy(LazyRelation.Proxy);
});
```

In the preceding code, we have told NHibernate that Employee association on Benefit should be treated as lazy and in particular, Proxy type.

 LazyRelation enumeration defines the other two lazy behaviors we discussed previously.

Next, we will write a test to load all the SeasonTicketLoan benefits having amount greater than 1000:

```
[Test]
public void LoadSeasonTicketLoanBenefitsHavingAmountGreaterThan1000()
{
    using (var transaction = Database.Session.BeginTransaction())
    {
        var seasonTicketLoans = Database.Session
                                    .QueryOver<SeasonTicketLoan>()
                                    .Where(s => s.Amount > 1000)
                                    .List<SeasonTicketLoan>();
        Assert.That(seasonTicketLoans.Count, Is.EqualTo(1));
        Assert.That(seasonTicketLoans[0].Employee, Is.Not.Null);

        transaction.Commit();
    }
}
```

If we inspect the actual value of the Employee property on the previous seasonTicketLoans[0] then we can see that it is of type EmployeeProxy, which is a type generated by NHibernate at runtime.

```
[Test]
▶ | 0 references
public void ManyToOneLazyLoadingTest()
{
    using (var transaction = Database.Session.BeginTransaction())
    {
        var seasonTicketLoans = Database.Session.QueryOver<SeasonTicketLoan>()
                            .Where(s => s.Amount > 1000)
                            .List<SeasonTicketLoan>();
        Assert.That(seasonTicketLoans.Count, Is.EqualTo(1));
        Assert.That(seasonTicketLoans[0].Employee, Is.Not.Null);
                        ▷ 🔧 seasonTicketLoans[0].Employee {EmployeeProxy} ⇥

        transaction.Commit();
    }
}
```

Proxy versus NoProxy

To understand the difference between `Proxy` and `NoProxy`, we will have to assume that `Employee` has one more entity inheriting from it. Suppose we have `FormerEmployee` inheriting from `Employee`. If we also consider the NHibernate's dynamically generated `EmployeeProxy` type, then we get the following class diagram:

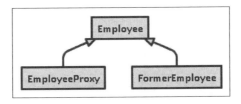

When a benefit entity is loaded, the `Employee` association is lazily loaded and set to an instance of type `EmployeeProxy`. NHibernate has not yet gone to database to check whether the actual entity is of the `Employee` type or the `FormerEmployee` type. If you are expecting an instance of `FormerEmployee` and downcast the loaded instance to that type, you would be greeted with an exception because the actual type held in there is `EmployeeProxy`.

This is where `NoProxy` plays its role. In the previous example, when the lazy setting was set to `Proxy` and the `Benefit` instances was loaded from database, its type was set to actual type – `SeasonTicketLoan` in this case. It was the `Employee` property that was set to proxy type `EmployeeProxy`. But when lazy setting on the `Employee` association is set to `NoProxy`, then NHibernate will load a proxy instance of the `Benefit` class first -, which is `SeasonTicketLoanProxy`. Now because the parent object is a proxy, NHibernate is capable of intercepting it. When you access the `Employee` property on this proxy, NHibernate will go to database and load the correct instance of `Employee` and return it.

NHibernate lets you intercept different operations that it performs so that you can run your custom logic before NHibernate finishes its own operation. One such interception, called property load interception, will let you run your logic before/after value of a property is loaded from database. Implementation of `NoProxy` uses property load interception. What that means for you, the user of NHibernate is that the `NoProxy` option will work only if the association uses property. If your association uses field then `NoProxy` would not work.

Lazy properties

Besides lazy collections and lazy single-ended associations, NHibernate also supports lazy properties. One or more mapped properties of an entity can be declared lazy by using the syntax shown next:

```
Property(e => e.EmployeeNumber, mapper => { mapper.Lazy(true);});
```

In the preceding syntax, the `EmployeeNumber` property on the `Employee` class is mapped as lazy. Value of a lazy property is loaded from database when the property is accessed for the first time. If a class has more than one lazy property then all lazy properties are loaded at once when any of the lazy property is accessed.

Why use lazy loading?

In the introduction of lazy loading, we discussed how lazy loading can avoid whole databases being loaded into memory on retrieval of a single entity. Well, that is a great benefit of lazy loading but there is another more apparent benefit that lazy loading brings to the table.

Suppose you are working on a business requirement with makes an employee a member of a community. Assume that you load this employee by its ID. Ideally, you would only want to load the `employee` and its `Communities` collection. In absence of lazy loading, you would have to resort to writing a detailed query to load only the parts you need.

Now, suppose you have another requirement that involves loading employee by its ID and the `Benefits` collection on the `employee` instance. The query you used for the previous requirement cannot be used here because that query did not load the `Benefits` collection. You have two options now – one, write a new query to load employee and its `Benefits` collection and two, update the previous query so that it loads both the `Communities` and `Benefits` collection of `employee` instance. Neither of these solutions are ideal. The first solution is not scalable as you would end up writing similar queries with slight variations in details that they load. The second solution leads to unnecessary loading of collection items that may not be required.

Lazy loading handles such situations quite nicely. You write one query to retrieve employee by its ID and use it in both the requirements. When the code for the first requirement navigates to the Communities collection, it is loaded. When the code for the second requirement accesses the Benefits collection, it is loaded at that point. Neither do you have to write duplicate querying code nor load unnecessary collection items.

Lazy properties are slightly different. If an entity has lazy properties, then NHibernate ends up making two database trips, once to load the non-lazy properties of the entity and second time to load the lazy properties of the entity. This behavior may actually result in unnecessary round trips to database. So do not use lazy properties unless you are absolutely sure that you need lazy behavior. One situation where you might want lazy property is when the property holds large amount of data which is not needed to be fetched all the time along with other properties on the same entity. SQL types such as BLOB, CLOB, TEXT, and Binary are examples of such properties. Making such properties lazy, you can save large amount of data coming out of database every time the entity is loaded.

Lazy loading gotcha's

While lazy loading is a great feature, it is very easy to get into issues if lazy loading is used without care. There are some gotchas around lazy loading that we will look into briefly in this section. Knowing these will help you avoid problems and frustration while working with lazy loading.

Keeping the session open

Any database interaction that NHibernate does, requires an open session to communicate with database. With lazy loading, the associated entities are loaded at the point of them being accessed for the first time. For this to work, it is mandatory that the session in which the parent entity was loaded is still around in usable state. Lazy loading, specifically the proxies used by NHibernate, rely on the original session object in order to load the proxied entities. So make sure that you do not close the session object until the parent object is in use if you know that lazy loading will be triggered at some point later.

Chapter 8, Using NHibernate in Real-world Applications, we will look at some guidelines and recommended patterns that can help with this situation.

Being aware of the select N+1 problem

Use of lazy loading leads to a performance problem often called as **select N+1 problem**. This is not much of an issue if the lazy collections have small number of items in them. For collections having large number of items, select N+1 problem can result in unnecessary loading of entities and significant performance degradation. Choosing right **fetching strategy** or correct **batching settings** can help with addressing select N+1 issues to some extent. We will look at fetching strategies next and in the next chapter we are going to look at select N+1 problem in detail along with batching.

Using lazy loading together with the right fetching strategy

select N+1 problem can be addressed by fetching strategies, but their role is not limited to fixing select N+1 problem only. Lazy loading used in combination with right fetching strategy can offer the best optimization of your data access code. Always consider using lazy loading in unison with right fetching strategy. Again, in the next chapter, we will look at this aspect in little more detail.

Using automatic properties

Lazy properties only work if they are declared as automatic properties. If a property is declared using backing fields and you try to access the field directly, then you may get unexpected results.

Eager fetching

You can disable lazy loading in mapping and that would load all collections/associations eagerly all the time. But as stated earlier, eagerly loading associations all the time is not a good idea. However, at times you do need to load a particular association eagerly. For this reason, NHibernate lets you specify, during the query, that a particular association should be loaded eagerly. Let's take a look at examples of different querying mechanisms to see how to eagerly load associations.

HQL

To eagerly load associations in HQL, you need to add keyword `fetch` after the `join` keyword, as shown next:

```
select e from Employee as e join fetch e.Benefits where e.Firstname =
:firstName
```

Preceding HQL query loads all employee instances with matching first name and also loads their `Benefits` collection in the same select eagerly.

Criteria

Criteria API offers a method named `SetFetchMode` that can be used to tell NHibernate of our intent to load a particular association eagerly. Following example loads employee records having first name as John and also loads the `Benefits` collection eagerly in the same `SELECT` statement:

```
var employees = Database.Session.CreateCriteria<Employee>()
                    .Add(Restrictions.Eq("Firstname", "John"))
                    .SetFetchMode("Benefits", FetchMode.Join)
                    .List<Employee>();
```

`SetFetchMode` takes two parameters. First is the name of the association property for which `fetch` mode is specified. Second parameter is the actual fetch mode specified using the `FetchMode` enum. The `FetchMode` enum has following values:

- `Default`: Default is `Select`.
- `Lazy`: Load the association lazily. This will use a separate `SELECT` statement to load the association when accessed.
- `Eager`: Load the association eagerly. This will use left outer join to load the association at the same time as root entity is loaded.
- `Select`: Same as `Lazy`.
- `Join`: Same as `Eager`.

QueryOver

QueryOver offers a nice lambda syntax for eager loading of associations. Following code listing shows the previous query written using QueryOver:

```
var employees = Database.Session.QueryOver<Employee>()
.Where(x => x.Firstname == "John")
.Fetch(e => e.Benefits).Eager.List<Employee>();
```

The `Fetch` method takes in a lambda to which you can pass the association property that you want to load eagerly followed by a call to `Eager`. This also works in the opposite way. If the association has laziness disabled and you want to load the association lazily in this query, then you can call `Lazy` after the call to the `Fetch` method, as shown next:

```
.Fetch(e => e.Benefits).Lazy
```

If you want to eagerly fetch more than one association/collection, you just need to repeat the call to the `Fetch` method, passing association/collection that you want fetched eagerly. Following fetches both `Benefits` and `Communities` eagerly:

```
var employees = Database.Session.QueryOver<Employee>()
                    .Where(x => x.Firstname == "John")
                    .Fetch(e => e.Benefits).Eager
                    .Fetch(e => e.Communities).Eager
                    .List<Employee>();
```

Although it is not recommended to load multiple levels of objects eagerly, if there is a requirement to do so, then that is supported as well. If you want to eagerly fetch the `Communities` collection and then eagerly fetch the `Members` collection that is present on the `Communities` collection, then you can do it as follows:

```
var employees = Database.Session.QueryOver<Employee>()
.Where(x => x.Firstname == "John")
.Fetch(e => e.Communities).Eager
.Fetch(e => e.Communities.First().Members).Eager.List<Employee>();
```

LINQ

Similar to QueryOver, LINQ offers a `Fetch` method that can be used to eagerly load associations/collections. But unlike QueryOver, this method can only be used to eagerly load associations/collections that would have been otherwise loaded lazily. Following is the same query written using LINQ:

```
var employees = Database.Session.Query<Employee>()
                    .Where(x => x.Firstname == "John")
                    .Fetch(e => e.Benefits)
                    .ToList();
```

Unlike QueryOver, there is no need to call anything after call to the `Fetch` method. If you need to eagerly load multiple collections then just place call to `Fetch` multiple times.

LINQ also has a `FetchMany` method which needs an explanation. While `Fetch` is capable of eagerly loading both single-ended associations and collections, `FetchMany` only deals with collections. But if you intend to eagerly fetch child association/collection on the collection that you have loaded eagerly, then you must use `FetchMany`. Let's look into an example. If we want to eagerly load the `Communities` collection on `Employee` and then eagerly load the `Members` collection on that `Communities` collection, then we must use `FetchMany`, as shown next:

```
var employees = Database.Session.Query<Employee>()
                    .Where(x => x.Firstname == "John")
```

```
.FetchMany(e => e.Communities)
.ThenFetch(c => c.Members);
```

Note the `ThenFetch` call that we are seeing for the first time. The `ThenFetch` method is used to tell NHibernate that association/collection from second level also needs to be loaded eagerly.

 Selective eager loading in queries looks like a good option to disable lazy loading temporarily. But there is a flip side to this approach. The SQL that is generated for eager loading may be Cartesian product of tables involved. Cartesian products are not very good at performance and may return more number of records than we expect by giving duplicate entities in the result. Future queries come in handy if want eager loading without side effects such as Cartesian products. We will look at future queries in the next chapter.

Pagination and ordering of results

Sometimes you do not want to use the results of a query as is. You might want to narrow down the number of records that a query is fetching or order them on a particular column. In this section, we will see how to manipulate the result set of a criteria query.

Narrowing down the number of records returned by a query

Many times we are only interested in a subset of records that can be returned by a query. On a criteria query or QueryOver, you can limit the maximum number of records returned by calling the `SetMaxResults()` method as follows:

```
using (var transaction = database.Session.BeginTransaction())
{
    employees = database.Session.CreateCriteria<Employee>()
                        .CreateCriteria("ResidentialAddress")
                        .Add(Restrictions.Eq("City", "London"))
                        .SetMaxResults(10)
                        .List<Employee>();
    transaction.Commit();
}
```

If the database server supports limiting results then NHibernate would make use of it to limit the number of results. For instance, preceding code when run against a SQLite database would generate the following SQL (shortened to save text):

```
SELECT      this_.Id                AS Id0_1_,
            /*other columns here*/
FROM        Employee this_
INNER JOIN Address address1_
ON          this_.Id=address1_.Employee_Id
WHERE       address1_.City = @p0 limit @p1;
 @p0 = 'London' [Type: String (0)],
 @p1 = 10 [Type: Int32 (0)]
```

Note the part `limit @p1` in bold which is responsible for returning only first 10 records as specified in our query. Not every relational database would support this construct. Even among the databases that support it, exact syntax for limiting the result set could be different. But NHibernate has handled it for you transparently. NHibernate can do this through its implementation of dialects. If you remember the discussion on dialects in *Chapter 4*, *NHibernate Warm-up*, then you would know that it is through dialect that NHibernate supports database specific features. This is one such example of that.

`SetMaxResults` is also supported by HQL and gives exact same result as criteria query. QueryOver and LINQ provide a different method named `Take` which achieves the same result. Following is an example of LINQ query which limits the number of results `20`:

```
var employees = Database.Session.Query<Employee>()
                    .Where(e => e.Firstname == "John")
                    .Take(20);
```

Now that we know how to limit number of records coming out of a query, the next logical extension of that is to be able to write queries that you can use in pagination scenarios. In pagination, you not only want to limit the records returned but also want to be able to specify at what number the returned result set should start. For instance, if you are building search employee functionality. Someone searched on employee's country of residence and hundreds of results are returned. It would not be wise to display hundreds of results to user in a grid that takes forever to load. You want to display the results in blocks of, say, 20. So you paginate them with 20 results on each page. Every time user navigates to the next or previous page, you ask NHibernate to load the next/previous result set. So if user is on page 1, then you display results from 1 to 20, on page 2 from 21 to 40, and so on. You can do this in criteria query by telling it to return maximum of 20 results starting from 21.

We have seen how to declare "maximum results" part. To declare the starting result set, you call a method `SetFirstResult()` on criteria query. For fetching records from 21 to 40, our query would look as follows:

```
using (var transaction = database.Session.BeginTransaction())
{
    employees = database.Session.CreateCriteria<Employee>()
                        .CreateCriteria("ResidentialAddress")
                        .Add(Restrictions.Eq("City", "London"))
                        .SetMaxResults(20)
                        .SetFirstResult(21)
                        .List<Employee>();
    transaction.Commit();
}
```

The preceding code will send the following SQL to a SQLite database:

```
SELECT this_.Id AS Id0_1_,
/*other columns here*/
FROM Employee this_ INNER JOIN Address address1_
ON this_.Id=address1_.Employee_Id
WHERE address1_.City = @p0 limit @p1 offset @p2;
@p0 = 'London' [Type: String (0)],
@p1 = 20 [Type: Int32 (0)],
@p2 = 21 [Type: Int32 (0)]
```

This time we can see that NHibernate has sent additional SQL to tell database server to paginate the results for us. As long as the database supports pagination, NHibernate will defer pagination to database server, else it would paginate the results in-memory.

As with `SetMaxResults`, `SetFirstResult` is supported by HQL and produces exactly the same results. The corresponding method for QueryOver and LINQ is `Skip`. Following code listing shows a pagination example implemented in QueryOver:

```
employees = Database.Session.QueryOver<Employee>()
                    .Where(x => x.Firstname == "John")
                    .Take(20)
                    .Skip(20)
                    .List<Employee>();
```

Note the subtle difference between `SetNextResult` and `Skip`. In former, you are specifying the first record number of the result set that you want returned. In the latter, you are telling "what is the size of the block that you want skipped". This is usually the last record number from the previous batch.

If the dialect that you are using does not support pagination natively, you can continue to use the pagination feature of NHibernate. If that is the case, NHibernate would carry out the pagination operation in memory. All the qualifying records will be loaded into memory and then iterated in order to return what is specified. But remember that this may result in poor performance and high memory usage. Most relation database servers offer pagination support natively but always check if the one you are using does support it.

Ordering the results

Even after pagination, things may become frustrating when a search result returns hundreds of pages and people have to wade through pages of results to locate the record they are looking for. Being able to sort the results on a particular field can come to the rescue in such situations. Again, NHibernate has you covered here as well with its support for ordering result sets. Criteria query has a method `AddOrder()` that can be used to specify how you would like the results to be ordered. Employee records sorted by first name in alphabetically ascending order can be queried as follows:

```
using (var transaction = database.Session.BeginTransaction())
{
  employees = database.Session.CreateCriteria<Employee>()
  .Add(Restrictions.Eq("Firstname", "John"))
  .AddOrder(Order.Asc("Firstname")).List<Employee>();

  transaction.Commit();

}
```

As with limiting the results, NHibernate would defer to database server for ordering the results. Most database technologies will have support for ordering result sets and the syntax is more or less same across all. Following is SQL generated by the preceding code for SQLite database:

```
SELECT this_.Id AS Id0_0_,
/*other columns removed*/
FROM Employee this_
WHERE this_.Firstname = @p0
ORDER BY this_.Firstname ASC;
@p0 = 'John' [Type: String (0)]
```

Again, note the SQL in bold where ordering is carried out at database server level. As with pagination, ordering of results works the same way for HQL as it does for criteria. For QueryOver and LINQ, it works slightly differently.

QueryOver offers a method named `OrderBy` which takes in a lambda of the property by which you want to order. You can then call either of the properties named `Asc` or `Desc` to specify the direction in which to order the results. Following is how you can sort employee records on the `Firstname` property:

```
employees = Database.Session.QueryOver<Employee>()
                        .Where(x => x.Firstname == John")
                        .OrderBy(x => x.Firstname).Desc
                        .List<Employee>();
```

LINQ takes a different approach. There is a method named `OrderBy` which takes in a lambda similar to QueryOver but always orders in ascending order. If you want to order in descending order then another method named `OrderByDescending` is available. Following is the same example written in LINQ:

```
var employees = Database.Session.Query<Employee>()
        .Where(e => e.Firstname == "John")
        .OrderByDescending(e => e.Firstname);
```

Retrieving entities by identifiers

If you recall the unit tests that we wrote in the previous chapters, we commonly used a method named `Get<T>` on `ISession` to retrieve a persistent instance of an entity by its id. Following is relevant part of that code:

```
using (var transaction = session.BeginTransaction())
{
  var employee = session.Get<Employee>(id);
  transaction.Commit();
}
```

You might be wondering what the reason behind providing this method is. All we are doing is querying an entity by its primary key. Why not use criteria query, QueryOver, or LINQ to query entities by primary key? Well, you can use those methods when you are not querying by identifier, but if you are querying by identifier then `Get<T>` has some optimizations built in that make it a preferred choice over any other querying method. Even other querying methods will use `Get<T>` internally if they need to load an entity by identifier.

Get<T> will first check whether an entity is present in the identity map of the session, and it would then check the second level cache for existence of the entity there. If an entity is not found in both identity map and second level cache, then it issues SQL to fetch the entity from database. Do you see the difference? There is an element of optimization that Get<T> applies that other querying methods do not. If there is a chance that an entity is present in first or second level cache then you can save a database roundtrip and few CPU cycles by using Get<T>.

ISession has another method named Load<T> which is syntactically same as Get<T> with a subtle difference in how it works internally. Get<T> would go from first level cache to second level cache to database looking for the entity and if not found, it returns a null. On the other hand, Load<T> works similarly to how lazy loading works. Load<T> does not hit the database immediately. It only returns a proxy of the entity with its identity set to the one passed to it. If you try to access any other properties of the entity returned by Load<T> then actual loading of the entity from database is triggered. Because NHibernate does not check if the ID that you passed to Load<T> is present in the database or not, it is possible to pass non-existing id to Load<T> and still get a proxy entity back. When NHibernate tries to load this entity from database, it figures out that there is no record in database with that id and throws NHibernate.ObjectNotFoundException.

Why use Load<T>?

By the sound of its behavior, Load<T> does not seem to add much value over Get<T>. But there are some situations where Load<T> results in more optimized behavior than Get<T> does. When an employee becomes member of a community, you may write code as follows:

```
object employeeId =null; //This is passed from some other code
var communities = Database.Session.Query<Community>()
        .First(c => c.Name == "London bikers");

var employee = Database.Session.Get<Employee>(employeeId);
communities.AddMember(employee);
```

In the preceding code, the employee instance loaded using Get<T> is not used for anything other than setting the relationship between Employee and Community. If we know the ID of the employee, then all we need in order to setup the relationship is a proxy employee instance with its id set. Load<T> offers exactly that. We could save an additional database roundtrip by using Load<T> in such similar situations.

So to summarize:

- Use Get<T>/Load<T> over querying by primary keys. Get<T>/Load<T> is optimized.

- If you need to access properties of the loaded entity (other than ID) then use Get<T>.

- If you do not intend to access properties of the loaded entity but only use it as a proxy to satisfy an association then use Load<T>.

 If entity is not marked as lazy, then Load<T> and Get<T> do not behave differently. Calling Load<T> for non-lazy entities results in immediate loading of the entity. This is because NHibernate never proxies entities marked as non-lazy.

Polymorphic queries

Polymorphic queries extend the polymorphic behavior of classes into the persistence layer. What I mean by this is – polymorphism gives us a base type variable that can hold a reference to a derived type and invokes methods from derives types at runtime, NHibernate is capable of loading correct instance of derived type when queried by base type. For instance, if you try to load a Benefit entity by ID from database, but the benefit record in the database corresponds to SkillsEnhancementAllowance, then NHibernate is capable of determining what the actual derived type the record needs to be mapped to (SkillsEnhancementAllowance in this example) and instantiates the correct entity type. We have seen this in *Chapter 3, Let's Tell NHibernate About Our Database* during mapping of inheritance hierarchy of classes. Let me take a moment to show you a unit test from that chapter which showed polymorphic nature of the ISession.Get<T> method:

```
public void MapsSkillsEnhancementAllowance()
{

object id = 0;
using (var transaction = Session.BeginTransaction())
{
  id = Session.Save(new SkillsEnhancementAllowance
  {
    Name = "Skill Enhacement Allowance", Entitlement = 1000,
    RemainingEntitlement = 250
  });
  transaction.Commit();
}

Session.Clear();

using (var transaction = Session.BeginTransaction())
```

```
{
    var benefit = Session.Get<Benefit>(id);
    var skillsEnhancementAllowance = benefit as
    SkillsEnhancementAllowance;
    Assert.That(skillsEnhancementAllowance, Is.Not.Null);

    transaction.Commit();
    }
}
```

In the preceding code listing, we persisted an instance of
`SkillsEnhancementAllowance` into database. We then asked NHibernate to
load an instance of `Benefit` from database using the id that we received when
the `SkillsEnhancementAllowance` instance was saved. But the type of the entity
that NHibernate loaded is `SkillsEnhancementAllowance` which is what we
had persisted.

The polymorphic nature of queries is not limited to the `Get<T>` and `Load<T>` methods
on `ISession`. All querying methods available in NHibernate support polymorphic
queries. Moreover, there is nothing special that you need to do to enable polymorphic
querying. This is default behavior of NHibernate. If you load an `Employee` instance
from database that has a collection of `Benefit` entities on it and then you iterate
through the collection and check the types of each item in collection, you will notice
that NHibernate has hydrated correct entity types as they should be. It does not
matter if the `Employee` instance was loaded using criteria query or LINQ.

Before we close on this topic, let me show you another flavor of polymorphic queries.
Suppose you want to load employees who have opted for season ticket loan. In
native SQL world, you would have joined to the `SeasonTicketLoan` table to get
the employees having a record in that table. This is possible to do using LINQ,
as shown next:

```
var employees = from e in Database.Session.Query<Employee>()
join b in Database.Session.Query<SeasonTicketLoan>()
on e equals b.Employee select e;
```

Following is another way to write this query using lambda syntax and utilizing
polymorphic capabilities of NHibernate:

```
var employeeQuery = Database.Session.Query<Employee>()
.Where(e => e.Benefits.Any(b => b is SeasonTicketLoan));
```

While both queries give us the same result, the former joins the `Employee` table directly with `SeasonTicketLoan`, giving us a short and faster SQL. Depending on the inheritance mapping strategy used, the latter may involve outer joins with multiple `Benefit` tables. It will load all matching records in memory and then filter out the ones needed. This goes back to the point I made that there are multiple ways of writing a query and you need to see which one works best for you.

Summary

There are multitude of different ways of retrieving data in NHibernate. These can be mainly divided into two types. First type consists of `ISession.Get<T>` and `ISession.Load<T>`, which you can use when you know the id of the entity you want to retrieve. Both of these can be the fastest ways of retrieving an entity from database. These are used by NHibernate internally. Second type of data retrieval methods in NHibernate are geared towards complex situations that go beyond loading entities by their id. HQL, Criteria API, QueryOver, and LINQ, all let you write complex queries in an intuitive way using object-oriented APIs. These let you load entities by properties other than ID or even combination of properties, join two or more entities, and so on. NHibernate does a lot of heavy lifting for you when it comes to writing complex queries, making the job of writing queries very easy. Querying capabilities of NHibernate are not limited to only complex queries. You can aggregate results, project results into different C# types, order or paginate results, and so on.

Data retrieval is the last major concept that you needed to learn before you can dive into more advanced and interesting topics. In this chapter, we have tried to cover most important areas of data retrieval features offered by NHibernate. But data retrieval is a complex topic and if one wants, an entire book can be written on NHibernate features around this area. While that is beyond the scope of this book, this chapter has touched upon basic building blocks that you will need to master the topic. I encourage readers to explore this area more as they use NHibernate in their work or hobby projects more and more.

In next few chapters, we will step away and try to look at bigger picture and invest our time in learning how to use NHibernate in real life projects, guidelines around using NHibernate most effectively and efficiently, recommended design patterns while working with NHibernate, and so on. Going through these chapters will help you connect the dots and get an overall picture of how to best fit NHibernate into architecture of your application.

7
Optimizing the Data Access Layer

So far we have covered all the basic concepts of NHibernate. You have officially learnt to use NHibernate if you have followed all the previous six chapters so far. From this chapter onwards, we will talk more about "how" rather than "what". These next few chapters will concentrate on practical advice to use NHibernate in different situations. Particularly in this chapter, we will talk about optimizing your data access layer.

Though this chapter talks about optimization and mostly performance optimization (and memory optimization in some cases), do not feel inspired to go and apply these techniques/guidelines to your current project right away. Performance optimization is a relative thing. What is good performance for one project may not be good for another. Besides your use of NHibernate, performance is also driven by lot of other factors such as design of database schema, presence of proper indexes, size of the database, actual SQL queries, hardware specification of the server, kind of software the server is running, and so on. I always tell my teams that software should not be designed for performance but to meet the functional requirements and other strategic non-functional requirements such as testability, modularity, and so on. When it comes to performance, you should first baseline the performance and then optimize it. Features/techniques/guidelines discussed in this chapter are good set of knowledge to have. Read them, understand them, and think how you can use them, but do not use them without understanding the nature of the performance problem you are dealing with.

Baseline and optimize

Trying to optimize any software without determining a baseline is like shooting in the dark. You may hit the target but not before you have spent significant time hitting the wrong thing. Same goes for use of NHibernate. Before you think of optimizing your data access layer, first measure how it is performing. You can use various different tools to measure performance of your data access layer. NHProfiler from www.hibernatingrhinos.com is one of the best tools that I have come across so far. Besides showing basic details such as the actual SQL sent to server and time taken to execute each SQL statement, NHProfiler shows some interesting information about your queries. I particularly like the analysis tab that groups queries by various parameters such as number of time it is run, time it took to execute, and so on.

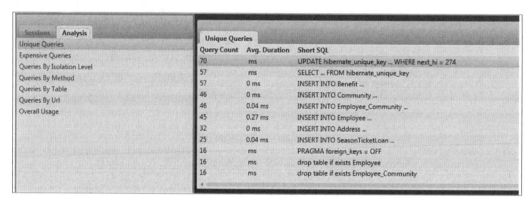

Another feature I like is the session usage information. Following is a snapshot of the **Session Usage** tab giving summary of a session. It shows basic information about the session, such as how long it took to run all queries, how many entities were loaded, and so on. But it also shows alerts which is NHProfile's way of telling you how you can optimize your queries.

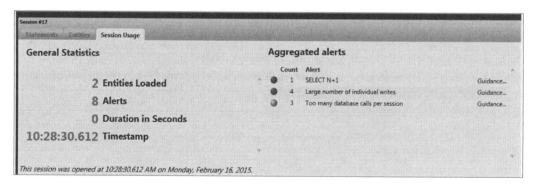

Once you have measured the performance, it is time to determine if there is a need to improve any aspect of the performance. It is important to understand what is fast and what is slow for your application. If you come to the conclusion that there is a genuine need to tune the performance then the first thing I would recommend you do is find out nature of read queries versus write queries in the application. The reason behind doing so is that the factors that affect the performance of read queries are different from the factors that affect write queries. For instance, an index on the database table makes read queries by indexed column faster but makes the writes into the table slower. Most of the features/guidelines discussed in this chapter apply either to read queries or to write queries but not both. Once you know the read versus write behavior in your application, it would be easy to find out where the performance lag is coming from. If it is coming from read queries (which is the case most of the times in my experience) then you know precisely how to tackle them.

Organization of the chapter

This chapter is organized as a series of features, techniques, guidelines, gotchas, and so on. These do not appear in any particular order. Most of these are useful when dealing with performance tuning, but some are useful when dealing with issues such as memory consumption and other nasty issues you may face. I have not specifically put them into different categories. My aim is not to steer you towards performance tuning but to make sure you know these techniques and are able to use them when needed.

> The techniques/features that are presented here are most basic that you will find on this topic. As your experience with NHibernate grows and you become more expert you will figure out that there are several avenues for optimization that are applicable to very specific situations. It is not in the scope of this book to talk about all such optimization techniques. Our discussion here mainly concentrates on NHibernate features that help with optimization than tricks/tweaks that people have used on their projects to squeeze an extra millisecond out of their queries.

Main features that we are going to talk about in this chapter are batching, fetching strategies, future queries, and so on. There are satellite ideas revolving around these main topics that we will look at as well. In terms of guidelines, we will talk about avoiding eager fetching, avoiding select N+1 problem, and so on. Let's get started with a discussion on batching then.

Batching

Total execution time of a NHibernate query constitutes of three things:

- Time it takes to send the query to remote database server
- Time it takes to execute actual SQL on the database server
- Time it takes to return the results to client, process the results on client, and hydrate the entities

Depending on what kind of queries you are writing, you may be spending a lot of time sending your queries to remote database server. In such a situation, you can batch multiple SQL statements together and send them to database server for execution in one roundtrip. Batching does not impact the time it takes to execute actual SQL on the server, but reduces the network time as you are doing a single database interaction against several you would have done in absence of batching. NHibernate offers different ways of batching queries that can be used in different scenarios.

As we discussed in the beginning, NHibernate queries can be generally divided into two buckets – read queries and write queries. For write queries, SQL commands are sent to database either when transaction is committed or when session is flushed. Read queries are more instantaneous. First, SQL command is sent to database when terminal method such as List<T> is called on the query. If lazy loading is enabled, further SQL commands are sent as our code interacts with loaded entities. For read queries, there is no one point in time (such as commit of transaction, and so on.) when all the accumulated operations are sent to database at once. One thing that is common in both types of queries is that each SQL command results in a database roundtrip making whole data access chatty and slow. You can overcome this issue by batching multiple SQL statements together. NHibernate supports batching for both type of queries.

Batching the write queries using ADO.NET batching

NHibernate uses ADO.NET under the hood for its database interaction. ADO. NET inherently supports the concept of batching SQL queries. If you are inserting or updating large number of entities in a single transaction, then you can utilize underlying ADO.NET batching to bundle up the INSERT/UPDATE statements to reduce the number of roundtrips to database. NHibernate lets you configure ADO. NET batch size either at session factory level or at session level. Let's go over an example to see how this works.

In the following code, we are inserting 100 employee instances having their `ResidentialAddress` property set and one community instance added to the `Communities` collection:

```
[Test]
public void InsertLargeNumberOfEmployeeRecords()
{
  using (var transaction = Database.Session.BeginTransaction())
  {
    for (int i = 0; i < 100; i++)
    {
      var employee = new Employee
      {
        DateOfBirth = new DateTime(1972, 3, 5),
        DateOfJoining = new DateTime(2001, 5, 28),
        ResidentialAddress = new Address()
      };
      employee.AddCommunity(new Community());

      Database.Session.Save(employee);
    }

  transaction.Commit();
  }
}
```

Note that we have not set meaningful values for different properties of the entities that we are saving. That is not needed for the preceding test. Date fields are populated because MS SQL Server 2012 was used for this test and it cannot work with the `DateTime` type of fields if they are left empty.

When this code is run, a total of 424 SQL statements would be sent to database. Of this, 24 statements are produced during the process of ID generation for entities to be inserted. Remaining 400 are produced for actual insert operation of 100 records into each `Employee`, `Address`, `Employee_Community`, and `Community` table. We would now turn on ADO.NET batching in our configuration using the following line of code:

```
SetProperty(Environment.BatchSize, "1");
```

Preceding property works in two ways. If it is not set or set to zero, it would mean that batching is disabled. If set to any number greater than 0, it would mean that batching is turned on and batch size is equal to the number set in configuration. This is configuration of batch size at session factory level. This configuration applies to all session instances created from that session factory.

If you want different batch size for each session, then you can change the batch size at session level by calling the `SetBatchSize` method on `ISession`. Change to batch size made by calling this method is local to that session and any new sessions created would inherit their batch size from the session factory configuration.

Following image illustrates what happens when we change the batch size from **0** to **50** and then to **100**:

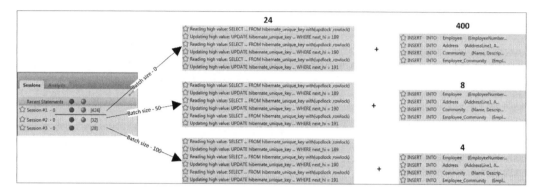

The first image on the left shows summary of each session. The number in square brackets next to each session is the number of database roundtrips that each session did. First **24** statements of each session are from ID generation logic so we are going to ignore those in this discussion. These cannot be batched as they run in their own transaction and possibly more than one transaction. Ignoring these roundtrips, we can see that first session did a total of **400** roundtrips while next two did **8** and **4** respectively. First session did not use any batching. Second session used a batch size of 50. NHibernate put 50 statements into a batch thus making 8 database roundtrips. The last session used batch size of 100 resulting in only 4 database roundtrips.

While this example is a bit contrived to prove the point, note the reduction in the number of roundtrips to database. In scenarios where database is on a different server or a different network, this can bring about huge savings in the time spent in sending SQL to remote server.

Limitations of batching

Write batching sounds like a quick win but this feature is not supported on all databases. Currently native batching is only supported on MS SQL Server, Oracle, and MySQL.

Besides that, write batching does not work in the couple of situations described next:

- When you are relying on databases to generate identifier values, for example, using identity columns as primary keys or using database sequences. Use of database identities means that NHibernate needs to go to database after every insert to read the identifier value which prevents batching. So if you are using database identities and you want to use batching then best option is to choose a different ID generation strategy if you can.

- Second situation is more of a NHibernate limitation. Batching works only if the entity being saved is inserted into one table. This does not include the tables for associated entity. This limitation poses a problem when an entity is part of an inheritance hierarchy. If the inheritance hierarchy is mapped using "table per subclass" or "table per concrete class" strategy then two tables are involved in saving of any derived entity. For instance, when the Leave class is saved, a record is inserted into base table Benefit and table Leave. Batching does not work in this case and if you are saving 100 instances of the Leave entity then there would be 100 database roundtrips. This obviously can be fixed if you use "table per hierarchy" strategy which puts everything into a single table.

Memory consumption and batching

Let me contrive the above example further to prove another point. What would happen if instead of persisting 100 instances of employee entity, you are asked to persist 100K instances? Most likely, you would be waiting for a long time to see your 100K records inserted into the database.

> I am using this example just to prove a point. NHibernate or any ORM is not a tool to carry out bulk insert kind of operations. There are tools available that are built for these kinds of operations and are more efficient at bulk insert than ORMs. Readers are recommended to use such tools instead of NHibernate.

If you use code similar to the one we used previously, with batching enabled and set to an appropriate number, you may get the work done in reasonable time but it is highly likely that you would be greeted with an out of memory exception. That is because every entity that is persisted is also kept in memory by session. Depending on the specification of the server, you would soon fill up the memory available to your application. One simple solution to resolve this issue is to flush the in-memory entity state to database at regular intervals and clear the session to reduce memory consumption. But I would not rely on this solution as clearing the session at right time is very important. Flushing/clearing the session at wrong time may result in issues. A better solution is to use stateless sessions. Stateless sessions are discussed in detail in *Chapter 11, A Whirlwind Tour of Other NHibernate Features*.

Since we are on the topic of persisting large number of entities using NHibernate, let me bring another characteristic of this situation to your attention. When we call `ISession.Save`, NHibernate does some checks on the entity being passed to the `Save` method. While doing these checks, NHibernate has to go through the graph of entities that it has stored in session. If there is a large number of entities stored in session then these checks take long time, resulting in save operation becoming slow. The flushing solution we discussed just now may help here. But if there is no reliable way of flushing the session then the gains you get out of batching are quickly outweighed by losses from slow execution of the `Save` method.

Read batching using future queries

ADO.NET batching capability can be used for write queries very easily but the same concept does not work for read queries. Design of read queries poses some challenges when it comes to batching them. Specifically, the following two characteristics of read queries highlight why batching of read queries is difficult:

- Lazy loading defers execution of some of the queries to later time thus reducing the opportunity for batching multiple related queries together

- Read queries need to be executed instantaneously, the moment terminal methods such as `ToList<T>` are called on them

Deferred query execution offered by lazy loading is a feature we want to use more often than not. So there is no point in turning off lazy loading in favor of ability to batch queries. Second issue is a bit different. If we have multiple related queries which are not dependent on each other then can we do something to have them sent to database in one batch? By not being dependent on each other, I mean, you do not need to have a prior query executed in order to execute a later query. Future queries were introduced in NHibernate to handle situations exactly like this.

Future queries work the same way as lazy loading by deferring the query execution to future time. Let's use an example to understand this better. Suppose we want to build a summary section where we want to display total number of employees, total number of communities, and top 5 communities by number of members. We can write something as the following using LINQ in order to build this summary section:

```
var employees = Database.Session.Query<Employee>();

var communities = Database.Session.Query<Community>();

var topCommunities = Database.Session.Query<Community>()
        .OrderByDescending(c => c.Members.Count())
        .Take(5);

var benefits = Database.Session.Query<Benefit>();
```

I have used an example to show you how future queries can be used to batch together completely unrelated queries. Another practical example where you can find future queries very useful is when you want to show paginated search results. You would like to return matching records on current page along with the total number of records that match the search criteria. You would write two different queries for this but can batch those using future queries.

Preceding code would send three SELECT statements to database at three different times when each of following methods are called:

```
employees.Count()
communities.Count()
topCommunities.ToList();
```

Since these methods are called at different times, each SELECT statement is sent to database independently of each other, causing more network traffic. This can be significant for remote database servers. These statements are related with each other and satisfy a single UI requirement that displays the summary section. There is no need to execute these queries independently of each other. There is no side-effect if these queries are bundled together and sent to database all at once. That is what future queries offer. Using future queries you can tell NHibernate to bundle a set of queries and send to database in one batch. You can convert any LINQ query to a future query by calling method ToFuture() in the end. Following is how our previous queries would look like when converted to future queries:

```
var employees = Database.Session.Query<Employee>().ToFuture();

var communities = Database.Session.Query<Community>().ToFuture();

var topCommunities = Database.Session.Query<Community>()
.OrderByDescending(c => c.Members.Count()).Take(5).ToFuture();

var benefits = Database.Session.Query<Benefit>().ToFuture();
```

Call to the ToFuture() method must be placed in the end. ToFuture returns IEnumerable<T>. NHibernate has a special type NHibernate.Impl. DelayedEnumerator<T> which implements IEnumerable<T>. Actually, it is this type that NHibernate returns. Internally, NHibernate keeps track of all the DelayedEnumerator<T> instances so that if query execution is triggered on any one of them, queries for rest of the DelayedEnumerator<T> instances are also sent to database for execution in the same roundtrip. The effect we get is similar to what we got with write batching. The only difference is that we cannot tell how many statements we want to bundle together. All the future queries that are associated with the session would be executed at once when one of them is triggered.

This looks good so far. But there still is a small problem with the preceding code. The first future query gets us the count of employees in the database and the SELECT statement generated for it is as follows:

```
SELECT  employee0_.id            AS  Id0_,
        employee0_.firstname     AS  Firstname0_,
        employee0_.lastname      AS  Lastname0_,
        employee0_.emailaddress  AS  EmailAdd5_0_,
        employee0_.dateofbirth   AS  DateOfBi6_0_,
        employee0_.dateofjoining AS  DateOfJo7_0_,
        employee0_.isadmin       AS  IsAdmin0_,
        employee0_.password      AS  Password0_
FROM    employee employee0_;
```

All we are after here is the count of employees but as you can see, we are loading the whole Employee table in memory and then counting the rows. That is because we are calling the Count() method on a future query (after the call to the ToFuture() method). Part of the query till ToFuture() is executed as a database query, everything after that is executed in-memory on the results loaded.

Why not place the call to Count() before ToFuture() then? Well, we cannot. ToFuture() is an extension method on IQueryable<T>, so it can only be called on IQueryable<T>. Methods such as Count() and ToList() change the IQueryable<T> to IEnumerable<T>/int and hence it is not possible to call ToFuture() after these methods are called.

Ideally, we would want the following SQL to be generated:

```
SELECT Cast(Count(*) AS INT) AS col_0_0_
FROM employee employee0_;
```

Fortunately, you can do this with future queries. If your query returns a scalar value then you can utilize companion method ToFutureValue. This method takes a lambda expression as input and returns an instance of IFutureValue<T>. Following example demonstrates how we can use this method to get count of employees:

```
var employees = Database.Session.Query<Employee>()
        .ToFutureValue(e => e.Count());
```

In the preceding method, we have passed `e.Count()` as argument to the `ToFutureValue` method. NHibernate would use that to build the SQL. `ToFutureValue` returns an `IFutureValue<T>` instance. In our case, `T` is an integer hence `IFutureValue<int>` would be returned. When the query is executed, you can access the result of the query via the `Value` property present on the `IFutureValue<T>` instance, shown as follows:

```
Assert.That(employees.Value, Is.EqualTo(3));
```

Future queries are supported in QueryOver as well but the method signature is slightly different. There is a generic signature in QueryOver's version of future queries. In LINQ you had `ToFuture`, in QueryOver you have `ToFuture<T>`. `ToFutureValue` is same for QueryOver and works in exactly the same way.

> Future queries is just a wrapper over another feature called **MultiQuery**. MultiQuery lets you write queries that NHibernate should batch together and send to database for execution in single roundtrip. MultiQuery is only supported for HQL and criteria. Future queries is the only way to use MultiQuery in QueryOver and LINQ. Since I have been encouraging the use of LINQ more and more, I do not intend to cover MultiQuery separately. Avid readers may choose to explore this topic on their own.

Batching lazy collections

Lazy collections are loaded as you access them. Also, the SQL statements required to load the lazy collections are generated internally by NHibernate. Future queries do not help in this situation. But NHibernate has a special batching support for lazy collection. If you are loading multiple lazy collections, then you can tell NHibernate to load a bunch of them together instead of one by one as they are accessed. Let's see how this works. Following code loads a bunch of employees who live in London. It then iterates through each of the loaded employee instance and accesses the `Benefits` collection on them.

```
var employees = Database.Session.Query<Employee>()
.Where(e => e.ResidentialAddress.City == "London");

foreach (var employee in employees)
{
  foreach (var benefit in employee.Benefits)
  {
    //do something with benefit here
  }
}
```

As we loop through employee instances and access the `Benefits` collection on each instance, a `SELECT` statement similar to the following is issued:

```
SELECT *--all columns from Benefit table
FROM benefit benefits0_
--join with other concrete benefit tables
WHERE benefits0_.employee_id =@p0;
@p0 = 11 [TYPE: Int32 (0)]
```

The actual `SELECT` statement is quite big and hence a shortened version highlighting more relevant part is presented here.

For our example, three employee instances having IDs 11, 12, and 13 are loaded. Correspondingly, three `SELECT` statements are sent to database in separate roundtrip as the `Benefits` collection on each instance is accessed. This is not very efficient and we can tell NHibernate to be forward looking and fetch more than one collection when it hits the database to load first collection. This is called batching of lazy collections. Following code listing depicts how to batch loading of three `Benefits` collection together:

```
Set(e => e.Benefits,
mapper =>
{
  mapper.Key(k => k.Column("Employee_Id"));
  mapper.Cascade(Cascade.All.Include(Cascade.DeleteOrphans));
  mapper.Inverse(true);
  mapper.BatchSize(3);
},
relation => relation.OneToMany(mapping =>
mapping.Class(typeof(Benefit))));
```

Preceding code snippet is from mapping of the `Employee` entity where the `Benefits` collection on the `Employee` entity is mapped. As part of one-to-many and many-to-many collection mapping, we can call method `BatchSize` to tell NHibernate to pre-fetch collections in a batch. The size of the batch is passed as parameter to the `BatchSize` method. After declaring a batch size, we get the following single `SELECT` statement in place of three we had observed earlier:

```
SELECT *
--all columns from Benefit table
FROM benefit benefits0_
--join with other concrete benefit tables
WHERE benefits0_.employee_id IN ( @p0, @p1, @p2 );
@p0 = 11 [Type: Int32 (0)],
@p1 = 12 [Type: Int32 (0)],
@p2 = 13 [Type: Int32 (0)]
```

Note how NHibernate changed the WHERE clause from matching a single employee ID to matching three employee IDs in one go, thus saving us two database roundtrips. If we had 10 employee instances, then NHibernate would load their benefits collection in batches of 3, 3, 3, and 1. These batches are loaded as they are accessed and not all at once. So if you had 10 employee instances, then first batch would be loaded when the benefits collection on the first instance is accessed. Second batch would be loaded when the benefits collection on the fourth instance is accessed, and so on.

> The SELECT statement generated with batching turned on uses the IN clause. The IN clauses may perform badly in some situations. So always compare performance with and without batching to confirm whether you are actually gaining anything out of batching lazy collections. Optimal size of batch is also a factor that plays an important role here. So play with multiple settings before you come to a conclusion.

Fetching strategies

Lazy loading is about "when associated entities are loaded". There is another angle to loading associated entities which is about "how associated entities are loaded". The latter is controlled by a feature called **fetching strategy**. A simple example here would help. Suppose you want to retrieve all benefit records for a particular employee. There are different ways of doing this. For instance, following are two different SQL queries that I can think of to retrieve benefit records:

- You can use a join between Employee and Benefit table
- You can just select from the Benefit table using a WHERE clause that limits the records by matching foreign key column Employee_Id to the ID of the employee record

NHibernate supports three different ways of fetching associations. Through fetching strategy you can tell NHibernate which way it should use for a particular association. From optimization point of view, this is a good lever to use. Fetching strategy is declared as part of mapping. It works globally once set in mapping. Eager fetching that we looked at in the previous chapter gives similar control over how associated entities are fetched from database. Eager fetching is local to a query, unlike fetching strategies. Also, eager fetching only gives you two options – lazy (select) and eager (join). Fetching strategy gives us a third option – subselect.

Let's take a look at different strategies and what difference they bring about to loading of associated entities.

Select fetching

Select fetching uses an independent SELECT statement to load associated entities. This is default fetching strategy where none is declared explicitly. If you want, you can still declare it explicitly. Following is how you declare it during mapping of an association:

```
Set(e => e.Communities, mapper =>
{
  //.. other mappings..//
  mapper.Fetch(CollectionFetchMode.Select);
},
relation => relation.ManyToMany(mtm =>
{
  //.. other mappings..//
}));
```

Preceding code is from mapping of the Communities collection on the Employee entity. The CollectionFetchMode enumeration defines different fetching strategies that we are going to discuss next.

Select fetching underpins lazy loading. We have discussed lazy loading at length in the previous chapter. Section *Avoid select N+1 problem* of this chapter discusses select fetching in more detail. In order to avoid repetition, I intend not to spend more time here explaining how select fetching works. Let's look at other fetching strategies.

Join fetching

You may not want to issue multiple SELECT statements to load associations of an entity. You may rather prefer a SQL join that returns the root entity and associated entities in a single SELECT statement. If that is the case then you have got join fetching at your disposal. Enabling join fetching is not much different from enabling select fetching. You use CollectionFetchMode.Join for this purpose. Following is a shortened version of code showing how to enable join fetching:

```
//.. other mapping code
mapper.Fetch(CollectionFetchMode.Join);
//.. other mapping code
```

Since join fetching would use SQL join between root entity table and associated entity table, both the root and associated entities are loaded at the same time using single SELECT statement. This effectively stops lazy loading of associations. This is true even if you have explicitly enabled lazy loading. If you intend to use lazy loading then do not enable join fetching. Eager fetching that we discussed in the previous chapter and join fetching are exactly the same. The only difference between them is that one is local to the query and the other is global and declared in the mapping. So everything that applies to eager fetching also applies to join fetching.

Eager fetching does not come without its own problems – specifically, the problem of duplicate records being loaded. In section *Avoid eager fetching* we will discuss this problem and solution to the problem. Another point worth mentioning is the behavior when lazy loading is enabled and join fetching is specified at the same time. Do you remember from lazy loading discussion of the previous chapter, that NHibernate uses special collection wrapper types and proxies when lazily loading collections and single-ended associations? If you are using join fetching even after enabling lazy loading, NHibernate would continue to return collection wrapper types and proxies even though associations are not loaded lazily. This should not make much of a difference to your code but it is worth keeping in mind.

Subselect fetching

Subselect fetching offers a middle ground between join fetching and select fetching. Select fetching results in multiple SELECT statements being sent to database. Join fetching does the job in single SELECT but results in duplication of root entity.

Subselect uses two SELECT statements:

- One to load all the root entities
- Second one to load associated collection entity for all root entities

This is difficult to understand without a proper example. Let's use the same code we used in the *Batching lazy collections* section. This code loads employees living in London and then accesses the Benefits collection on each employee instance in a foreach loop.

```
var employees = Database.Session.Query<Employee>()
.Where(e => e.ResidentialAddress.City == "London");

foreach (var employee in employees)
{
  foreach (var benefit in employee.Benefits)
  {
```

```
        //do something with benefit here
    }
}
```

If the `Benefits` collection on `Employee` is configured to use subselect fetching then we would get the following two SELECT statements when the preceding code is run:

```
SELECT *
-- columns from Employee table
FROM    employee employee0_
        INNER JOIN address address1_
                ON employee0_.id = address1_.employee_id
WHERE   address1_.city = 'London' /* @p0 */

SELECT *
--columns from Benefit table
FROM    benefit benefits0_
WHERE   benefits0_.employee_id IN
  (SELECT employee0_.id
        FROM    employee employee0_
                INNER JOIN address address1_
                ON employee0_.id = address1_.employee_id
                WHERE   address1_.city = 'London' /* @p0 */)
```

The first SELECT would load all the employees residing in London. The second SELECT statement, which is triggered when the `Benefits` collection on the first employee instance is accessed, loads the associated benefits for all the employees that were loaded in the previous SELECT statement. Note that the second SELECT uses the modified version of the first SELECT in its WHERE clause – which is also called subselect.

Following code enables subselect fetching on the `Benefits` collection of `Employee`:

```
Set(e => e.Benefits, mapper =>
{
  mapper.Key(k => k.Column("Employee_Id"));
  mapper.Cascade(Cascade.All.Include(Cascade.DeleteOrphans));
  mapper.Inverse(true);
  mapper.Fetch(CollectionFetchMode.Subselect);
},
relation => relation.OneToMany(mapping =>
mapping.Class(typeof(Benefit))));
```

Subselect fetching does not disable lazy loading but it does pre-fetch all associations when the first association is accessed. This gives a batching-like effect. But be careful with this option. Once this is enabled globally, there is no way to turn this off in individual queries. For small collection sizes, this may work well but you cannot predict when the collection will grow in size in production.

Choosing the right fetching strategy

Reality is that there is no one right fetching strategy. More than one factor are at play in deciding what results in optimal data access operation. Fetching strategy just happens to be one of the factors. So do not try to stick to one strategy that may have worked for you in a particular situation. Try different strategies in combination with lazy loading, batching, and so on. Also try to figure out how your collections might be accessed at different points in code. Use all of that knowledge to choose the right strategy for a particular data access requirement.

Next two sections are more of guidelines around two problems that NHibernate beginners tend to overlook. We will try to understand the problem and look at different ways of fixing the problems.

Avoiding the select N+1 problem

We had briefly mentioned select N+1 problem in the previous chapter. Select N+1 is bad from both performance and memory consumption point of view. We are going to discuss how we can avoid this problem. Before we get our hands dirty, let's spend some time trying to understand what is select N+1 problem.

What is the select N+1 problem?

It is easier to understand select N+1 problem if we read it in reverse – 1+N select. That is right. Let's see how.

Suppose you want to load all employees living in London and then for every employee iterate through the benefits that they are getting. Following is one way of doing that using a LINQ query:

```
[Test]
public void WithSelectNPlusOneIssue()
{
  using (var transaction = Database.Session.BeginTransaction())
  {
```

```
var employees = Database.Session.Query<Employee>()
.Where(e => e.ResidentialAddress.City == "London");

foreach (var employee in employees)
{
  foreach (var benefit in employee.Benefits)
  {
    Assert.That(benefit.Employee, Is.Not.Null);
  }
}
transaction.Commit();
  }
}
```

Let me state one thing about the preceding code before we continue with our discussion. I have inserted a not so meaningful assert in there because I needed some work to be done on each `benefit` instance in the `Benefits` collection. In real life, this could be some business operation that needs to be performed on the loaded `benefit` object. With that clear, let's get back to our discussion.

If you notice, the `Benefits` collection is lazily loaded as we iterate through the loaded employee instances. When the previous code is run, we get the following SQL. This is a stripped down version only showing the parts relevant to this discussion.

```
SELECT        employee0_.id AS id0_,
              //...other columns...//
FROM          employee employee0_
INNER JOIN address address1_
ON            employee0_.id=address1_.employee_id
WHERE         address1_.city=@p0;
@p0 = 'London' [Type: String (0)]


SELECT            benefits0_.employee_id AS employee4_1_,
                  benefits0_.id          AS id1_,
                  //...other columns...//
FROM              benefit benefits0_
LEFT OUTER JOIN leave benefits0_1_
ON                benefits0_.id=benefits0_1_.id
LEFT OUTER JOIN skillsenhancementallowance benefits0_2_
ON                benefits0_.id=benefits0_2_.id
LEFT OUTER JOIN seasonticketloan benefits0_3_
ON                benefits0_.id=benefits0_3_.id
WHERE             benefits0_.employee_id=@p0;
@p0 = 11 [Type: Int32 (0)]
```

```
SELECT              benefits0_.employee_id AS employee4_1_,
                    benefits0_.id           AS id1_,
                    //...other columns...//
FROM                benefit benefits0_
LEFT OUTER JOIN     leave benefits0_1_
ON                  benefits0_.id=benefits0_1_.id
LEFT OUTER JOIN     skillsenhancementallowance benefits0_2_
ON                  benefits0_.id=benefits0_2_.id
LEFT OUTER JOIN     seasonticketloan benefits0_3_
ON                  benefits0_.id=benefits0_3_.id
WHERE               benefits0_.employee_id=@p0;
@p0 = 12 [Type: Int32 (0)]


SELECT              benefits0_.employee_id AS employee4_1_,
                    benefits0_.id           AS id1_,
                    //...other columns...//
FROM                benefit benefits0_
LEFT OUTER JOIN     leave benefits0_1_
ON                  benefits0_.id=benefits0_1_.id
LEFT OUTER JOIN     skillsenhancementallowance benefits0_2_
ON                  benefits0_.id=benefits0_2_.id
LEFT OUTER JOIN     seasonticketloan benefits0_3_
ON                  benefits0_.id=benefits0_3_.id
WHERE               benefits0_.employee_id=@p0;
@p0 = 13 [Type: Int32 (0)]
```

There are a total of four SELECT statements in the preceding SQL. First one is to retrieve employees living in London. We got three instances of such employees having ID 11, 12, and 13. The next three SELECT statements are to fetch the Benefits collection for each employee instance. Do you see the pattern here? We have got one SELECT that returns N records and then for each of those N records we get an additional SELECT. So we end up getting $1 + N$ SELECT statements. That is select $N+1$ problem for us. Or read in the reverse order $1 + N$ SELECTs problem.

Why select N+1 is a problem?

Following are the three reasons why select N+1 is not a good thing:

- In terms of algorithmic complexity, we have got complexity of order $O(N)$. For a small number of N, it is fine to send multiple SELECT statements to database but as N increases, then sending hundreds of SELECT statements to database could have significant impact on application's behavior.

- While the N SELECT statements are bad, what is worse is that each of those SELECT statements are sent to database in a separate roundtrip. Imagine what would happen to network traffic for a large number of N.

- Those N SELECT statements are not the best in class. They are querying on foreign key that is present on the table. If this key is not indexed then you are doing a full table scan to get your results. For a large value of N, doing full table scan hundreds of times in succession is not a good idea.

How do we fix the select N+1 problem?

Select N+1 has multiple problems and there are multiple solutions to it. Not every solution addresses every problem of select N+1 but you can choose the right solution depending on severity of issue at hand. For example, you can use the following batching solution to bundle up number of SELECT statements in a batch and have them sent to database in one roundtrip, thus reducing cost of remote calls. Let's see what each solution offers and in which situation it can be used:

- **Eager fetching**: We have covered eager fetching in the previous chapter. With eager fetching you can fetch collections along with root entity at the same time. Using this option would disable lazy loading and you may end up fetching a large number of collection items even when they are not needed. Though eager fetching solves the select N+1 problem completely, I recommend using caution with eager fetching when lazily loading multiple collections or collections having large number of items in them. We will see the reason for it in the *Avoid eager fetching* section of this chapter.

- **Fetching strategies**: Join fetching and subselect fetching both fix the select N+1 problem. Join fetching, being same as eager fetching, poses same issues around lazily loading multiple collections and collections having large number of items in them. So use join fetching wisely. Subselct offers pre-fetching which may result in unnecessarily loading the collections that we may never access in the code. If you want pre-fetching a small number of collections at a time then use batching of lazy collection we discussed in this chapter.

- **Batching**: In the batching section at the beginning of this chapter, we saw how the SELECT statements generated out of lazy loading of collections can be batched together. This solution does not reduce the number of SELECT statements that are generated but lets you reduce the number of database roundtrips, thus saving the cost of remote calls.

- **Extra Lazy**: We have briefly touched upon extra lazy option in the previous chapter. Extra lazy adds smartness to loading of indexed collections. If you have got an indexed collection and your code accesses a particular item of that collection using index, then NHibernate can fetch only that one item instead of the whole collection if the collection is set to use extra lazy behavior. From the previous chapter we know how to set extra lazy behavior on a collection. Beyond that, this is a very simple concept which we will not explore in any detail beyond this point.

- **Caching**: This is easiest to understand. By turning on caching and making sure that collection items are cached as they are loaded, we can reduce the number of database roundtrips by having the collection items loaded from cache. We will discuss caching in *Chapter 11, A Whirlwind Tour of Other NHibernate Features,* where we talk about features of NHibernate that you do not use routinely.

As with fetching strategies, there is no right solution to the select N+1 problem. My best bet would be to use lazy loading with batching turned on. If I need a particular collection to be eagerly loaded then I will use future queries. This is what we discuss next.

Avoiding eager fetching

While eager fetching of collections looks like a simple and quick solution to select N+1 problem, it does introduce an issue. Since eager fetching uses left outer joins, it results in Cartesian product of matching row in root table and collection table. Following unit test illustrates this behavior. We have three employees stored in-memory database. All three employees live in London. Two of the three employees are members of a community and the third employee is member of two communities. The query in the following unit test loads all employees living in London and also eagerly fetches their `Communities` collection. I expect to get three employee instance back.

```
[Test]
public void QueryOver()
{
  using (var transaction = Database.Session.BeginTransaction())
  {
    Address residentialAddress = null;
    var employees = Database.Session.QueryOver<Employee>()
            .JoinAlias(e => e.ResidentialAddress,
            () => residentialAddress)
```

```
                    .Where(() => residentialAddress.City == "London")
                    .Fetch(e => e.Communities).Eager
                    .List<Employee>();

            Assert.That(employees.Count, Is.EqualTo(3));
            transaction.Commit();
        }
    }
```

If you run this test, you will note that we get four records from database and the test fails. Why did that happen? If we look at the SQL that is issued by the preceding query, which is shown next, we realize that there is a join between the Employee and Community tables:

```
SELECT              this_.id AS id0_2_,
                    //... employee columns
                    residential_.id AS id2_0_,
                    //... address columns
                    communitie4_.employee_id AS employee1_4_,
                    community5_.id          AS community2_4_,
                    //... community columns
FROM                employee this_
INNER JOIN          address residential_
ON                  this_.id=residential_.employee_id
LEFT OUTER JOIN     employee_community communitie4_
ON                  this_.id=communitie4_.employee_id
LEFT OUTER JOIN     community community5_
ON                  communitie4_.community_id=community5_.id
WHERE               residential_.city = @p0;@p0 = 'London' [Type: String
(0)]
```

To LC: Format the following part of the above in Code Highlight

```
LEFT OUTER JOIN     employee_community communitie4_
ON                  this_.id=communitie4_.employee_id
LEFT OUTER JOIN     community community5_
ON                  communitie4_.community_id=community5_.id
```

The left outer join between Employee and Community makes the employee who is member of two communities appear in the result twice. So we get a total of 4 records – 2 each for the employees who are member of one community and 2 for employee who is member of 2 communities. If we had 1000 qualifying employees and each a member of 2 communities, we would have got back 2000 results. The problem amplifies even more if we eagerly fetch more than one collection in the same query. In that case, the original Cartesian product would be multiplied by the number of the items in the new collection.

This is such a common problem that NHibernate has provided a neat fix for this. The fix is in the form of a result transformer. Result transformer operates on the results loaded from database and transforms them into a different form. A result transformer is represented by interface `IResultTransformer`. Various different implementations of this interface are available to satisfy different result transformation requirements. The one we are interested in here is called `DistinctRootEntityResultTransformer`. This implementation takes the query results which may contain duplicates due to Cartesian product, de-duplicates the root entity, and places the collection items under the correct instance of root entity. If we change the query from the previous unit test to something as follows, then the test would pass:

```
Address residentialAddress = null;
var employees = Database.Session.QueryOver<Employee>()
.JoinAlias(e => e.ResidentialAddress, () => residentialAddress)
.Where(() => residentialAddress.City == "London")
.Fetch(e => e.Communities).Eager
.TransformUsing(Transformers.DistinctRootEntity).List<Employee>();
```

We have registered a result transformer to be used with this query by placing a call to method `TransformUsing` just before we call the terminal method `List<Employee>`. The parameter passed to this method is an instance of `IResultTransformer` that we want to be used. We have used factory class `Transformers` which make easy to work with all in-built transformers. `Transformers.DistinctRootEntity` is what would give us the unique results.

I have used QueryOver example as it is explicit about use of transformers. LINQ possesses the same problem with Cartesian products but you would never see it because it transparently applies `DistinctRootEntityResultTransformer` for you all the time.

So are we saying that `DistinctRootEntityResultTransformer` fixes the problem introduced by eager fetching? In a way yes, but the solution is not most elegant. Result transformers do their transformation in memory. That means we are loading all the results out of a Cartesian product into memory first and then processing them before they are returned to our code. Cartesian product has a tendency to grow too large too soon. There could be situation when a Cartesian product inadvertently returns hundreds of thousands of records which would kill your application, both memory-and-CPU wise. For these reasons it is best to avoid eager fetching if you can. What to do when we do not want collections lazily loaded because of select N+1 issue and we also do not want them to be eagerly fetched due to Cartesian product issue? Solution is to use future queries.

Future queries to the rescue

We have seen that future queries let us bundle multiple queries together and have them executed in one database roundtrip. We can use future queries to give us the effect of eager loading without side-effects from Cartesian products. Suppose we want to write the same query we saw previously, and in addition to the `Communities` collection also load the `Benefits` collection. Following code snippet shows how we can do it using future query:

```
Address residentialAddress = null;
var employees = Database.Session.QueryOver<Employee>()
    .JoinAlias(e => e.ResidentialAddress, () => residentialAddress)
    .Where(() => residentialAddress.City == "London")
    .Future<Employee>();

Database.Session.QueryOver<Employee>()
    .JoinAlias(e => e.ResidentialAddress, () => residentialAddress)
    .Where(() => residentialAddress.City == "London")
    .Fetch(e => e.Communities).Eager
    .Future<Employee>();

Database.Session.QueryOver<Employee>()
    .JoinAlias(e => e.ResidentialAddress, () => residentialAddress)
    .Where(() => residentialAddress.City == "London")
    .Fetch(e => e.Benefits).Eager
    .Future<Employee>();
```

The important parts are in bold in the preceding code. We have used the base query to retrieve employees living in London and turned that into a future query by calling `Future<Employee>` in the end. The next two queries may seem like repetition of the first query but if you look carefully, they are eagerly fetching the `Communities` and `Benefits` collections. These queries are also marked as future queries but their results are not stored in any local variable. The results are discarded. Internally, NHibernate still tracks and executes these queries when the first query is executed. This is what happens internally.

The first query is executed and the results from that query are kept in identity map of session. Second query is not any different from its non-future version. Following SQL is emitted for the second query:

```
SELECT this_.*,
       community5_.*,
FROM   employee this_
       INNER JOIN address residential1_
               ON this_.id = residential1_.employee_id
```

```
                LEFT OUTER JOIN employee_community communitie4_
                        ON this_.id = communitie4_.employee_id
                LEFT OUTER JOIN community community5_
                        ON communitie4_.community_id = community5_.id
        WHERE  residential_.city = 'London';
```

 This is an intentionally shortened version of actual SQL generated when the future query is run.

This is still a Cartesian product between `Employee` and `Community`. NHibernate uses only part of this result to populate the `Communities` collection on the `employee` instances, that it stored in the identity map populated using the results from the first query. Everything else from this query is discarded. The same is repeated for the results of the third query.

Two things to note here – we have not avoided the Cartesian products altogether but there is not significant processing of the results in memory. Also, in case of eager fetching multiple collections, we got a big Cartesian product involving all the collections. With future queries we get small Cartesian products involving only root entity and one collection at a time. This significantly reduces the data coming back from database and also the amount of processing required on the data.

Using extra-lazy for lazy collections

Extra lazy behavior was mentioned in the previous chapter. It is worthwhile to mention two benefits that extra lazy behavior brings to the table.

Suppose you have loaded a bunch of employees from database to be displayed on UI, along with number of benefits that they are entitled to. When you call `employee.Benefits.Count()` as in the following code, NHibernate would load the `Benefits` collection into memory and then count the number of items:

```
var employees = Database.Session.Query<Employee>()
.Where(e => e.ResidentialAddress.City == "London");

foreach (var employee in employees)
{
  Assert.That(employee.Benefits.Count(), Is.GreaterThan(0));
}
```

But if you enable extra lazy behavior on mapping of the Benefits collection then the preceding code would result in the following SQL being sent to database:

```
SELECT Count(id)
FROM benefit
WHERE employee_id =@ p0;
@p0 = 11 [TYPE: Int32 (0)]

SELECT Count(id)
FROM benefit
WHERE employee_id =@ p0;
@p0 = 12 [TYPE: Int32 (0)]

SELECT Count(id)
FROM benefit
WHERE employee_id =@ p0;
@p0 = 13 [TYPE: Int32 (0)]
```

Instead of loading all benefit instances into memory, NHibernate smartly issues a SELECT COUNT() statement which defers the operation of counting the records to database server. We not only reduce in-memory processing of records but also save on the amount of data returned from the server.

Another advantage extra lazy behavior brings about is to do with indexed collection. We do not have any examples of indexed collection in our domain mode. Items of an indexed collection can be accessed using integer indices. Because NHibernate knows about those indices, NHibernate can issue a SQL only to load the item that you have accessed, instead of bringing in the whole collection and wasting time on processing loads of data that you are not accessing.

Summary

Most developers like optimizing their code. They like making their code run faster. A seasoned professional usually does not run after optimization. He/She keeps delivering functionalities with an eye open to how his/her code is doing. At the same time, a seasoned professional also keeps their toolbox ready so that the moment he/she spots a problem they know which tool from their toolbox should be used to fix the problem. This chapter has tried to help you with knowing what to add to your toolbox. Learning the features/guidelines presented in this chapter is one step taken in the direction of becoming a seasoned professional. This chapter by no means is an encyclopedia of advice on how to tune performance of NHibernate.

This chapter gives an idea of different knobs that are available to you and what happens when these knobs are turned in different directions. The features presented in this chapter are basic and form the part of fundamental understanding of NHibernate. You may not get the right level of optimization by following just the features mentioned here. There are several different tweaks and tricks that you can apply. These tricks and tweaks will be unique to your problem. As you develop more expertise in the area of optimization and understand how NHibernate works internally, you will find it easier to get to the right level of optimization.

We have hit another important milestone. In the next chapter, we will be looking at using NHibernate in a real life web application. We will look at interesting topics such as how to use sessions and transactions effectively in a web application, how to structure the application, and so on. The next chapter will be more about practical advice about developing real life applications with NHibernate.

8
Using NHibernate in a Real-world Application

We have learned a lot of concepts and features of NHibernate. But we have learned all of them in isolation so far. While I enjoyed talking about them, it would be more interesting to see how to actually make use of NHibernate capabilities in a real-life application. And that is what I intend to do in this chapter.

There are two main objectives of this chapter. First one is to understand how NHibernate-based data access layer fits into the overall architecture of a web application and how it interacts with other components of an architecture. Second objective is to look closely at concepts such as repository pattern, unit of work, and session context. Repository pattern is a very commonly used pattern for abstracting away complex data access concepts and making the working with ORMs such as NHibernate easy. Unit of work is another time tested concept around executing related work items together as a unit. Session context is something specific to NHibernate and aids in management of session objects created by the application. On surface these concepts look simple and I want to show you that they are indeed simple.

This chapter uses an ASP.NET MVC web application as a primary example for walkthrough. I choose this as I believe that majority of software development happens in web space these days. Even desktop applications are becoming more of an UI wrapper powered by web service backends containing all the domain logic. In any of these scenarios, the data access layer operates under web context. So I believe it is important to understand how NHibernate fits into a web scenario. At the same time, also remember that most NHibernate features are generic and not specific for a particular type of application being built. Where things are different for a desktop application versus a web application, I will try to provide as much information as I can.

The approach we are going to take for this chapter is similar to a hands-on workshop. We will try to work through couple of functional requirements. While we progressively build these features, we will introduce new concepts such as unit of work, repository patterns, and session context at appropriate times. This approach, in my opinion, is more effective in understanding what problems are solved by these features. We will begin by spending some time talking about what kind of application we are going to build. We will then discuss some architectural principles that we will use while building these features. Once we have a common understanding of what approach we are going to take, we will jump into the actual coding of features.

What kind of application are we building?

As I just said, we will be building a web application. But we will try to lay out some details beyond that. So the web application that we are building will be based on ASP.NET MVC. We will have conceptual layers in this application such as business/domain layer, data access layer, presentation, and so on. But these layers will all be in the same process at runtime. We will not have each layer running in its own process like a standard 2-tier or 3-tier application. However, everything that we discuss here can be extended and applied without many changes to 2-tier or 3-tier applications separated by process boundaries.

Architectural principles we will follow

Building an extensible, testable, and maintainable data access layer is a topic very close to my heart. I cannot claim to be an expert on the topic but I have had a fair amount of success with implementing clean data access layer code using NHibernate on different projects. What has helped me get better over time is few architectural or design principles that I have discovered during this journey. I would like to introduce these principles to you briefly as I am going to base most conversations in this chapter and next on these principles. At first, some of the principles sound unnecessarily complex but my experience with these is that in the long run these are always beneficial.

No anaemic domain model

An anaemic domain model does not have much in terms of behavior. You have got classes with relationships between them which correctly represent the business domain. But inside these classes you have got bunch of getter/setter properties and nothing more. Then you have got another set of classes called domain services or manager classes which contain all the domain logic. This not only defeats the purpose of object-oriented programming but also leaves your domain entities as pure data containers and nothing more. We would rather add any business behavior related to an entity on that entity directly. That does not mean that we want to cram every aspect of a business operation into one method on a single class. We may still have classes that handle different aspects of validations, classes that interact with external services, and so on. But core domain logic for any business operation will sit within the relevant domain entity.

We will still have an application service layer in various different forms whose job is to expose the domain logic to consumers. But this layer is thin and only delegates the task to domain layer.

The onion architecture

Most software developers of my age or older have worked on one or more project that embraced layered architecture. Following diagram shows what I mean by layered architecture:

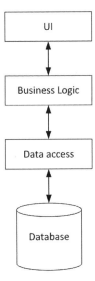

To summarize layered architecture:

- Every major concern of the application such as data access, business logic, application service, and UI is modeled as a layer.

- Layers have compile time and runtime dependency from top to bottom. UI layer depends on application service layer which in turn depends on business logic layer, and so on.

- Any layer directly depends on the layer right below it and indirectly depends on all the layers below it. For instance, UI layer indirectly depends on data access layer.

Thousands of software projects are executed following this architecture but lately the development community has started realizing the problems that this style introduces in long run. I would like to mention the following two problems with this architectural style which are important from data access point of view:

- **Tight coupling**: Every layer is tightly coupled to the layer directly below it. Tight coupling in any form is bad. It limits your opportunities to update the software by making small progressive changes. Such a situation makes the software get outdated too quickly. Tight coupling also comes in the way of unit testing. If you are not doing unit testing then you are missing one of the most important skills required to deliver quality software with confidence. If you are following TDD then you know what I mean.

- **Domain is not at the heart of the application**: In layered architecture, domain layer or business layer is not independent. It depends on and is tightly coupled to data access layer which is tightly coupled to a particular database schema. Any changes in database schema or data access layer may have an impact on business logic. Core of your application is business logic and that should be free of any external elements such as database or UI.

Let me introduce **onion architecture** to you which solves both of these problems. The term onion architecture was first coined by Jeffrey Palermo in 2008 on his blog at `http://jeffreypalermo.com/blog/the-onion-architecture-part-1/`. Following figure depicts onion architecture in a nutshell:

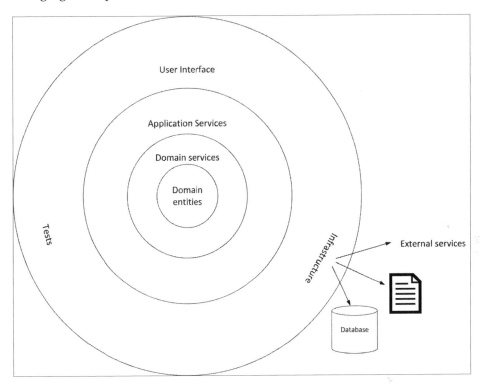

To summarize onion architecture:

As against layers, each major component is modeled around concentric circles:

- Compile time dependencies go from the outermost circle to the innermost circle
- Domain or business logic is at the centre and hence not dependent on any other components
- Infrastructure components such as UI and data access sit on outermost circle and no other component depends on them

If you come from layered architecture background then you may find this little hard to digest at first go. But have patience to go through this chapter with me and I hope to convince you why this is better architecture than layered. Two important concepts that help in working with onion architecture style are **Inversion of Control (IoC)** and externalization of infrastructure. Next section talks in detail about IoC. Externalization of infrastructure lets you identify and remove dependency on pieces of code that are external to our domain model. An example of this is database and data access layer. From onion architecture perspective, database is a place where we store our entities. It is just one step in overall domain logic. Domain logic does not care where and how the entities are stored as long as it can retrieve them back or persist them. Business operations depend on application's ability to retrieve and persist data but do not need to know how it is done or even be dependent on the components that actually persist or retrieve data.

In the preceding figure, there are two layers - application service and domain service. It is important to understand the precise difference between the two. A domain service is where we can add any business logic that cannot be fitted into domain layer. CRUD operations are not usually business logic and they should not be part of domain services. An application service is what external clients/consumers use to talk to your system. Think of WCF or web API-based service layer when you think of application services.

Dependency inversion

I would like to quote very nice description of dependency inversion principle that appears in Bob Martin's article on object oriented design available at http://butunclebob.com/ArticleS.UncleBob.PrinciplesOfOod. Dependency inversion can be summarized in two simple sentences:

- High-level modules should not depend upon low-level modules. Both should depend upon abstraction.

- Abstractions should not depend upon details. Details should depend upon abstractions.

In the previous definition, a high-level module refers to the module that contains the business logic. High-level module is identity of your software. Low-level module is things such as UI, file operations, database access, and so on. Dependency inversion principle states that business logic should not depend on details such as file operations, database access, and so on. This is in line with what onion architecture gave us. But there is one more thing that dependency inversion says – both high-level modules and low-level modules should depend on abstraction. What does that mean?

Suppose you have got a `Vehicle` class that depends on an `Engine` class besides some other classes. The `Vehicle` class has a method `Start` that encapsulates the logic for starting the vehicle. Starting the vehicle involves performing some checks on different parts of the vehicle and if everything is fine, then calling the `Fire` method on the `Engine` class. `Vehicle` is a high-level module. It contains the logic for starting the vehicle. `Engine` is a low-level module which provides the torque needed to push the vehicle forward. We may choose to swap one engine for another if we need to. That is the nature of low-level module. They provide a capability that can be replaced if needed.

Following is how this implementation would look like in a world without dependency inversion:

```
public class Engine
{
  public void Start()
  {
    //Start the engine here
  }
}

public class Vehicle
{
  private readonly Engine engine;
  public Vehicle()
  {
    engine = new Engine();
  }

  public void Start()
  {
    //Perform other checks
    engine.Start();
  }
}
```

We have got the `Vehicle` class, a high-level module, dependent on the `Engine` class, a low-level module. Dependency inversion principle says that this is not right. There are several reasons for why this is not right. This book is not about design principles and hence I will not go into details of those. But there is one reason that I will talk about here. Because of the way our dependencies are structured, it is not possible to swap out one engine for another without modifying the high-level module `Vehicle`. This is because the `Vehicle` module is dependent on a concrete `Engine` class. The `Vehicle` class is also controlling and instantiating the `Engine` class, the dependency.

If we introduce an abstraction that represents an engine, then things start looking a bit better. Suppose we introduce the following interface:

```
public interface IEngine
{
  void Start();
}
```

With the preceding abstraction in place, we could change our original code to the following:

```
public class Engine : IEngine
{
  public void Start()
  {
    //Start the engine here
  }
}

public class Vehicle
{
  private readonly IEngine engine;
  public Vehicle()
  {
    engine = new Engine();
  }

  public void Start()
  {
    //Perform other checks
    engine.Start();
  }
}
```

We still have got one tiny problem in the preceding code. Though the Vehicle class now depends on IEngine, it is instantiating an instance of the Engine class in its constructor. That keeps the dependency of the Vehicle class on the Engine class as is. Ideally, we should be passing an instance of IEngine to the constructor of the Vehicle class, as shown next:

```
private readonly IEngine engine;
public Vehicle(IEngine engine)
{
  this.engine = engine;
}
```

The Vehicle class now depends on IEngine. We have completely removed dependency of Vehicle on Engine. We now also get flexibility to choose which implementation of IEngine we want to pass into the Vehicle class. Now we can inject an instance of engine into the Vehicle class and Vehicle is no more dependent on Engine. We have inverted the dependencies.

 Dynamically injecting the dependencies through constructor is also called dependency injection. There are tools called IoC containers (Inversion of Control, another word for dependency inversion) that let you configure which dependencies should be injected where and then handle the actual dependency injection at runtime automatically for you. There are several such tools available and Autofac is one of my favorites.

The second statement in dependency inversion principle is not easy to understand at first. What it means is, the abstraction that you use to make the modules depend on, should not know anything about modules that depend on it. Let's elaborate that by extending the previous example. Suppose we have two engine implementations, PetrolEngine and DieselEngine. A petrol engine needs a spark plug but a diesel engine does not. If we add a property on the IEngine abstraction to hold spark plug then that would be a violation of dependency inversion principle. Spark plug is a detail that one of the implementations of IEngine needs. IEngine itself does not need spark plug and hence we should not add it to the IEngine interface.

Next principle is not a standard per say. This is something I have been following and seeing good results when used in incremental development environments or TDD settings.

Explicitly declaring the capabilities required

"Explicitly declaring the capabilities required" is more of a coding style that one can follow. Following this style brings about multiple advantages listed as follows:

- In the context of designing a class, lets you concentrate on what the class should be doing and abstracting the details that do not belong to the class.
- With experience, above leads to single responsibility principle.
- Offers a different way of looking at and thinking about dependencies. This helps in guiding you through your design incrementally instead of doing full design in one big sweep.
- Lets you concentrate on domain logic at hand than how multiple classes and dependencies would play out at runtime.
- Helps in identifying and pushing out concepts that do not belong to domain layer.

Let me reuse the vehicle example from the previous section to expand on this principle. Suppose you are asked to build a vehicle. You are working on "start vehicle" functionality and on outset you know roughly what is needed in order to implement the functionality. Now instead of thinking more about all those semi-complete details, you concentrate on domain logic of starting a vehicle and begin coding it in the `Vehicle` class. The first stab of this could be something as follows which is nothing but comments that guide us through implementation:

```
public class Vehicle
{
  public void Start()
  {
    //Check all parts are functioning ok
    //If all parts are ok start the engine else return
    //confirm that vehicle has started
  }
}
```

This is a good start. We have got a class that represents a vehicle and a method on it which when called will start the vehicle. As for starting of the vehicle goes, we now know that it is a three-step process. Let's look at the first step – check all parts are functioning ok. Is the `Vehicle` class capable of confirming that all parts are functioning ok? Maybe it is. But is `Vehicle` the right class to make that check? I think not. This is not a responsibility of the `Vehicle` class. This is a capability that needs to be offered to the `Vehicle` class in order for it to successfully start the vehicle. So the `Vehicle` class explicitly declares that it needs this capability. This explicit declaration is through a dependency injected via constructor. Moreover, the `Vehicle` class does not care how the actual check is performed. All it cares for is that the check is performed and it is supplied with the results in a format that it can understand. So the required capability needs to be declared in the form of an abstraction. Let's say we declare this capability using an interface `IConfirmVehiclePartsFunctioningOk`:

```
public interface IConfirmVehiclePartsFunctioningOk
{
  bool AreAllPartsOk();
}
```

The beauty of the preceding code is that it is such a simple piece of code to understand. We do not know and care (at this point of time), how many parts are involved in starting a vehicle and how they are checked. All we do is call the `AreAllPartsOk` method on the injected dependency and use the Boolean value returned to determine what to do next. With the previous dependency injected, following is how the `Vehicle` class would look like:

```
public class Vehicle
{
```

```
private readonly IConfirmVehiclePartsFunctioningOk
partsConfirmer;

public Vehicle(IConfirmVehiclePartsFunctioningOk partsConfirmer)
{
   this.partsConfirmer = partsConfirmer;
}

public void Start()
{
   If(partsConfirmer.AreAllPartsOk())
   {
      //Start the engine
      //confirm that vehicle has started
   }
 }
}
```

Same goes for the other steps - starting the engine and confirming if the vehicle has started. You need to ask yourself whether this logic belongs to the Vehicle class. If yes, go ahead and code it; if not, then explicitly declare this as a capability that the Vehicle class needs. Next time someone looks at the Vehicle class, they would know what external components the Vehicle class needs in order to function correctly. We also get all the advantages of dependency inversion principle that we just discussed. Following is the complete Vehicle class code with all capabilities declared:

```
public class Vehicle
{
   private readonly IConfirmVehiclePartsFunctioningOk
   partsConfirmer;
   private readonly IEngine engine;


   public Vehicle(IConfirmVehiclePartsFunctioningOk partsConfirmer,
               IEngine engine)
   {
      this.partsConfirmer = partsConfirmer;
      this.engine = engine;
   }

   public void Start()
   {
      if(partsConfirmer.AreAllPartsOk())
      {
```

```
        engine.Start();
        ConfirmVehicleStarted();
    }
}

public void ConfirmVehicleStarted()
{
    //confirm that vehicle has started
}
}
```

Confirming that vehicle has started is not pushed out as a capability required. This shows that though everything can be pushed out as a capability required, not everything needs to be pushed out. Always ask yourself, whether that particular piece of logic belongs to the class you are building. This will also help maintain single responsibility that the class delivers.

Unit of work

Unit of work is a programming concept that enables grouping database operations and executing them together as one unit. A unit of work implementation is expected to offer a guarantee that all database operations specified in the unit finish successfully. If any operation does not finish for any reason then unit of work should provide a way to roll back the changes made to the database state. Concept of unit of work is very important from business point of view. It is not desirable to leave the database in an inconsistent state when a business operation cannot be finished for any reason.

At relational database level, unit of work is equivalent of a transaction. You put all your SQL statements inside of the BEGIN TRANSACTION and END TRANSACTION statements. Database server then guarantees that either all SQL statements are executed or none are executed, leaving the database state intact. While this is good from theoretical point of view, this is no good when it comes to practical use. The main issue with this pattern is that it forces you to execute all state affecting operations together into a transaction. In code we do not have a notion of SQL statements or transaction. All we do in code is create new entities or update/delete exiting entities. NHibernate tracks the changes we are making to entities and issues appropriate SQL statements. Moreover, we do not make changes to entities in one place. During execution of a particular business operation, there may be several updates to state of different entities and these updates may be coded in multiple difference places. How can we make sure that these changes are treated as a unit of work? NHibernate's ISession and ITransaction interfaces are to the rescue here.

`ITransaction` implementation of NHibernate makes use of transaction capability of database to provide a better implementation of unit of work. And `ISession` intelligently tracks changes being made to entities and puts all the resulting SQL commands inside of unit of work provided by `ITransaction`. Following code snippet shows a very simple version of `ITransaction` and `ISession` working together to provide a unit of work pattern:

```
var session = //acquire session instance
try
{
  session.BeginTransaction();

  //different business operations here

  session.Transaction.Commit();
}
catch (Exception)
{
  if(session.Transaction.IsActive)
      session.Transaction.Rollback();
}
```

We begin a new transaction by calling the `BeginTransaction` method on `ISession`. This internally signals NHibernate that any database updates that result out of entity state changes from this point onwards need to be considered as part of a unit of work. The transaction created is held in an instance of `ITransaction`. This is returned to our code and internal copy is saved by `ISession` and made available to use via the `Transaction` property. We choose to discard the returned copy because we want to use the one on `ISession`. We then go on making series of changes to entities using the same `ISession` instance. When we are done, we call the `Commit` method on transaction to tell NHibernate that it should go ahead and synchronize with database the changes made to entities. At this point, NHibernate generates required SQL statements, wraps them in a database transaction statement, and sends to database for execution. If any error occurs at any point, we can call the `Rollback` method. This would roll back any changes that may have been made but not committed.

> If a transaction is disposed without calling the `Commit` or `Rollback` method, then NHibernate automatically calls the `Rollback` method. This also means that there is actually no need to call the `Rollback` method explicitly because we would not call the `Commit` method when there is an error and straight away dispose the transaction. NHibernate can then call `Rollback`. But it is better to explicitly call `Rollback` as a good coding practice and help future developers of your application understand things better.

Here I have used a `try...catch` block to show how to roll back database operations in case of errors. This is not required. You can use any mechanism to detect that an error has occurred and transaction is still active before you roll back the transaction.

I want to bring to your attention the following two important aspects that may not have been conveyed accurately by the preceding code:

- Calls to `BeginTransaction`, `Commit`, and `Rollback` do not need to appear in the same method or even in the same class. They can appear anywhere in your code as long as they are called. This gives tremendous flexibility when writing your code without forcing yourself to compromise on code quality/ design and still being able to use unit of work.

- Use of NHibernate transactions is orthogonal to using `ISession` to save, update, or delete entities. You continue to use `ISession` for these operations as you would have used it whether a transaction is in force or not. Transaction aspect can be handled independently and completely outside of your domain logic code.

Though `ISession` and `ITransaction` offer an implementation of unit of work, lot of developers choose to write their own implementation in order to have better control. We will look at both ways in this chapter.

That completes our list of architectural principles which may be useful in designing better applications using NHibernate. We would now move into implementing some simple features using our NHibernate knowledge and keeping these principles in mind. We may not go through end-to-end implementation of these features. We would mainly concentrate on parts that affect data access layer and its use in other layers.

Feature 1 – onboarding an employee

In our problem statement, we did not clearly define what happens when a new employee joins. We would detail that out now so that we have something meaningful to work with. Let's say, the following needs to happen when a new employee joins:

- Employee is awarded 21 sick leaves and 24 paid leaves
- A skill enhancement allowance of £1,000 is allocated
- Employee record is saved in database

First two items are clearly a part of business logic. We can say that this logic can live within the Employee class. Third item is not a domain concern but more of an infrastructure concern. So we would want to push it out to one of the outer layers of onion architecture. It is difficult to say which layer this items belongs to exactly. So instead of trying to answer that question now, let's work with what we have got and see where that takes us.

First of all, we would need a controller and an action defined on the controller that accepts a POST request for onboarding a new employee. We will not go into the details of controllers since it is not very important for our discussion. Besides, if you have used ASP.NET MVC for some time, you would know enough about writing controller actions. Now let's go back to the two items that we said to be fitting for business logic. We would implement this business logic in the Employee class in the form of a public method. In this method we create new instances of appropriate Benefit entities, set property values, and add them to the Benefits collection on Employee. Following is how this code looks:

```
public virtual void Onboard()
{
  AddBenefit(new Leave
  {
    AvailableEntitlement = 21,
    Type = LeaveType.Sick
  });

  AddBenefit(new Leave
  {
    AvailableEntitlement = 24,
    Type = LeaveType.Paid
  });

  AddBenefit(new SkillsEnhancementAllowance
  {
    Entitlement = 1000,
    RemainingEntitlement = 1000
  });
}
```

There are two missing pieces now. We need somewhere to call this method from and then persist this employee instance of database. Call to the Onboard method can be placed in controller action but hosting the persistence logic inside controller action is wrong. First of all, it is not the responsibility of controller action to carry out this coordination logic. Second, we will be promoting an anti-pattern called thick controller. A controller's job is to coordinate between model and view. When controllers start housing more logic than that, then they start becoming thick and hence the name thick controller. Thick controllers are like monolithic software - difficult to test, maintain, and change.

We need something that sits between domain entities and UI layer. During the introduction of onion architecture, we talked about domain services. Domain services is where we can write business logic that cannot be fitted into domain layer. Let's introduce a domain service layer and see where that takes us. We begin by adding a new project into our solution and name this as DomainService. This is a usual class library project. This project depends on the Domain project. We then add a class EmployeeOnboardingService to this project with a method Execute, as shown next:

```
using Domain;

namespace DomainService
{
  public class EmployeeOnboardingService
  {
    public void Execute(Employee employee)
    {
      employee.Onboard();
      //Persit employee instance
    }
  }
}
```

You may be wondering that we are adding layers unnecessarily. But as we progress, it will become clearer that a domain service layer brings benefits that are not possible to achieve without such a layer. Also, the business logic we have got now is very simple. It is possible for you a feel that all these layers are not needed for such a simple logic. But remember, this is just an example and in real life you may be dealing with logic that is more complex than this.

This has taken us a few steps further but we still do not seem to have solved the original problem of where do we write code to actually persist the employee instance to database. We could call `ISession.Save` from the preceding code but that would mean the `EmployeeOnboardingService` class needs to take dependency on `ISession`. That would further lead to the `DomainService` layer taking dependency on NHibernate. This goes against the onion architecture. The `DomainService` layer should not be dependent on infrastructure code, NHibernate in this case. So how do we solve this conundrum? The answer is in inversion of control and explicitly declaring required capabilities. The `EmployeeOnboardingService` class requires a capability to persist employee instance to database. It does not need to bother itself with who offers that capability or how is it actually fulfilled. If made available, it just uses that capability.

At this point, allow me to detour into discussion of a design pattern called **repository pattern**. Thoughtful implementation of repository pattern can provide the capability that the `EmployeeOnboardingService` class needs right now.

Repository pattern

On one hand, using design patterns is a good thing whereas on the other hand, too many patterns from the start could lead to unnecessary complexity and too much code to maintain. But some software problems and their solutions in a particular design pattern are so widely used that they have gone through good test of time. Repository pattern is one such design pattern to address common issues around data access. I am not saying that repository pattern is the best solution to the problem but it is the easiest one to get started. Repositories have their own shortcomings and come with their own problems. We would look at these and alternatives in the next chapter. For now, I want to introduce you to this pattern so that you can make an educated choice.

Repository pattern abstracts away the details of specific database operations and the persistence API used to carry out those operations. This includes infrastructure code or any interaction with the database. If I need to save an entity, I give that entity to a repository and trust that repository would save the entity in database for me. The simplest implementation of such a repository could be as follows:

```
public class Repository<T> where T :EntityBase<T>
{
  public void Save(T entity)
  {
    //Code to persist entity to database
  }
}
```

Here we have added a generic parameter T so that the Save method is typesafe. We have also added a constraint that T must be a type that inherits from EntityBase<T>. This limits the types that can be passed to domain entities only.

Right now there is nothing in the Save method. Let's try to add some code to persist the supplied entity instance to database. We would need to get hold of current session object for that. Since ISession is a capability that this class needs, we would add a constructor that takes ISession as a parameter and stores it in a field. Following is how our repository looks now:

```
public class Repository<T> where T :EntityBase<T>
{
  private readonly ISession session;

  public Repository(ISession session)
  {
    this.session = session;
  }

  public void Save(T entity)
  {
    session.SaveOrUpdate(entity);
  }
}
```

Nothing complex here. We have added a call to ISession.SaveOrUpdate and passed the supplied entity parameter. Now that our basic repository skeleton is ready, next question is where in our architecture should we add repository?

Where does the repository belong?

We started with EmployeeOnboardingService needing a repository. We now have a repository that we can use but can we put the repository class next to the service class? The answer is clearly a no but let's contemplate why:

- Repository<T> is abstracting away NHibernate behavior. This qualifies Repository<T> as infrastructure code. Following onion architecture principle, we do not want any infrastructure code in domain or domain service layer. So it better fits into the Persistence project of our solution.

- The `Repository<T>` class is a concrete implementation. As per IoC principle no class should depend on a specific implementation but on a more generic contract. By that logic it would not be prudent to make the `EmployeeOnboardingService` class take dependency on the `Repository<T>` class. Moreover, if we have decided to keep the `Repository<T>` class in the `Persistence` project, then the `EmployeeOnboardingService` class does not know about it (no compile time dependency) and hence cannot take a dependency on it.

Taking the preceding two points into consideration, we would need to create an interface out of the `Respository<T>` class so that `EmployeeOnboardingService` can take a dependency on that interface. We also need to move this interface into the `DomainService` project so that it is visible from that project. We would leave the `Repository<T>` in the `Persistence` project. Following is how the code looks now:

```
namespace DomainService.Capabilities
{
   public interface IRepository<T> where T : EntityBase<T>
   {
     void Save(T entity);
   }
}

namespace Persistence
{
   public class Repository<T> : IRepository<T>
   where T :EntityBase<T>
   {
     //Same as before
   }
}
```

Note that nothing has changed inside the class `Repository<T>` other than it implementing interface `IRepository<T>`. A shorter version of this class is presented here to save space. Also, the interface `IRepository<T>` is moved in a namespace `DomainService.Capabilities`. This is because `IRepository<T>` exposes a capability that domain service layer needs. This goes in line with what we discussed in the beginning. Every layer explicitly declares (using interfaces or abstract classes) the capabilities that they need someone else to provide.

We have a basic repository implementation in place which looks finished for what we need now. Let's go back to finishing the employee onboarding functionality.

Back to onboarding an employee

A repository is the capability that our domain service class needs and it can express this requirement by taking dependency on the IRepository<T> interface from the DomainService.Capabilities namespace. We add the following code to the EmployeeOnboardingService class to satisfy the dependency requirement:

```
private readonly IRepository<Employee> employeeRepository;

public EmployeeOnboardingService(
IRepository<Employee> employeeRepository)
{
   this.employeeRepository = employeeRepository;
}
```

Here we have added a new constructor that takes a parameter of type IRepository<Employee> and saves the supplied value in a private field.

Let's use this repository capability to finish the onboarding logic:

```
public void Execute(Employee employee)
{
   employee.Onboard();
   employeeRepository.Save(employee);
}
```

A call to the IRepository<Employee>.Save method is all we need to save the employee instance. This all looks fine and dandy but what about unit of work? What about executing the whole operation as single unit? We might just implement unit of work somehow and be done with it but there are some peripheral concepts around unit of work that are interesting and important to understand.

Unit of work

You might argue that we do not need unit of work in the previous situation as we are only saving a single entity using one call to ISession.Save. But remember that saving an employee instance results in multiple database records being inserted, and ideally, the whole operation of inserting these multiple records in database should be an atomic operation. Unit of work guarantees the atomicity we need. Before we bring a notion of unit of work, I would like to spend some time talking about scope of unit of work in this particular situation. A unit of work has to begin somewhere and end somewhere. Determining where unit of work begins and ends is crucial to robustness of data access layer.

Scope of unit of work for web applications

Web application design is an interesting topic. This book is not on web application design hence I will not spend too much time on it. But there is one aspect of web application design that is critical in deciding the scope of unit of work. Is your web application designed in such a way that every request performs a task that in itself can qualify as single business operation? Or in other words, does your web application handle any request that constitutes multiple business operations that can be finished independently of each other? If you do, then you are probably doing it wrong or you are making it difficult on yourself. Consider the following scenario.

You have a web application which takes some input from end user and then works on that input. Application performs two tasks, namely A and B, with those inputs. This is not clear to the user from the UI that they see but that is what happens behind the scenes. If both tasks A and B finish, then you take your users to a nice looking success page. But what if task A finishes but task B fails? Since your users do not know that there is task A and task B, you cannot tell them, "sorry folks, task B failed and you would need to provide the input again". Let's say you could do that; then what about task A that finished? If task A updated some database records (or inserted new ones), are you going to revert those operations? If you do not revert the operations, how would you ensure that next time the user provides the same input, you only perform task B because task A was finished already? Are you going to design your application as a state machine so that you remember where users left off last time?

You can see that there are too many questions and too many things to think about. I do not need to tell you that such a design would need lot of code to support it and even after that there would still be edge cases that would make your application fail over. So a decent and reliable design that you can implement with least amount of code is the one that wraps a single business operation in a web request. Such a design is also better from error recovery point of view. Now if you are going to code a single business operation per request, then we can safely say that if nothing goes wrong with processing of that request then the business operation can be called to have finished successfully. If there is any error during processing of the request then business operation fails. Any database changes made during a successful business operation should be committed at the end of the operation. The scope of unit of work needs to span across the whole business operation. In this design, a request wraps one business operation so we can say that scope of unit of work can span the whole request.

Session per request

We know that ISession can act as unit of work. We have also established that a good design of web application extends the scope of unit of work to full request processing. So an instance of ISession for every incoming request, with its inherent unit of work capability, seems to fit nicely here. You open a new session at a point where incoming request first hits your code. At the same time, you begin a transaction. You use that session whenever you need to interact with database during processing of that request. The last point in your code before request leaves is where you decide whether you should commit the transaction and close the session or rollback the transaction and then close the session. Sounds like it can work. Rather, this is a pattern so famous that it is recognized by its own name "session per request" and NHibernate supports it natively through an implementation of contextual sessions which is what we learn next.

Contextual sessions

In order to implement "session per request" kind of pattern, we need an ability to hold on to a session as long as the request is being processed. In other words, the scope of session needs to be limited by lifetime of the request in whose context the session was created. Such sessions can be called contextual sessions. There are two mechanisms that let us have contextual sessions. One of the mechanisms is natively supported by NHibernate whereas the other mechanism is offered by most famous IoC containers. We will look at the native NHibernate offering in detail and leave the IoC container mechanism for our avid readers to explore on their own.

NHibernate's implementation of contextual sessions hinges around the following three operations:

- Seamlessly store a session object
- Seamlessly retrieve previously stored session object
- Mark beginning and end of a context in which session object needs to be used

The way this works is – when a new request comes in, you create a new session by calling the OpenSession method on session factory. You then tell NHibernate that a new context starts here and NHibernate stores the session object created. NHibernate has defined a class named NHibernate.Context.CurrentSessionContext. This class provides a method Bind which is used to signal NHibernate of beginning of context. From this point onwards, if you need this session object then you can call the GetCurrentSession method on session factory. After the request is processed, your context ends and you can call the Unbind method on CurrentSessionContext to tell NHibernate that the context has ended and it no longer needs to hold on to the session object.

It is possible that the previous text has left you even more confused and hence we will look at a code listing which should explain this in a better way. Following code listing shows implementation of a class `SessionManager` which we can use whenever we need access to current session object:

```
using NHibernate;
using NHibernate.Context;

namespace Persistence
{
  public class SessionManager
  {
    private static readonly ISessionFactory sessionFactory;

    static SessionManager()
    {
      sessionFactory = new DatabaseConfiguration()
                    .BuildSessionFactory();
    }

    public static ISession GetCurrentSession()
    {
      if (CurrentSessionContext.HasBind(sessionFactory))
      {
        return sessionFactory.GetCurrentSession();
      }

      var session = sessionFactory.OpenSession();
      CurrentSessionContext.Bind(session);
      return session;
    }

    public static void Unbind()
    {
      CurrentSessionContext.Unbind(sessionFactory);
    }
  }
}
```

First and the most important thing about the preceding code is that the `GetCurrentSession` method is made `static` so that it can be called from anywhere. There is no need to instantiate the `SessionManager` class in order to get instance of session. We would look at code inside the `GetCurrentSession` method line by line. Before that, note that there is a static constructor where session factory is built.

The first line in `GetCurrentSession` is an `if` condition which calls `CurrentSessionContext.HasBind` and passes the session factory to it. We are seeing this method for the first time. This method returns true if an existing session has been tracked by the context already. In that case, we just call `sessionFactory.GetCurrentSession()` to return that tracked session. If no session is tracked, then we open a new session by calling `sessionFactory.OpenSession()`. The next line passes this newly created session to the `CurrentSessionContext.Bind` method to tell the session context that it should track this session.

So first call to `SessionManager.GetCurrentSession` will open a new session, add it to context, and return it. Subsequent calls to this method would return the same session object.

When processing of the request finishes, you can tell NHibernate to forget about the session object by calling the `SessionManager.Unbind` method. This method internally calls the `CurrentSessionContext.Unbind` method which takes session factory as input.

This looks good so far. But the following two questions are still unanswered:

- When `SessionManager.GetCurrentSession` is called from multiple threads for multiple requests, do we get a new session object or the same session object? How does `CurrentSessionContext` ensure that every web request gets its own session object?

- We kept referring to beginning of request processing and end of request processing in the above discussion. Those are the two points from where the earlier code would be called. But where is beginning of request and end of request for an ASP.NET MVC application, for example?

Answer to the first question lies in the implementation of `CurrentSessionContext`. There are more than one implementations of `CurrentSessionContext`. You can configure which one you want to use for you application. We would discuss this next. Second question is more of an ASP.NET MVC detail and has nothing to do with NHibernate. After we discuss the configuration of `CurrentSessionContext`, we would turn our attention to this aspect.

Configuring CurrentSessionContext

Implementation of `CurrentSessionContext` is pluggable. What that means is that you can inherit from this class and have your own implementation of contextual sessions. You can then choose to have storage of contextual sessions managed in a better and thread-safe way so that no two web requests get hold of the same session object. The good news is that NHibernate provides an implementation which does exactly that. NHibernate implements a class `WebSessionContext` which uses `HttpContext` to store the session. This stored instance of session is available to use throughout the processing of the request. During NHibernate configuration you can declare that you want to use `WebSessionContext` as your current session context class. Following code shows how to do this:

```
public class DatabaseConfiguration : Configuration
{
  public DatabaseConfiguration()
  {
    this.CurrentSessionContext<WebSessionContext>();
  }
}
```

Note that there is other NHibernate configuration in the preceding class which is not shown here in order to save space. If you remember from *Chapter 4, NHibernate Warmup*, programmatic configuration of NHibernate is done using the `NHibernate.Cfg.Configuration` class. You can instantiate this class directly. Here I have preferred to inherit from that class and declared the entire configuration inside the inherited class. The `Configuration` class exposes a method `CurrentSessionContext<T>`. This method is used to tell NHibernate which implementation of contextual session we want to use. Since our application is a web application, we have used `WebSessionContext` here but the following different implementations are available to use in different situations. Remember that all these implementations do the exact same thing – track session by storing them somewhere. Where they differ is the storage mechanism that is used which makes them suitable to be used in different kind of applications/setups.

- `CallSessionContext`: This uses `CallContext` to track current session. `CallContext` is a specialized collection class available in .NET which provides set of properties and data slots that are carried along with execution code path. These data slots are unique to each logical thread. When the execution path involves a remote call, `CallContext` is transparently copied over to the remote side.

- `ThreadStaticSessionContext`: This implementation uses a static variable local to current thread for tracking current session. It uses the `ThreadStatic` attribute of .NET in doing so. This implementation is most useful in desktop applications such as WinForms or other multi-threaded but non-web applications.

- `WcfOperationSessionContext`: If you are working with WCF services then you can use this implementation to track your current session. This implementation uses `OperationContext` offered by WCF to store the current session instance.

If the previous OOTB implementations do not help with your situation then you can always implement your own. But I am yet to come across a situation where this is needed. Now let's look into implementing session per request using contextual sessions.

Implementing session per request using the contextual sessions

To implement "session per request" pattern, you need to be able to create a new session when a new request comes in, then use that session throughout the request processing and in the end, dispose the session. .NET provides hooks that you can use to intercept requests when they come in and leave. All web/service frameworks of .NET provide such hooks. The idea is to use these hooks to create a new session when a new request comes in and dispose the session when the request processing is done. Let's quickly run through different options available for hooking into request pipeline to implement "session per request".

Using the HTTP module

HTTP modules are one of the oldest mechanisms of building pluggable components that are capable of intercepting incoming and outgoing requests. An HTTP module is a class that implements the `IHttpModule` interface. An HTTP module has a `Init` method to which an instance of `HttpApplication` is passed. `HttpApplication` exposes events to which we can subscribe. In this case, we can subscribe to `BeginRequest`, which is invoked at the beginning of every incoming request, and `EndRequest`, which is invoked at the end of processing of every request. Following code listing shows the simplest implementation of such an HTTP module:

```
public class DatabaseSessionModule : IHttpModule
{
  public void Init(HttpApplication context)
  {
```

```
      context.BeginRequest += Context_BeginRequest;
      context.EndRequest += Context_EndRequest;
   }

   private void Context_EndRequest(object sender, System.EventArgs e)
   {
var session = SessionManager.GetCurrentSession();
session.Close();
session.Dispose();
   }

   private void Context_BeginRequest(object sender, System.EventArgs e)
   {
var session = SessionManager.GetCurrentSession();
   }

   public void Dispose()
   {

   }
}
```

Configuring an HTTP module is outside the scope of this book so I will jump straight into the part that is of interest to us. We have added two methods to subscribe to the `BeginRequest` and `EndRequest` events. In method `Context_BeingRequest`, we create a new session object which would be tracked by NHibernate's contextual session implementation and is available throughout the request processing. In `Context_EndRequest`, we would close and dispose that session.

Using hooks in the global.ascx file

If you have developed web applications using .NET then you know that there is a `global.ascx` file in every web application. This file contains the entry point of your application. The code-behind file for this also has options to set up some hooks that are called by frameworks on some events. This is very similar to HTTP module. Like HTTP modules, two events that are of interest to us are `Application_BeginRequest` and `Application_EndRequest`. `Application_BeginRequest` is called at the beginning of every incoming request and `Application_EndRequest` is called in the end, after every request is processed. Rest of the logic is exactly same as for HTTP module. Following code listing shows the relevant part of `global.ascs.cs`:

```
public class MvcApplication : HttpApplication
{
   protected void Application_Start()
```

```
{
  //Other MVC specific code
}

protected void Application_BeginRequest(object sender, EventArgs e)
{
  var session = SessionManager.GetCurrentSession();
}

protected void Application_EndRequest(object sender, EventArgs e)
{
  var session = SessionManager.GetCurrentSession();
  session.Close();
  session.Dispose();
}
}
```

Using the action filters of ASP.NET MVC or Web API

This is the newest and most configurable option of all. Action filters, like HTTP modules, intercept incoming and outgoing requests. Unlike HTTP modules, the scope of action filters is limited to MVC or Web API part of the application. Besides that, action filters provide nice control over which of the incoming requests should be intercepted by a particular action filter. You can also have global action filters which apply to all requests. Following code listing shows how to implement "session per request" using action filter:

```
public class RequiresDatabaseSession : ActionFilterAttribute
{
  public override void OnActionExecuting(ActionExecutingContext
  filterContext)
  {
    var session = SessionManager.GetCurrentSession();
  }

  public override void OnActionExecuted(ActionExecutedContext
  filterContext)
  {
    var session = SessionManager.GetCurrentSession();
    session.Close();
    session.Dispose();
  }
}
```

This is just like any other MVC action filter. If you have used action filters before then you know that action filters provide various event handlers which are called by MVC framework at appropriate times. Two of such event handlers are `OnActoinExecuting` and `OnActionExecuted`. Former is called before the code from controller action is executed and the latter is called after the controller action is executed. We have acquired an instance of session during `OnActionExecuting` and released it during `OnActionExecuted`.

WCF

WCF offers hooks in the form of pluggable message inspectors. This works similar to MVC action filters in that you can specify which WCF endpoints you want to apply a particular message inspector to. As the name suggests, a message inspector is capable of intercepting and inspecting incoming and outgoing messages. In this case, we would need to implement a specific message inspector called dispatch message inspector. Dispatch message inspector needs to implement the following interface:

```
public interface IDispatchMessageInspector
{
  public object AfterReceiveRequest(
  ref System.ServiceModel.Channels.Message request,
  IClientChannel channel, InstanceContext instanceContext;

public void BeforeSendReply(
  ref System.ServiceModel.Channels.Message reply,
  object correlationState;

}
```

Barring the details of the parameters that are going into the methods, this is a very simple interface. You have got two methods on this interface. `AfterReceiveRequest` is called when service receives a client request for processing. At this point we would open a new session. `BeforeSendReply` is called after we are done servicing the request and a response is about to be sent to the client. It is in this method that we would close and dispose the session.

I do not intend to go into the details of full implementation of a dispatch message inspector for WCF. This is left as a self-exercise for readers.

 In every implementation, we are opening a new session as soon as a request is received. This is in line with "session per request" but it is not really needed. You can defer opening of a new session till a time when session is first needed during request processing.

Next, we would extend the previous examples to add unit of work implementation.

Unit of work implementation

We have talked about unit of work in quite some detail so far. You probably have a very clear picture of what unit of work does. In this section, we would quickly look at couple of different ways of implementing unit of work.

Unit of work spanning the whole HTTP request

In earlier section when we talked about unit of work, we also discussed how ISession inherently offers unit of work when all interaction with ISession is done inside a transaction. All we needed to do was place a call to BeginTransaction after a session is opened. The same concept can be combined with "session per request" implementation to provide a complete unit of work pattern making most of NHibernate's capabilities. Let's take a look at the following code listing:

```
public override void OnActionExecuting(ActionExecutingContext
filterContext)
{
    var session = SessionManager.GetCurrentSession();
    session.BeginTransaction();
}
```

This is exactly the same code that we saw earlier. We have only added an extra line of code to open a new transaction every time a new session is created. We are effectively adding any database interaction done using this session to a transaction, thus making that interaction a part of unit of work.

The BeginTransaction statement sends a SQL command to database to being a SQL transaction. This command is sent to database immediately. So you have an open database transaction as long as your request is being processed. If your request takes a long time to process, then transaction remains open for a long time. This may have negative impact on other SQL queries that are waiting to be executed. I tend to see this as a positive thing because it really forces me to ensure that 1) a single request is not taking long time to execute and 2) my requests (and overall application) are designed so that we do not have less requests doing bulky jobs but more requests doing small, meaningful chunks of work. But if you are worried about this, you can always move the call to BeginTransaction inside SessionManager and remove the call to GetCurrentSession from OnActionExecuting. If you do that, make sure that you call BeginTransaction only when a new session is being created.

The transaction that we started needs to be committed at some point (or everything rolled back if anything goes wrong). Let's take a look at modified code of OnActionExecuted which achieves this:

```
public override void OnActionExecuted(ActionExecutedContext
filterContext)
{
    var session = SessionManager.GetCurrentSession();
    var transaction = session.Transaction;

    if (transaction.IsActive)
    {
        if (filterContext.Exception != null)
        {
            transaction.Rollback();
        }
        else
        {
            transaction.Commit();
        }
    }
    session.Close();
    session.Dispose();
}
```

There are two interesting things to note here. First, we get hold of the transaction that is attached to the current session (this is same transaction that we started in OnActionExecuting), and if there is any exception thrown during the execution of controller action then we rollback the transaction. Second, if there was no error during execution of action then we commit the transaction. We close and dispose the session before leaving the method.

This same implementation can be extended to other ways of implementing contextual session that we saw using the HTTP module or hooks in global.asax.

Note that the scope of an action filter is limited to controller action only. If you have got some logic in a different action filter or in an HTTP module, then any database interaction from that place would not be part of the unit of work that is initiated from this action filter. You are effectively not doing "session per request" in that situation. There is nothing wrong in doing so as long as you know that there are multiple units of work at play and one or more of units of work may be committed to database even if a latter unit of work fails because of some error. Make sure that such a situation does not leave your database in an inconsistent state.

Unit of work with custom scope

Sometimes we may not want to put all database interactions within a request in a single unit of work. For those times, the above implementation does not work and we need to implement a custom unit of work which can be invoked from anywhere. I have been using the following simple implementation with some success:

```
public class UnitOfWork
{
  private readonly ITransaction transaction;

  public UnitOfWork(ISession session)
  {
    transaction = session.BeginTransaction();
  }

  public void Commit()
  {
    if(transaction.IsActive) transaction.Commit();
  }

  public void Rollback()
  {
    if(transaction.IsActive) transaction.Rollback();
  }
}
```

Whenever you need to add database activities in a unit of work, you just instantiate a new instance of the UnitOfWork class and pass the session object that you are using. You can then call either Commit or Rollback depending on whether you want to commit your changes or discard them.

This is a very simple implementation that should give you an idea of what can be done. I have skipped some basic validations such as checking that session is not null, making sure that transaction has not started already on the session object, and so on. Feel free to add that logic if you happen to use unit of work with custom scope. Another thing you could do is to make the above class disposable by implementing the IDisposable interface. You can then call the Rollback method from the Dispose method of IDisposable and thus forever end the need to call Rolllback manually. Personally, I use such an implementation very sparingly.

That concludes our long discussion on managing session and unit of work. We discussed multiple concepts and implementations which may be confusing. Important take-away from this discussion is to understand the role that session and unit of work play when it comes to integrity of critical business data. Let's continue our journey of implementing other features.

Feature 2 – updating the details of an employee

Next feature we are going to implement is updating details of an employee. Possible updates to an employee entity could be changes to properties such as first name, last name, and so on, or addition or removal of one or more benefits or communities. Remember that all updates work in almost the same way so it is more important to understand how updates work than what is being updated.

NHibernate offers multiple different mechanisms for making changes to persistent entities. Before we look into actual implementation of modification of an employee record, I want to spend some time discussing two important concepts that dictate how this feature could be implemented. Clarity around these two concepts should help you determine which mechanism you can use to update entities:

- **Partial updates versus full updates**: When you want to change values of some of the properties on a persistent entity, then that will need a partial update. An example of this would be updating first name or last name on employee. Contrast that with a situation when you want to modify every other property on an entity. That would be a full update. I have rarely seen business requirements that need full updates. Most business logics require a partial update.

- **Updating detached entities versus updating persistent entities**: In *Chapter 5, Let's Store Some Data into the Database*, we learned about entity states, particularly about detached entities. Detached entities are the entities which are present in database and in application memory but are not associated with any session object. On the other hand, persistent entities are present in both database and application memory and are also associated with session object. Being associated with a session is an important characteristic because then session is capable of tracking changes made to the entity.

Persistent entities can be updated using transitive persistence feature of NHibernate. To work with detached entities, we can make use of the `Update` and `Merge` methods available on `ISession`. Let's look into both the options in little more detail.

Updates using transitive persistence

In *Chapter 6, Let's Retrieve Some Data from the Database,* we discussed transitive persistence. Any changes made to a persistent entity are automatically tracked by session. These changes are synchronized with database either when transaction is committed or session is flushed. Nature of transitive persistence makes it suitable for both partial and full updates. We would implement a partial update where we update residential address of an employee. As with onboarding of an employee, we would add a domain service class where we would implement update employee logic. Following code shows the basic skeleton of that class:

```
public class UpdateEmplyeeService
{
  public void Execute(int employeeId, Address newAddress)
  {
  }
}
```

We have got the `Execute` method that takes two parameters. First one is an identifier of the employee entity whose residential address needs to be updated. Second parameter is the new residential address. We want to use transitive persistence to update the residential address. For that, we first need to load the persistent instance of employee from database. As we have done during employee onboarding feature, we would delegate this task to repository. Let's assume that we have a `GetById` method available on repository then `UpdateEmployeeService` can take a dependency on `IRepository<Employee>` and use the repository to load the persistent instance. Once we have persistent instance available then updating any detail is as easy as setting the relevant property to new value. Following is how the complete code looks:

```
public class UpdateEmplyeeService
{
  private readonly IRepository<Employee> repository;

  public UpdateEmplyeeService(IRepository<Employee> repository)
  {
    this.repository = repository;
  }

  public void Execute(int employeeId, Address newAddress)
  {
    var employee = repository.GetById(employeeId);
    employee.ResidentialAddress = newAddress;
  }
}
```

One important thing to remember here is that the previous mechanism works when the session that loaded the persistent entity is still open while entity is being updated (in other words, the entity being updated has not become detached). Our "session per request" implementation ensures that the session is kept open during processing of the request. Also note that the updates made to the `employee` instance are synchronized with database when transaction is committed. In our case, that happens at the last moment towards the end of request processing and hence actual database update happens at the point only.

For the sake of completeness, following is the implementation of the `GetById` method on the `Repository<T>` class:

```
public T GetById(int id)
{
   return session.Load<T>(id);
}
```

Note the use of the `Load<T>` method instead of the `Get<T>` method. If you recall from *Chapter 5, Let's Store Some Data into the Database*, `Load<T>` would not go to database to load the entity but only return an in-memory proxy instance with identifier set to what was passed to the method. On the other hand, `Get<T>` would actually hit the database to load the entity. There is no need to load the entity in order to update some properties on it.

> We made an assumption that identifier of the entity to be updated is known. We then used the identifier value to retrieve the persistent instance of the entity. Loading the persistent instance and having some method on repository to do is the important point here. You could have used any other property on the previous `employee` in place of identifier.

Updating the detached entities

Transitive persistence only works with persistent entities and is capable of performing both partial and full updates. Transitive persistence should be your preferred mechanism for implementing entity updates. We will see why after we look at the other mechanism for updating entities.

> I encourage you to avoid detached entities if you can. I want to cover this topic so that you know how to deal with detached entities. But the code samples that I would use will be primitive with just enough details required to support the theory.

NHibernate supports synchronizing changes made to detached entities through two different methods available on `ISession`. We have briefly looked at both of these methods in *Chapter 6, Let's Retrieve Some Data from the Database*, but let's look at them again with little more detail. First method is `Merge`. This method takes in a detached instance of an entity, associates it with session, and returns the persistent instance of the entity. Internally, NHibernate checks if the entity being asked to merge exists in session. If it does, then NHibernate will update the entity in session with the property values from the entity being passed. It then returns the entity in session. After this point, because you are dealing with a persistent entity, any changes made to the properties of the entity would be tracked by NHibernate. If the entity was not present in the session, then NHibernate will load the entity from database and then carry out the merge operation. Following code listing shows this in action:

```
using (var tx = Session.BeginTransaction())
{
  var emp = new Employee
  {
    Id = (int) id,
    Firstname = "Hillary"
  };
  emp.AddBenefit(new Leave
  {
    AvailableEntitlement = 25,
    RemainingEntitlement = 23,
    Type = LeaveType.Paid
  });
  var emp2 = Session.Merge(emp);

  emp2.EmailAddress = "Hillary.Smith@organisation.com";
  tx.Commit();
}
```

Here, we have got an instance of the `Employee` class with its identifier set to some value and some other properties set. We pass this instance to the `Merge` method which returns another instance of the `Employee` class. If a record is present in database with identifier value of original instance, then this new instance represents that record in database. At the same time, state of the entity in the session is overwritten with state of the entity that we passed to the `Merge` method. We then updated the `EmailAddress` property of the persistent instance. In the end, we commit the transaction, at which point, all the changes made to the persistent entity are synchronized to database. Preceding code would generate the following SQL:

```
INSERT INTO Benefit (NAME, Description,
Employee_Id, Id)
VALUES (@p0, @p1, @p2, @p3 );
```

```
@p0 = NULL, @p1 = NULL, @p2 = 11, @p3 = 65537

INSERT INTO Leave
(Type, AvailableEntitlement, RemainingEntitlement, Id)
VALUES (@p0, @p1, @p2, @p3);
@p0 = 0, @p1 = 25, @p2 = 23, @p3 = 65537

UPDATE Employee
SET Firstname = @p0,
        Lastname = @p1,
        EmailAddress = @p2
WHERE  Id = @p3;
@p0 = 'Hillary', @p1 = NULL, @p2 = 'Hillary.Smith@organisation.com',
@p3 = 11

DELETE
FROM SeasonTicketLoan
WHERE Id = @p0;
@p0 = 65536

DELETE
FROM Benefit
WHERE Id = @p0;
@p0 = 65536
```

A major issue with Merge is that it always attempts to do a full update. What that means is, if you try to merge an entity with only few properties set to a value you want to update to and leave the remaining properties to null, then Merge will update those null properties as well thinking you intend to update those properties to null values. Following unit test explains this in detail:

```
[Test]
public void PartialUpdatesUsingMergeResultInInconsistentState()
{
  object id = 0;
  using (var tx = Session.BeginTransaction())
  {
    id = Session.Save(new Employee
    {
      Firstname = "John",
      Lastname = "Smith"
    });

    tx.Commit();
  }
```

```
Session.Clear();

using (var tx = Session.BeginTransaction())
{
  var emp = new Employee
  {
    Id = (int)id,
    Firstname = "Hillary"
  };
  var emp2 = Session.Merge(emp);

  emp2.EmailAddress = "Hillary.Smith@organisation.com";
  tx.Commit();
}

Session.Clear();

using (var tx = Session.BeginTransaction())
{
  var employee = Session.Get<Employee>(id);
  Assert.That(employee.Lastname, Is.Null);
  tx.Commit();
}
}
```

In this test, we first saved an employee instance having only the `Firstname` and `Lastname` properties set to some value. We then created another instance in-memory having its `Firstname` property set to a new value and the `Id` property set to the identifier of the previously saved instance. We then merged this new instance by passing it to the `Merge` method. Instance returned by the `Merge` method, `emp2`, is the new persistent instance. We update the `EmailAddress` property on this instance hoping that it would be persisted to database. When the changes are synchronized to the database, NHibernate checked that the original entity has `Lastname` but merged entity has `Lastname` set to null so it generates following SQL statement to update `Lastname` to null along with `Firstname` and `EmailAddress` being updated to correct value.

```
UPDATE employee
SET Firstname = @p0,
        Lastname = @p1,
        EmailAddress = @p2
WHERE  Id = @p3;
        @p0 = 'Hillary',
        @p1 = NULL,
        @p2 = 'Hillary.Smith@organisation.com',
        @p3 = 11
```

So use `Merge` carefully as it may result in properties set to null inadvertently, resulting in subtle issue and data loss.

Why transitive persistence is better

We have seen how using detached entities for update operations may lead to subtle defects resulting in data loss at times. The `Merge` and `Update` methods work perfectly fine only when they are passed with a fully hydrated entity. In other words, they only work reliably in case of full updates. Reality of building software for businesses is that on most occasions we need to deal with partial updates. For instance, in case of employee benefit management system, do you think we would have one screen where all details of an employee including employee's name to her benefits and communities can be updated? I highly doubt that. An elegant user journey would be the one where end user can add a benefit to an employee independently of updating any other details on the employee's profile. In order to facilitate such a use case using detached entities, you would need to pass all details of the employee from UI to backend so that backend can have a fully hydrated employee instance without having to go to database. This is not only a contrived way of fulfilling simple task but is also inefficient. Instead of passing the whole employee profile from UI to backend, why not just pass the identifier and load the detail from database? And if you are loading the `employee` instance from database then why not use transitive persistence?

Feature 3 – searching employees

The last feature that we are going to look at is an ability to search employees in the system. I have seen largest number of variations in the implementation of search features across different systems. The variations are in the way it works, the way results are displayed to end user, and also the complexity of the actual search. Let's begin with the most simple search.

The purpose of this section is not to show you how to implement a search functionality. If you have gone through *Chapter 6, Let's Retrieve Some Data from the Database*, then you know that implementing search feature comes down to building some queries using `ISession` and utilizing pagination features offered by `ISession`. The intent of this section is to show you some limitations of repository pattern. So we will run through the simplest implementation without beating around the bush and discuss issues with repository pattern in the end.

We will implement a feature to search employees by their name. Let's say the search function does not specify first name or last name. Whatever end user enters is checked against employees' first name and last name both. The only restriction that we will apply to keep this simple is that the end user should not enter multiple words. Or in other words, no spaces are allowed. For instance, if you enter John, then search function will return employees having first name or last name as John. Let's move on to the implementation then.

First thing we need is a controller action which would take the input from the end user. This controller action would then pass this input to the next layer. Let's keep this consistent and add a domain service class as the next layer. Let's say we add the following domain service class:

```
public class EmployeeSearchService
{
  public IEnumerable<Employee> Search(string name)
  {
    //Query the database and return results
  }
}
```

So we have got a Search function that takes a string parameter for name to match against the first and last names of employees present in database. SearchEmployeeService needs a capability to run that query against database and return the results. Let's add the capability on IRepository<T> and make SearchEmployeeService take dependency on IRepository<T>. Following code listing depicts this:

```
public class EmployeeSearchService
{
  private readonly IRepository<Employee> repository;

  public EmployeeSearchService(IRepository<Employee> repository)
  {
    this.repository = repository;
  }


  public IEnumerable<Employee> Search(string name)
  {
```

```
        return repository.FindAll(name);
    }
}

public interface IRepository<T> where T : EntityBase<T>
{
    void Save(T entity);
    void Update(int id, Employee employee);
    T GetById(int id);
    IEnumerable<Employee> FindAll(string name);
}
```

We have added a `FindAll` method on `IRepository<T>` that takes name as a parameter and returns list of the `employee` instance found having matching first name or last name. Let's turn our attention now to implementing the `FindAll` method. If we use LINQ then it is not very difficult. Following is the simplest implementation of this method:

```
public IEnumerable<Employee> FindAll(string name)
{
    return session.Query<Employee>()
                .Where(e => e.Firstname == name || e.Lastname == name)
                .ToList();
}
```

This seems to get the work done but there are some issues with the previous approach.

- The `FindAll` method on `IRepository` is specific to the `Employee` class. This makes generic `Repository<T>` unusable by other entities. A solution to this is to implement an `Employee` specific repository but then we would soon add dozen more repository classes that we would need to maintain.

- Right now we have got two methods on `IRepository`. One returns an entity by its identifier and second returns list of employees with matching name. As your application grows, these two methods will not be enough. You might need to retrieve employees by their employee number, country/city of residence, email address, and so on. Imagine how would your repository classes look with loads of such methods stacked on to them.

- We have not yet addressed other concerns around search which are pagination and sorting. If we add pagination and sorting in the preceding query, then the `FindAll` method becomes too specific to search functionality and cannot be used in other scenarios where we might not need pagination or sorting, for example, to get the count of employees having a particular first name. A solution to this problem could be to not place a call to terminal method `ToList` within `FindAll` and return an `IQueryable<T>` instead of an `IEnumerable<T>` so that the `EmployeeSearchService` can then add pagination and sorting as it sees fit. But development community is divided on this approach. A large number of seasoned developers consider returning an `IQueryable<T>` from repository as a leaky abstraction. I will not go into that debate or pros and cons of either approach as I believe that there is a better solution in the form of a different querying pattern to this problem.

I can go on listing few more issues with our implementation, but let me take a moment and come back to the point I am trying to convey here. There is nothing wrong with implementation of search query and there is no way you can avoid having multiple different ways of querying entities, but stacking everything on to a repository is not wise. Call it a limitation of repository pattern but lot of developers have learned through their experience that building complex queries using repositories mostly results in code that is not testable or maintainable. Next chapter is dedicated to this aspect and solutions available so I will not waste any more space here discussing the issue at length.

That brings us to the end of this chapter. There was no new NHibernate feature that we learned in this chapter, baring contextual session obviously. But we tried to put our NHibernate knowledge into perspective and use it in real-life application.

Summary

We tried to bring a change in general style and tone of this chapter. I hope you felt it. This chapter was more about practical guidance and I felt I would make it sound more like so. Along with practical guidance and design principles, there were three main topics that we covered in this chapter. First and most important is contextual sessions. Contextual sessions can be used to effectively manage and reuse session object across multiple classes. If you are not using IoC containers, then session context is probably the best way to implement strategies such as "session per request", and so on. Next we talked about unit of work, another important concept. Unit of work lets you bundle different database operations under a transaction so that they are carried out atomically – either all operations succeed or all operations fail. Atomicity of database operations results in consistent state of data which is very important from functional point of view.

The last topic we covered was repository pattern. Study of NHibernate is incomplete without learning repository pattern. Repository pattern adds one more layer of abstraction on top of NHibernate but this abstraction plays in favor of developers because of simplicity of its design. Repository pattern is a time-tested and widely used pattern and hence less risky to begin with. Even if you are stuck at something, it is very easy to get help online.

Repository pattern does what it says on the tin. If you are new to NHibernate then it is best to use and get the job done. But that does not mean that it comes without any downsides. I come from a "clean and maintainable code" mind set and I always find these downsides of repository pattern a bit awkward to work with. In the next chapter, we would look into what these downsides are and what are the solutions. We would talk about separating read side from write side in the repository. Once the reads and writes are separated, we would look into some advanced querying patterns that make working with read side easier. If I have managed to get you excited then turn over the page.

One last thing, it is possible that some of you may not agree with every idea/advice that I have presented here. There are several ways of skinning this cat and I am all ears to hear your experience if you think you have approached the issue in a different way which is better that what I have discussed.

9

Advanced Data Access Patterns

We are coming to the end of our NHibernate learning experience. This is not the last chapter but the chapters after this are a bit disconnected from our journey so far. Previous chapters should have given you solid understanding of how to use NHibernate in a real-life application. We learned an important design pattern such as repository and other useful design principles. But we closed the chapter saying repository pattern has some downsides. In this chapter, we would dig deeper into that statement and try to understand what those downsides are and what can be done about them. In our attempt to address the downsides of repository, we would present two data access patterns, namely specification pattern and query object pattern. Specification pattern is a pattern adopted into data access layer from a general purpose pattern used for effectively filtering in-memory data. Query object pattern on the other hand, is a very specific pattern developed around querying data from a database. Query object pattern is often defined in a very abstract way and most people tend to come up with their own implementation. One that we would see in this chapter is something I have been using for some time.

Before we begin, let me reiterate – repository pattern is not bad or wrong choice in every situation. If you are building a small and simple application involving a handful of entities then repository pattern can serve you well. But if you are building complex domain logic with intricate database interaction then repository may not do justice to your code. The patterns presented in this chapter can be used in both simple and complex applications, and if you feel that repository is doing the job perfectly then there is no need to move away from it.

Problems with the repository pattern

A lot has been written all over the Internet about what is wrong with repository pattern. A simple Google search would give you lot of interesting articles to read and ponder about. In this section, we would spend some time trying to understand problems introduced by repository pattern.

Generalization

In the previous chapter, we implemented search employee functionality. We added a `FindAll` method on repository for that. From a clean code and maintenance point of view, this method has some issues that need to be addressed. `FindAll` takes name of the employee as input along with some other parameters required for performing the search. When we started putting together a repository, we said that `Repository<T>` is a common repository class that can be used for any entity. But now `FindAll` takes a parameter that is only available on `Employee`, thus locking the implementation of `FindAll` to the `Employee` entity only. In order to keep the repository still reusable by other entities, we would need to part ways from the common `Repository<T>` class and implement a more specific `EmployeeRepository` class with `Employee` specific querying methods. This fixes the immediate problem but introduces another one. The new `EmployeeRepository` breaks the contract offered by `IRepository<T>` as the `FindAll` method cannot be pushed on the `IRepository<T>` interface. We would need to add a new interface `IEmployeeRepository`. Do you notice where this is going? You would end up implementing lot of repository classes with complex inheritance relationships between them. While this may seem to work, I have experienced that there are better ways of solving this problem.

Unclear and confusing contract

What happens if there is a need to query employees by a different criteria for a different business requirement? Say, we now need to fetch a single `Employee` instance by its employee number. Even if we ignore the above issue and be ready to add a repository class per entity, we would need to add a method that is specific to fetching the `Employee` instance matching the employee number. This adds another dimension to the code maintenance problem. Imagine how many such methods we would end up adding for a complex domain every time someone needs to query an entity using a new criteria. With several methods on repository contract that query same entity using different criteria makes the contract less clear and confusing for new developers. Such a pattern also makes it difficult to reuse code even if two methods are only slightly different from each other.

Leaky abstraction

In order to make methods on repositories reusable in different situations, lot of developers tend to add a single method on repository that does not take any input and return an `IQueryable<T>` by calling `ISession.Query<T>` inside it, as shown next:

```
public IQueryable<T> FindAll()
{
    return session.Query<T>();
}
```

`IQueryable<T>` returned by this method can then be used to construct any query that you want outside of repository. This is a classic case of leaky abstraction. Repository is supposed to abstract away any concerns around querying the database, but now what we are doing here is returning an `IQueryable<T>` to the consuming code and asking it to build the queries, thus leaking the abstraction that is supposed to be hidden into repository. `IQueryable<T>` returned by the preceding method holds an instance of `ISession` that would be used to ultimately interact with database. Since repository has no control over how and when this `IQueryable` would invoke database interaction, you might get in trouble. If you are using "session per request" kind of pattern then you are safeguarded against it but if you are not using that pattern for any reason then you need to watch out for errors due to closed or disposed session objects.

God object anti-pattern

A god object is an object that does too many things. Sometimes, there is a single class in an application that does everything. Such an implementation is almost always bad as it majorly breaks the famous **single responsibility principle (SRP)** and reduces testability and maintainability of code. A lot can be written about SRP and god object anti-pattern but since it is not the primary topic of this book, I would leave the topic with underscoring the importance of staying away from god object anti-pattern. Avid readers can Google on the topic if they are interested.

Repositories by nature tend to become single point of database interaction. Any new database interaction goes through repository. Over time, repositories grow organically with large number of methods doing too many things. You may spot the anti-pattern and decide to break the repository into multiple small repositories but the original single repository would be tightly integrated with your code in so many places that splitting it would be a difficult job.

For a contained and trivial domain model, repository pattern can be a good choice. So do not abandon repositories entirely. It is around complex and changing domain that repositories start exhibiting the problems just discussed. You might still argue that repository is an unneeded abstraction and we can very well use NHibernate directly for a trivial domain model. But I would caution against any design that uses NHibernate directly from domain or domain services layer. No matter what design I use for data access, I would always adhere to "explicitly declare capabilities required" principle. The abstraction that offers required capability can be a repository interface or some other abstractions that we would learn in this chapter.

Specification pattern

Specification pattern is a reusable and object-oriented way of applying business rules on domain entities. The primary use of specification pattern is to select subset of entities from a larger collection of entities based on some rules. An important characteristic of specification pattern is combining multiple rules by chaining them together.

Specification pattern was in existence before ORMs and other data access patterns had set their feet in the development community. The original form of specification pattern dealt with in-memory collections of entities. The pattern was then adopted to work with ORMs such as NHibernate as people started seeing the benefits that specification pattern could bring about. We would first discuss specification pattern in its original form. That would give us a good understanding of the pattern. We would then modify the implementation to make it fit with NHibernate.

Specification pattern in its original form

Let's look into an example of specification pattern in its original form. A specification defines a rule that must be satisfied by domain objects. This can be generalized using an interface definition, as follows:

```
public interface ISpecification<T>
{
  bool IsSatisfiedBy(T entity);
}
```

`ISpecification<T>` defines a single method `IsSatisifedBy`. This method takes the entity instance of type `T` as input and returns a Boolean value depending on whether the entity passed satisfies the rule or not. If we were to write a rule for employees living in London then we can implement a specification as follows:

```
public class EmployeesLivingIn : ISpecification<Employee>
{
  public bool IsSatisfiedBy(Employee entity)
  {
    return entity.ResidentialAddress.City == "London";
  }
}
```

The `EmployeesLivingIn` class implements `ISpecification<Employee>` telling us that this is a specification for the `Employee` entity. This specification compares the city from the employee's `ResidentialAddress` property with literal string `"London"` and returns `true` if it matches. You may be wondering why I have named this class as `EmployeesLivingIn`. Well, I had some refactoring in mind and I wanted to make my final code read nicely. Let's see what I mean. We have hardcoded literal string `"London"` in the preceding specification. This effectively stops this class from being reusable. What if we need a specification for all employees living in Paris? Ideal thing to do would be to accept `"London"` as a parameter during instantiation of this class and then use that parameter value in the implementation of the `IsSatisfiedBy` method. Following code listing shows the modified code:

```
public class EmployeesLivingIn : ISpecification<Employee>
{
  private readonly string city;

  public EmployeesLivingIn(string city)
  {
    this.city = city;
  }

  public bool IsSatisfiedBy(Employee entity)
  {
    return entity.ResidentialAddress.City == city;
  }
}
```

This looks good without any hardcoded string literals. Now if I wanted my original specification for employees living in London then following is how I could build it:

```
var specification = new EmployeesLivingIn("London");
```

Did you notice how the preceding code reads in plain English because of the way class is named? Now, let's see how to use this specification class. Usual scenario where specifications are used is when you have got a list of entities that you are working with and you want to run a rule and find out which of the entities in the list satisfy that rule. Following code listing shows a very simple use of the specification we just implemented:

```
List<Employee> employees = //Loaded from somewhere
List<Employee> employeesLivingInLondon = new List<Employee>();
var specification = new EmployeesLivingIn("London");

foreach(var employee in employees)
{
  if(specification.IsSatisfiedBy(employee))
  {
    employeesLivingInLondon.Add(employee);
  }
}
```

We have a list of employees loaded from somewhere and we want to filter this list and get another list comprising of employees living in London.

Till this point, the only benefit we have had from specification pattern is that we have managed to encapsulate the rule into a specification class which can be reused anywhere now. For complex rules, this can be very useful. But for simple rules, specification pattern may look like lot of plumbing code unless we overlook the composability of specifications. Most power of specification pattern comes from ability to chain multiple rules together to form a complex rule. Let's write another specification for employees who have opted for any benefit:

```
public class EmployeesHavingOptedForBenefits :
ISpecification<Employee>
{
  public bool IsSatisfiedBy(Employee entity)
  {
    return entity.Benefits.Count > 0;
  }
}
```

In this rule, there is no need to supply any literal value from outside so the implementation is quite simple. We just check if the Benefits collection on the passed employee instance has count greater than zero. You can use this specification in exactly the same way as earlier specification was used.

Now if there is a need to apply both of these specifications to an employee collection, then very little modification to our code is needed. Let's start with adding an And method to the ISpecification<T> interface, as shown next:

```
public interface ISpecification<T>
{
  bool IsSatisfiedBy(T entity);
  ISpecification<T> And(ISpecification<T> specification);
}
```

The And method accepts an instance of ISpecification<T> and returns another instance of the same type. As you would have guessed, the specification that is returned from the And method would effectively perform a logical AND operation between the specification on which the And method is invoked and specification that is passed into the And method. The actual implementation of the And method comes down to calling the IsSatisfiedBy method on both the specification objects and logically ANDing their results. Since this logic does not change from specification to specification, we can introduce a base class that implements this logic. All specification implementations can then derive from this new base class. Following is the code for the base class:

```
public abstract class Specification<T> : ISpecification<T>
{
  public abstract bool IsSatisfiedBy(T entity);

  public ISpecification<T> And(ISpecification<T> specification)
  {
    return new AndSpecification<T>(this, specification);
  }
}
```

We have marked Specification<T> as abstract as this class does not represent any meaningful business specification and hence we do not want anyone to inadvertently use this class directly. Accordingly, the IsSatisfiedBy method is marked abstract as well. In the implementation of the And method, we are instantiating a new class AndSepcification. This class takes two specification objects as inputs. We pass the current instance and one that is passed to the And method. The definition of AndSpecification is very simple.

```
public class AndSpecification<T> : Specification<T>
{
  private readonly Specification<T> specification1;
  private readonly ISpecification<T> specification2;
```

```
public AndSpecification(Specification<T> specification1,
ISpecification<T> specification2)
{
   this.specification1 = specification1;
   this.specification2 = specification2;
}

public override bool IsSatisfiedBy(T entity)
{
   return specification1.IsSatisfiedBy(entity) &&
   specification2.IsSatisfiedBy(entity);
}
}
```

AndSpecification<T> inherits from abstract class Specification<T> which is obvious. IsSatisfiedBy is simply performing a logical AND operation on the outputs of the ISatisfiedBy method on each of the specification objects passed into AndSpecification<T>.

After we change our previous two business specification implementations to inherit from abstract class Specification<T> instead of interface ISpecification<T>, following is how we can chain two specifications using the And method that we just introduced:

```
List<Employee> employees = null; //= Load from somewhere
List<Employee> employeesLivingInLondon = new List<Employee>();
var specification = new EmployeesLivingIn("London")
                                    .And(new
EmployeesHavingOptedForBenefits());

foreach (var employee in employees)
{
   if (specification.IsSatisfiedBy(employee))
   {
     employeesLivingInLondon.Add(employee);
   }
}
```

There is literally nothing changed in how the specification is used in business logic. The only thing that is changed is construction and chaining together of two specifications as depicted in bold previously.

We can go on and implement other chaining methods but point to take home here is composability that the specification pattern offers. Now let's look into how specification pattern sits beside NHibernate and helps in fixing some of pain points of repository pattern that we discussed at the beginning of this chapter.

Specification pattern for NHibernate

Fundamental difference between original specification pattern and the pattern applied to NHibernate is that we had an in-memory list of objects to work with in the former case. In case of NHibernate we do not have the list of objects in the memory. We have got the list in the database and we want to be able to specify rules that can be used to generate appropriate SQL to fetch the records from database that satisfy the rule. Owing to this difference, we cannot use the original specification pattern as is when we are working with NHibernate. Let me show you what this means when it comes to writing code that makes use of specification pattern.

A query, in its most basic form, to retrieve all employees living in London would look something as follows:

```
var employees = session.Query<Employee>()
            .Where(e => e.ResidentialAddress.City == "London");
```

The lambda expression passed to the `Where` method is our rule. We want all the `Employee` instances from database that satisfy this rule. We want to be able to push this rule behind some kind of abstraction such as `ISpecification<T>` so that this rule can be reused. We would need a method on `ISpecification<T>` that does not take any input (there are no entities in-memory to pass) and returns a lambda expression that can be passed into the `Where` method. Following is how that method could look:

```
public interface ISpecification<T> where T : EntityBase<T>
{
    Expression<Func<T, bool>> IsSatisfied();
}
```

Note the differences from the previous version. We have changed the method name from `IsSatisfiedBy` to `IsSatisfied` as there is no entity being passed into this method that would warrant use of word `By` in the end. This method returns an `Expression<Fund<T, bool>>`. If you have dealt with situations where you pass lambda expressions around then you know what this type means. If you are new to expression trees, let me give you a brief explanation. `Func<T, bool>` is a usual function pointer. This pointer specifically points to a function that takes an instance of type `T` as input and returns a Boolean output. `Expression<Func<T, bool>>` takes this function pointer and converts it into a lambda expression. An implementation of this new interface would make things more clear. Next code listing shows the specification for employees living in London written against the new contract:

```
public class EmployeesLivingIn : ISpecification<Employee>
{
    private readonly string city;
```

```
public EmployeesLivingIn(string city)
{
  this.city = city;
}

public override Expression<Func<Employee, bool>> IsSatisfied()
{
  return e => e.ResidentialAddress.City == city;
}
}
```

There is not much changed here compared to the previous implementation. Definition of IsSatisfied now returns a lambda expression instead of a bool. This lambda is exactly same as the one we used in the ISession example at the beginning of this section. If I had to rewrite that example using the preceding specification then following is how that would look:

```
var specification = new  EmployeeLivingIn("London");
var employees = session.Query<Employee>()
              .Where(specification.IsSatisfied());
```

We now have a specification wrapped in a reusable object that we can send straight to NHibernate's ISession interface. Now let's think about how we can use this from within domain services where we used repositories before. We do not want to reference ISession or any other NHibernate type from domain services as that would break onion architecture. We have two options. We can declare a new capability that can take a specification and execute it against the ISession interface. We can then make domain service classes take a dependency on this new capability. Or we can use the existing IRepository capability and add a method on it which takes the specification and executes it.

We started this chapter with a statement that repositories have a downside, specifically when it comes to querying entities using different criteria. But now we are considering an option to enrich the repositories with specifications. Is that contradictory? Remember that one of the problems with repository was that every time there is a new criterion to query an entity, we needed a new method on repository. Specification pattern fixes that problem. Specification pattern has taken the criterion out of the repository and moved it into its own class so we only ever need a single method on repository that takes in ISpecification<T> and execute it. So using repository is not as bad as it sounds. Following is how the new method on repository interface would look:

```
public interface IRepository<T> where T : EntityBase<T>
{
  void Save(T entity);
```

```
    void Update(int id, Employee employee);
    T GetById(int id);
    IEnumerable<T> Apply(ISpecification<T> specification);
}
```

The `Apply` method in bold is the new method that works with specification now.
Note that we have removed all other methods that ran various different queries and
replaced them with this new method. Methods to save and update the entities are
still there. Even the method `GetById` is there as the mechanism used to get entity
by ID is not same as the one used by specifications. So we retain that method.

One thing I have experimented with in some projects is to split read operations
from write operations. The `IRepository` interface represents something that is
capable of both reading from the database and writing to database. Sometimes,
we only need a capability to read from database, in which case, `IRepository` looks
like an unnecessarily heavy object with capabilities we do not need. In such a
situation, declaring a new capability to execute specification makes more sense.
I would leave the actual code for this as a self-exercise for our readers.

Specification chaining

In the original implementation of specification pattern, chaining was simply a
matter of carrying out logical AND between the outputs of the `IsSatisfiedBy`
method on the specification objects involved in chaining. In case of NHibernate
adopted version of specification pattern, the end result boils down to the same
but actual implementation is slightly more complex than just ANDing the results.
Similar to original specification pattern, we would need an abstract base class
`Specification<T>` and a specialized `AndSpecification<T>` class. I would just skip
these details. Let's go straight into the implementation of the `IsSatisifed` method
on `AndSpecification` where actual logical ANDing happens.

```
public override Expression<Func<T, bool>> IsSatisfied()
{
  var p = Expression.Parameter(typeof(T), "arg1");
  return Expression.Lambda<Func<T, bool>>(Expression.AndAlso(
         Expression.Invoke(specification1.IsSatisfied(), p),
         Expression.Invoke(specification2.IsSatisfied(), p)), p);
}
```

Logical ANDing of two lambda expression is not a straightforward operation. We need to make use of static methods available on helper class `System.Linq.Expressions.Expression`. Let's try to go from inside out. That way it is easier to understand what is happening here. Following is the reproduction of innermost call to the `Expression` class:

```
Expression.Invoke(specification1.IsSatisfied(), parameterName)
```

In the preceding code, we are calling the `Invoke` method on the `Expression` class by passing the output of the `IsSatisfied` method on the first specification. Second parameter passed to this method is a temporary parameter of type `T` that we created to satisfy the method signature of `Invoke`. The `Invoke` method returns an `InvocationExpression` which represents the invocation of the lambda expression that was used to construct it. Note that actual lambda expression is not invoked yet. We do the same with second specification in question. Outputs of both these operations are then passed into another method on the `Expression` class as follows:

```
Expression.AndAlso(
   Expression.Invoke(specification1.IsSatisfied(), parameterName),
   Expression.Invoke(specification2.IsSatisfied(), parameterName)
)
```

`Expression.AndAlso` takes the output from both specification objects in the form of `InvocationExpression` type and builds a special type called `BinaryExpression` which represents a logical AND between the two expressions that were passed to it. Next we convert this `BinaryExpression` into an `Expression<Func<T, bool>>` by passing it to the `Expression.Lambda<Func<T, bool>>` method.

This explanation is not very easy to follow and if you have never used, built, or modified lambda expressions programmatically like this before, then you would find it very hard to follow. In that case, I would recommend not bothering yourself too much with this.

Following code snippet shows how logical ORing of two specifications can be implemented. Note that the code snippet only shows the implementation of the `IsSatisfied` method.

```
public override Expression<Func<T, bool>> IsSatisfied()
{
   var parameterName = Expression.Parameter(typeof(T), "arg1");
   return Expression.Lambda<Func<T, bool>>(Expression.OrElse(
   Expression.Invoke(specification1.IsSatisfied(), parameterName),
   Expression.Invoke(specification2.IsSatisfied(), parameterName)),
   parameterName);
}
```

Rest of the infrastructure around chaining is exactly same as the one presented during discussion of original specification pattern. I have avoided giving full class definitions here to save space but you can download the code for this chapter to look at complete implementation.

That brings us to end of specification pattern. Though specification pattern is a great leap forward from where repository left us, it does have some limitations of its own. Next, we would look into what these limitations are.

Limitations

Specification pattern is great and unlike repository pattern, I am not going to tell you that it has some downsides and you should try to avoid it. You should not. You should absolutely use it wherever it fits. I would only like to highlight two limitations of specification pattern.

Specification pattern only works with lambda expressions. You cannot use LINQ syntax. There may be times when you would prefer LINQ syntax over lambda expressions. One such situation is when you want to go for theta joins which are not possible with lambda expressions. Another situation is when lambda expressions do not generate optimal SQL. I will show you a quick example to understand this better. Suppose we want to write a specification for employees who have opted for season ticket loan benefit. Following code listing shows how that specification could be written:

```
public class EmployeeHavingTakenSeasonTicketLoanSepcification
:Specification<Employee>
{
  public override Expression<Func<Employee, bool>> IsSatisfied()
  {
    return e =>  e.Benefits.Any(b => b is SeasonTicketLoan);
  }
}
```

It is a very simple specification. Note the use of `Any` to iterate over the `Benefits` collection to check if any of the `Benefit` in that collection is of type `SeasonTicketLoan`. Following SQL is generated when the preceding specification is run:

```
SELECT employee0_.Id          AS Id0_,
       employee0_.Firstname   AS Firstname0_,
       employee0_.Lastname    AS Lastname0_,
       employee0_.EmailAddress AS EmailAdd5_0_,
       employee0_.DateOfBirth AS DateOfBi6_0_,
```

```
            employee0_.DateOfJoining AS DateOfJo7_0_,
            employee0_.IsAdmin       AS IsAdmin0_,
            employee0_.Password      AS Password0_
   FROM     Employee employee0_
   WHERE    EXISTS
   (SELECT benefits1_.Id
    FROM    Benefit benefits1_
    LEFT OUTER JOIN Leave benefits1_1_
     ON benefits1_.Id = benefits1_1_.Id
    LEFT OUTER JOIN SkillsEnhancementAllowance benefits1_2_
     ON benefits1_.Id = benefits1_2_.Id
    LEFT OUTER JOIN SeasonTicketLoan benefits1_3_
     ON benefits1_.Id = benefits1_3_.Id
    WHERE   employee0_.Id = benefits1_.Employee_Id
    AND CASE
      WHEN benefits1_1_.Id IS NOT NULL THEN 1
         WHEN benefits1_2_.Id IS NOT NULL THEN 2
         WHEN benefits1_3_.Id IS NOT NULL THEN 3
         WHEN benefits1_.Id IS NOT NULL THEN 0
         END = 3)
```

Isn't that SQL too complex? It is not only complex on your eyes but this is not how I would have written the needed SQL in absence of NHibernate. I would have just inner-joined the `Employee`, `Benefit`, and `SeasonTicketLoan` tables to get the records I need. On large databases, the preceding query may be too slow. There are some other such situations where queries written using lambda expressions tend to generate complex or not so optimal SQL.

If we use LINQ syntax instead of lambda expressions, then we can get NHibernate to generate just the SQL we want as we would see in the next section. Unfortunately, there is no way of fixing this with specification pattern.

Query object pattern

You may not find much mention of query object pattern elsewhere. This pattern is very abstract and most people have their own interpretation and implementation of it. The one I am going to present here is an implementation that I have used successfully. At the heart of query object pattern is the concept that everything of a query (unlike only the filtering criteria in specification pattern) is abstracted away behind an interface so that it can be reused. The simplest form of this interface would look as follows:

```
public interface IQuery<T> where T : EntityBase<T>
{
   IEnumerable<T> Run(IQueryable<T> queryable);
}
```

`IQuery<T>` is a generic interface where `T` stands for the entity type which is being queried. The `Run` method on the interface is what runs the query and returns an `IEnumerable<T>` as a result. Now, unlike specification pattern, the `Run` method takes in an `IQueryable<T>` as input. This is where query object makes the difference. Because you have access to an `IQueryable`, you can write more specific and complete queries than just specifying the filtering criteria. Let's build a query object for employees living in London:

```
public class EmployeesLivingIn : IQuery<Employee>
{
  public IEnumerable<Employee> Run(IQueryable<Employee> employees)
  {
    return (from e in employees
            where e.ResidentialAddress.City == "London"
            select e).ToList();
  }
}
```

We have used LINQ syntax here to implement our query. Since we had an `IQueryable<T>` to work with, we could have written the query using lambda expression as well. That is one big advantage of this implementation of query object. There are times when you would want to use LINQ syntax only, for instance, when using theta joins. There would be other times when a query written using lambda expressions is more ideal. You are free to choose whatever way you want to go. Let's tidy up the previous query object a bit and then we would look into how to run this query from domain services layer. String literal London is hardcoded in the previous query, which we can externalize as we did with previous implementations. Following is how the query class looks after that change:

```
public class EmployeesLivingIn : IQuery<Employee>
{
  private readonly string city;

  public EmployeesLivingIn(string city)
  {
    this.city = city;
  }

  public IEnumerable<Employee> Run(IQueryable<Employee> employees)
  {
    return (from e in employees
    where e.ResidentialAddress.City == city select e)
          .ToList();
  }
}
```

Nothing new in the preceding code. How do we use this query object? Instantiating the EmployeesLivingIn class is not difficult but passing IQueryable<Employee> can be tricky. In absence of a query object, the preceding query could have been written as follows:

```
from e in session.Query<Employee>()
where e.ResidentialAddress.City == city
select e
```

The IQueryable<Employee> parameter that is passed into Run method is in reality what is returned by ISession.Query<Employee>. We need some component that can pass this value into the Run method. A domain service class cannot be that component because it has no knowledge of ISession or any other NHibernate type. For now, let's say that we add a QueryRunner class in the Persistence project. Definition of a QueryRunner class can be as simple as follows:

```
public class QueryRunner
{
  private readonly ISession session;

  public QueryRunner(ISession session)
  {
    this.session = session;
  }

  public IEnumerable<T> Run<T>(IQuery<T> query) where T :
  EntityBase<T>
  {
    return query.Run(session.Query<T>());
  }
}
```

This class takes a dependency on ISession and also has a method Run which takes in an instance of IQuery<T>. It then executes the Run method on the IQuery object by passing ISession.Query<T> as a parameter. That is simple. Now how do we make this class available to domain services? Well, we would use the design principle we learnt in the last chapter. Let's turn the tables around and say that domain service needs to execute a query. It has an instance of IQuery<T> and needs a capability to run the query contained in that query object. We know that this capability is offered by QueryRunner, so let's add the following interface into domain services project to make use of the capability offered by QueryRunner:

```
namespace DomainService.Capabilities
{
  public interface IRunQuery
```

```
  {
    IEnumerable<T> Run<T>(IQuery<T> query) where T :
    EntityBase<T>;
  }
}
```

This interface abstracts the behavior of QueryRunner and offers the capability that domain service needs. All that domain service needs to do at this point is to declare dependency on the IRunQuery interface. Inside domain service, we can choose to create an instance of query object that we need and pass it to the Run method on the IRunQuery interface.

Extending the query object pattern

The query object we saw earlier implemented a simple query involving a single entity. What if you want to write a query that involves more than one entity? If you are using lambda expressions then nothing changes. For instance, the query to fetch employees who have opted for season ticket loan can be written using lambda expression as follows:

```
public IEnumerable<Employee> Run(IQueryable<Employee> employees)
{
   return (from e in employees
           where e.Benefits.Any(b => b is SeasonTicketLoan)
           select e).ToList();
}
```

 Note that preceding code snippet only shows the Run method on query object to save space.

The problem with the preceding query is that it generates the same complex and inefficient SQL that specification pattern generated. Actually, this query is no different than the one we wrote for specification pattern. A better query using LINQ syntax can be written as follows:

```
return (from e in employees
join s in seasonTicketLoans on e equals  s.Employee
select e).ToList();
```

Preceding query when run generates the following SQL which uses an inner join involving only the `Employee`, `Benefit`, and `SeasonTicketLoan` tables:

```
SELECT  employee0_.Id            AS Id0_,
        employee0_.Firstname     AS Firstname0_,
        employee0_.Lastname      AS Lastname0_,
        employee0_.EmailAddress  AS EmailAdd5_0_,
        employee0_.DateOfBirth   AS DateOfBi6_0_,
        employee0_.DateOfJoining AS DateOfJo7_0_,
        employee0_.IsAdmin       AS IsAdmin0_,
        employee0_.Password      AS Password0_
FROM    Employee employee0_,
        SeasonTicketLoan seasontick1_
        INNER JOIN Benefit seasontick1_1_
            ON seasontick1_.Id = seasontick1_1_.Id
WHERE   seasontick1_1_.Employee_Id = employee0_.Id
```

Encapsulating this LINQ query inside a query object would require us to make changes to the query object. This query needs access to two `IQueryable` instances, specifically, `IQueryable<Employee>` and `IQueryable<SeasonTicketLoan>`. Our current query object infrastructure only supports a single `IQueryable` instance. Let's work out how we can extend our query objects to support this scenario. First of all, we would need an implementation of the `Run` method as follows:

```
public IEnumerable<Employee> Run(IQueryable<Employee> employees,
IQueryable<SeasonTicketLoan> seasonTicketLoans)
{
  return (from e in employees
          join s in seasonTicketLoans on e equals  s.Employee
          select e).ToList();
}
```

Looking at the preceding code, we can say that we would need a query interface as follows:

```
public interface IBenefitQuery<T1, in T2>
where T1 : EntityBase<T1>
where T2 : Benefit
{
  IEnumerable<T1> Run(IQueryable<T1> queryable1, IQueryable<T2>
  queryable2);
}
```

This interface is slightly different than the previous more generic interface. Parameter T2 is constrained to the Benefit type in here. This is because of limitation of C# generics. I could have defined an interface as follows but that would just not work:

```
public interface IQuery<T1, in T2>
where T1 : EntityBase<T1>
where T2 : EntityBase<T2>
{
    IEnumerable<T1> Run(IQueryable<T1> queryable1, IQueryable<T2> queryable2);
}
```

Preceding interface needs to have a class that directly inherits from EntityBase<T2> to be passed in second parameter. Since the SeasonTicketLoan class inherits from Benefit, passing a SeasonTicketLoan instance into the above interface does not work. Hence we need to use the implementation where T2 is constrained to Benefit.

Now that we have our new query interface ready, we would need to extend the IRunQuery interface to work with the new query. As shown in the following code snippet, we would add a new Run method on IRunQuery that would take IBenefitQuery<T1, T2> as input:

```
public interface IRunQuery
{
    IEnumerable<T> Run<T>(IQuery<T> query) where T : EntityBase<T>;
    IEnumerable<T1> Run<T1, T2>(IBenefitQuery<T1, T2> query)
    where T1 : EntityBase<T1>
    where T2 : Benefit;
}
```

Following is the implementation of this new method, which is very similar to the previous method:

```
public IEnumerable<T1> Run<T1, T2>(IBenefitQuery<T1, T2> query) where
T1 : EntityBase<T1> where T2 : Benefit
{
    return query.Run(session.Query<T1>(), session.Query<T2>());
}
```

And that is it. We have got a working and extended example of query object. You can scale this to any level you want really. If you need to write a query using LINQ syntax that needs access to three or more IQueryable instances, then you just add appropriate query interfaces, make required changes on the IRunQuery interface, and you are done.

The limitations of the query object pattern

Query object pattern is one of the easiest and cleanest querying pattern that I have come across so far. There is not much in terms of limitations or downsides except for that fact that there is no way of composing multiple query objects to form a composite query. Composition acts on the WHERE clause of a query and the only way to be able to combine two queries is by refactoring out the WHERE clause in its own class. This is what specification pattern offers. Query objects wrap the entire query and hence combining two or more queries together is not possible. But given the other advantages and simplicity offered by query object pattern, I personally tend to push back on the need to be able to chain multiple queries together. If the project you are working on is too complex or big and there is a significant reuse of queries, then it would make sense to use specification pattern and make full use of the composition benefits offered by it.

That brings us to the end of our quick tour of specification and query object patterns. Though I named the chapter as "advanced data access patterns", I honestly do not find these patterns to be advanced. I call them advanced as they involve bit of learning curve for people new to NHibernate. But now it should be clear to you that they are really simple to understand and implement. Rather, I would not want to keep calling them advanced and keep you from utilizing them in your projects under the name of "simplicity". These patterns are indeed simple, go use them.

Summary

Repository pattern has been around for long time but suffers through some issues. General nature of its implementation comes in the way of extending repository pattern to use it with complex domain models involving large number of entities. Repository contract can be limiting and confusing when there is a need to write complex and very specific queries. Trying to fix these issues with repositories may result in leaky abstraction which can bite us later. Moreover, repositories maintained with less care have a tendency to grow into god objects and maintaining them beyond that point becomes a challenge.

Specification pattern and query object pattern solve these issues on the read side of the things. Different applications have different data access requirements. Some applications are write-heavy while others are read-heavy. But there are a minute number of applications that fit into former category. A large number of applications developed these days are read-heavy. I have worked on applications that involved more than 90 percent database operations that queried data and only less than 10 percent operations that actually inserted/updated data into database. Having this knowledge about the application you are developing can be very useful in determining how you are going to design your data access layer.

For a read-heavy application, specification patterns and query object patterns are serious design patterns to consider. Specification pattern provides a highly reusable way of writing filter criteria. Queries written using specification pattern are not only highly reusable but are also highly testable. Lately, testability is becoming a more and more important characteristic to have for any software component. The only limitation of specification pattern is that it can only be used with lambda expressions. Query object pattern on the other hand can be used with both LINQ syntax and lambda expressions. Query object pattern goes beyond just filter criteria and encapsulates the whole query into an object which is reusable and testable like specification pattern. Because query pattern encapsulates the whole query, the extent to which it can be reused may not match that of specification pattern but I personally prefer it for the fact that it does not leak any aspect of query outside its object boundary.

That brings us to the end of our NHibernate journey. Not quite, but yes, in a way. We do not have any further chapter which builds upon concepts we learned in this chapter and introduces concepts that are logically next in order of learning. In the next chapter specifically, we would handle the interesting topic of working with legacy databases. Legacy databases can come in different shapes and forms. Legacy databases is more of a situation where there is lack of harmony between database schema and domain model. So in most aspects, legacy databases would give us trouble when we try to interact with them using NHibernate or tools such as NHibernate. While there are features in NHibernate that help in some of these situations, there also are some tricks and tips that might save you some time and energy. If you are working on such a database, then next chapter is for you.

10
Working with Legacy Database

So far, our approach to working with databases has been to start with a domain model, and then use NHibernate to generate appropriate database schema matching that domain model. Database schema generated this way is fit for purpose, and leads to a frictionless NHibernate experience. Even if you do not use NHibernate to generate database schema, you could build one that is closest to your domain model. This approach works great for green field applications and is most recommended approach. But if you are working with a legacy database, then what was simple so far may start showing its complex side. It is also worth noting that a legacy database, in the context of this chapter, is not just a database that is old, it is more of a situation that leads to the domain model differing from the database schema.

You could also be working with a database which is not legacy at all, but the application you are working on is not the only (or the primary) application using that database. For instance, you could be working on a small portal for a banking application. This portal of yours may be using the main banking application's database, which from the primary banking application's perspective is not legacy. You would not want to influence the design of domain model for your portal, driven by the design of that database. So you may end up designing a domain model which does not fit with the database available. Another legacy database situation could be that you are working in a team with dedicated DBAs, who are also the gatekeepers of database schema designs. They may have got their own rules about how tables are named and structured, and what level of normalization is used. Database schema that you generate from your domain model may not be accepted without changes, and you will almost always end up with a legacy-database kind of situation.

The main reason legacy databases become complex to work with is because business requirements, and hence the domain model, change at a higher rate than databases.

This leads to a situation where the domain model is vastly different from the underlying database. There is no magic switch in NHibernate that would make all the pains of working with legacy databases go away. But there are some features developed specifically to deal with one or more legacy situations. Besides that there are some tricks/trips that you can employ depending on the situation. In this chapter, we will take a look at those features, and learn how to use these features in different situations. Unlike previous chapters, this chapter does not follow an incremental approach where we start with something simple and keep enhancing it. Most features that we would discuss here are quite disconnected from each other. The same goes for examples and code samples. Wherever possible, I will try to use the employee benefits domain that we have been using throughout this book. But there may be situations where I would be forced to use a new example. Let's get started without much ado then.

Composite IDs

Using surrogate keys is becoming the norm these days. Database tables we have seen so far had simple surrogate primary keys. A single column named `Id`, of integer type, acted as primary key. In old databases, it is possible to have tables which use natural keys. Primary keys of such tables, at times, can be composed of more than one column. Such primary keys are called composite keys. Let's assume for a moment that the `Employee` table in our employee benefits application is such a legacy table and it does not have an `Id` column. In order to maintain the uniqueness of records in this table, we designate `Firstname` and `Lastname` columns to form a composite key.

You could argue that we should use `EmailAddress` column as primary key in this instance. Well, you can, but we just wanted to see an example of composite keys on a database that we know of, instead of introducing a whole new database schema.

A barebones `Employee` class for this example could look as follows:

```
public class Employee
{
    public virtual string FirstName { get; set; }
    public virtual string LastName { get; set; }
    public virtual DateTime DateOfJoining { get; set; }
}
```

An additional property `DateOfJoining` is added for the sake of having some state beyond the primary key of the table. Following code listing shows the mapping for this class, where `FirstName` and `LastName` properties form a composite ID for this entity.

```
public class EmployeeMapping : ClassMapping<Employee>
{
  public EmployeeMapping()
  {
    ComposedId(idMapper =>
    {
      idMapper.Property(e => e.FirstName);
      idMapper.Property(e => e.LastName);
    });
    Property(e => e.DateOfJoining);
  }
}
```

Instead of using the `Id` method, we have used the `ComposedId` method to specify which properties of the entity constitute the identifier. The signature for `ComposedId` is straightforward. It takes in a delegate accepting `IIdMapper`. This instance of `IIdMapper` is used to specify which properties on the `Employee` class participate in composite ID. In the previous chapters, when we were using a surrogate key, we also specified an identifier generation strategy to be used. Unfortunately, identifier generation strategies cannot be used with composite IDs. This is obvious; NHibernate does not know how to generate values for `FirstName` and `LastName` properties of an entity instance. Moreover, these properties contain information owned by business, and we do not want NHibernate to generate this information for us.

Saving entities with composite IDs is no different than saving any other entities. But retrieving such entities using `ISession.Get<T>` or `ISession.Load<T>` is different. Both of these methods take identifier value as input. But with composite IDs, there is more than one identifier value. How do we pass multiple identifier values into these methods? Solution is to create a default instance of the entity, set the values of properties forming the composite ID, and pass the instance of `ISession.Get<T>` or `ISession.Load<T>` method. The following unit test depicts this behavior:

```
[Test]
public void EmployeeIsSavedCorrectly()
{
  using (var tx = Session.BeginTransaction())
  {
    Session.Save(new Employee
    {
      FirstName = "firstName",
      LastName = "lastName",
      DateOfJoining = new DateTime(1999, 2, 26)
    });

    tx.Commit();
```

```
    }

    Session.Clear();

    using (var tx = Session.BeginTransaction())
    {
      var id = new Employee
      {
        FirstName = "firstName",
        LastName = "lastName"
      };
      var employee = Session.Get<Employee>(id);
      Assert.That(employee.DateOfJoining.Year, Is.EqualTo(1999));
      tx.Commit();
    }
  }
```

We are first saving an instance of Employee entity. There is nothing new in that part. We then create a new instance of Employee and set Firstname and Lastname properties to the same values that we had saved earlier. This instance is then passed into ISession.Get<Employee> to retrieve a matching instance of Employee. We then assert that the instance returned is the one we expected.

The preceding test would fail with NHibernate insisting that we must implement Equals and GetHashCode methods on Employee class. If you recall *Chapter 5*, *Let's Store Some Data in Database*, in which we discussed how implementing these methods is a good practice. With composite IDs, implementing these methods becomes mandatory. When you have a single integer type column as an identifier, NHibernate can compare the value in that column in order to determine equality of two instances of same type. But in case of composite IDs, NHibernate cannot do the comparison for us, and rather asks us to implement the logic by overriding Equals and GetHashCode methods. Let's add a very simple implementation of these methods to get going. The following code snippet shows the Employee class after these methods have been implemented.

```
    public class Employee
    {
      public virtual string FirstName { get; set; }
      public virtual string LastName { get; set; }
      public virtual DateTime DateOfJoining { get; set; }

      public virtual ICollection<Benefit> Benefits { get; set; }

      public override bool Equals(object obj)
      {
```

```
        var otherEmployee = obj as Employee;

        if (otherEmployee == null) return false;

        return string.Equals(Firstname, otherEmployee.Firstname) &&
               string.Equals(Lastname, otherEmployee.Lastname);
    }

    public override int GetHashCode()
    {
        var hash = 17;
        hash = hash*37 + Firstname.GetHashCode();
        hash = hash*37 + Lastname.GetHashCode();
        return hash;
    }

}
```

In the `Equals` method, we check if the `FirstName` and `LastName` properties on the object being compared have the same values as the current class. `GetHashCode` looks a bit verbose, but is actually very simple. The algorithm starts with a prime number, to which we add the hash code of every property that should be considered in equality. The resulting hash is multiplied by the same prime number every time hash code of the property is added. An algorithm like this has higher chances of generating a hash code that is least likely to collide with another hash code in the same application domain—an important prerequisite for a hash code. If you ran the test now, it would run and pass successfully.

> The rule that the hash code of an object must not change in its lifetime still applies. Prior implementation is not safe from that point of view. An implementation similar to what we used previously can be used here as well. We have used this implementation for the sake of simplicity.

Composite foreign key

A foreign key association based on composite ID is where it gets a bit tricky. There is one thing you need to keep in mind while mapping associations that use composite foreign keys. Composite foreign keys work only if the composite ID is mapped as a component. What it means is that the properties that constitute a composite ID must be moved into their own class, like we do with components.

We would extend our previous example to see how associations based on composite IDs work. Let's begin by moving `Firstname` and `Lastname` properties into their own class. Here is how the new `EmpoyeeId` class should look:

```
public class EmployeeId
{
  public virtual string Firstname { get; set; }
  public virtual string Lastname { get; set; }

  public override bool Equals(object obj)
  {
    var otherEmployee = obj as EmployeeId;

    if (otherEmployee == null) return false;

    return Firstname.Equals(otherEmployee.Firstname) &&
    Lastname.Equals(otherEmployee.Lastname);
  }

  public override int GetHashCode()
  {
    var hash = 17;
    hash = hash * 37 + Firstname.GetHashCode();
    hash = hash * 37 + Lastname.GetHashCode();
    return hash;
  }
}
```

Notice that we have not only moved the `Firstname` and `Lastname` properties, but also moved the implementation of `Equals` and `GetHashCode` methods from `Employee` class into this class. All identifier equality checks would now be based on `EmployeeId` class and hence it is important to have those methods implemented here.

We do not have any association on `Employee` entity that we can use. Let's add the usual benefits collection on `Employee`. The next code listing shows the minimal `Employee` and `Benefit` entity implementation:

```
public class Employee
{
  public virtual EmployeeId Id { get; set; }
  public virtual DateTime DateOfJoining { get; set; }
  public virtual ICollection<Benefit> Benefits { get; set; }

  public virtual void AddBenefit(Benefit benefit)
```

```
  {
    benefit.Employee = this;
    if(Benefits == null) Benefits = new List<Benefit>();
    Benefits.Add(benefit);
  }
}
public class Benefit
{
  public virtual int Id { get; set; }
  public virtual Employee Employee { get; set; }
}
```

This code should be familiar to you. It is exactly the same code we have been using in all the previous chapters. The only difference is that the identifier on Employee entity is not a simple integer type but a complex type EmployeeId. Let's take a look at the mapping of these entities. The following code snippet shows how the Employee entity, with its new composite id, is mapped:

```
public class EmployeeMapping : ClassMapping<Employee>
{
  public EmployeeMapping()
  {
    ComponentAsId(e => e.Id, idMapper =>
    {
      idMapper.Property(e => e.Firstname);
      idMapper.Property(e => e.Lastname);
    });
    Property(e => e.DateOfJoining);

    Set(e => e.Benefits, mapper =>
    {
      mapper.Key(k =>
      {
        k.Columns(colMapper => colMapper.Name("Firstname"),
                  colMapper => colMapper.Name("Lastname"));
      });
      mapper.Cascade(Cascade.All.Include(Cascade.DeleteOrphans));
      mapper.Inverse(true);
      mapper.Lazy(CollectionLazy.Extra);
    },
    relation => relation.OneToMany(mapping =>
            mapping.Class(typeof(Benefit))));
  }
}
```

We are familiar with most parts of the preceding mapping. The parts highlighted are relevant to the discussion of composite ID. Instead of using the `ComposedId` function, we have used the `ComponentAsId` function to map the properties on `EmployeeId` class as the identifiers. The next part is the `Set` mapping for the `Benefits` collection. Even in that, the only different part is the mapping of key columns. Normally we would have only one key column to map here, but due to the composite identifier, we have to map the two key columns—namely `Firstname` and `Lastname`. A slight downside here is that the mapping is not refactor-friendly. Let's take a look at the mapping of the other side of the association. The following code snippet shows the mapping of the `Benefit` entity:

```
public class BenefitMapping : ClassMapping<Benefit>
{
  public BenefitMapping()
  {
    Id(b => b.Id);

    ManyToOne(b => b.Employee, mapper =>
    {
      mapper.Columns(colMapper => colMapper.Name("Firstname"),
              colMapper => colMapper.Name("Lastname"));
    });
  }
}
```

Again, nothing new here except for the part where multiple columns are declared as part of the mapping of the many-to-one association.

At this point, you should be able to use the `Employee` to `Benefit` association as usual. The following unit test can be used to verify that the previous mapping works to our satisfaction:

```
[Test]
public void BenefitsAssociationIsSavedCorrectly()
{
  using (var tx = Session.BeginTransaction())
  {
    var employee = new Employee
    {
      Id = new EmployeeId
      {
        Firstname = "firstName",
        Lastname = "lastName",
      },
      DateOfJoining = new DateTime(1999, 2, 26)
```

```
  };
  employee.AddBenefit(new Benefit());

  Session.Save(employee);

  tx.Commit();
}

Session.Clear();

using (var tx = Session.BeginTransaction())
{
  var id = new EmployeeId
  {
    Firstname = "firstName",
    Lastname = "lastName"
  };

  var employee = Session.Get<Employee>(id);
  Assert.That(employee.DateOfJoining.Year, Is.EqualTo(1999));
  Assert.That(employee.Benefits.Count, Is.EqualTo(1));
  tx.Commit();
}
}
```

Components

We have seen components in *Chapter 3, Let's Tell NHibernate About Our Database*. We had seen that `ResidentialAddress` property on `Employee` class can be mapped as a component or as a one-to-one relation. When it is mapped as a component, all properties on the `Address` class are assumed to be present in the `Employee` table, while you get the freedom to use a separate class to represent an address. With one-to-one mapping, the `Address` class is mapped to its own table.

It is possible that the database that you are working with has modeled such instances in one of the two ways. If you want to model a domain concept using its own class, but state information in that class is not kept in its own table, then you can use components.

Since we covered components in *Chapter 3, Let's Tell NHibernate About Our Database* in detail; we would not discuss them in any more detail here. Just remember that components exist, and use them whenever you can.

Join-mapping to load data from multiple tables

Components address a situation where multiple domain classes need to be mapped to a single database table. If you have the exact opposite situation, where a single domain entity needs to be mapped to multiple database tables, then you can use joins. This feature comes with a caveat though—the tables being joined must have a one-to-one relation between them. You would soon agree that this caveat makes sense.

To understand this better, we would assume that in our employee benefits domain model, we do not have an `Address` entity, and all address fields are present on the `Employee` entity itself. Moreover, we would also assume that in the database, address fields are stored in a different table named `Address`, having a one-to-one relation with `Employee` table. For the sake of simplicity, we would ignore other fields on `Employee` entity. Following is how the `Employee` entity with details relevant to this discussion looks:

```
public class Employee
{
  public virtual int Id { get; set; }
  public virtual string AddressLine1 { get; set; }
  public virtual string AddressLine2 { get; set; }
}
```

We only have an `Id` field and a couple of more fields for address. We now want to map this entity such that fields related to address would come from a different table. If you are using mapping by code, then a function named `Join` is available to specify that some of the properties of this entity need to be fetched by joining another table. The following code listing shows this mapping:

```
public class EmployeeMapping : ClassMapping<Employee>
{
  public EmployeeMapping()
  {
    Id(e => e.Id);
    Join("tableName", joinMapper =>
    {
      joinMapper.Table("Address");
      joinMapper.Key(keyMapper => keyMapper.Column("Id"));
      joinMapper.Property(e => e.AddressLine1);
      joinMapper.Property(e => e.AddressLine2);
    });
  }
}
```

You are familiar with the most part of the preceding mapping code. The only new part is the call to `Join` method. Let's drill a bit into that method. The first parameter to this method is a string which is a default table name. I have just passed `tableName` here, as I intend to override this value later on, as we will see. The second parameter is a delegate that takes `NHibernate.Mapping.ByCode.IJoinMapper<T>` as its parameter. In this case, it happens to be `IJoinMapper<Employee>`. `IJoinMapper`, which has several methods available on it that you can use to control how the `Employee` and `Address` tables are joined. We have used three methods from this interface. First one, `Table`, is used to specify the name of the table to be joined. Second, `Key`, is used to specify the name of the key column on the table. This information is used by NHibernate internally, when querying the table or inserting records into this table. The last method, `Property`, is similar to the `Property` method available during usual class mapping. This method is used to map properties to columns on the table.

We have the following test to verify the behavior of such a mapping:

```
[Test]
public void AddressIsSavedCorrectly()
{
  object id = 0;
  using (var tx = Session.BeginTransaction())
  {
    id = Session.Save(new Employee
    {
      AddressLine1 = "address line 1",
      AddressLine2 = "address line 2"
    });

    tx.Commit();
  }

  Session.Clear();

  using (var tx = Session.BeginTransaction())
  {
    var employee = Session.Get<Employee>(id);
    Assert.That(employee.AddressLine1, Is.EqualTo("address line
    1"));
    tx.Commit();
  }
}
```

We are inserting an instance of `Employee` and then retrieving it by its `Id`. The following SQL statements are generated by NHibernate for the preceding code:

```
INSERT INTO Employee (Id)
VALUES
(@p0);
@p0 = 0

INSERT INTO Address (AddressLine1, AddressLine2, Id)
VALUES (@p0, @p1, @p2);
@p0 = 'address line 1', @p1 = 'address line 2', @p2 = 0

SELECT      employee0_.Id            AS Id0_0_,
            employee0_1_.AddressLine1 AS AddressL2_1_0_,
            employee0_1_.AddressLine2 AS AddressL3_1_0_
FROM        Employee employee0_
INNER JOIN Address employee0_1_
ON          employee0_.Id=employee0_1_.Id
WHERE       employee0_.Id=@p0;@p0 = 0
```

This is, as expected. You can notice that NHibernate used an inner join, as that is the default in this case. But if you want, you can change it to an outer join by specifying that the record in `Address` table is optional.

There is not much to join mapping. You can map properties from an entity to as many as tables as you want. But remember that this is not recommended if you are working on a green field project. This feature has only been made available to work with legacy databases. In an ideal world, it is expected to have a lesser number of tables than the number of entities in the domain model.

Working with database views

Views are one of the ways of putting related data from multiple tables under one container. If you have been using any mainstream RDMBS for some time, then it is possible that you have come across a view more than once. If not, a view is a simple SQL script where you specify which columns from which tables you want to appear in the view, and how those tables are related with each other. Once that script is executed, the database will create an object that holds information about the tables and columns involved in the view definition. After that, you can use the view like any other table with only one restriction; that you are only allowed to read from the view. You cannot update the data in the view (some RDBMS allows the updating of part of the data in a view, with some constraints, but let's ignore that for a moment). Reason for this is that, when you execute a `SELECT` statement against a view, the database server actually runs the original script that we used to build the view, and then applies the `SELECT` statement on the result of running the view scripts.

Internally, how *SELECTs* against views are executed can be different. Every RDMBS would have its own logic to run it, and it is more detailed than what was described in the previous few lines. But at a very high level, that is how views work.

If you are working on an application that reads data from a legacy database but never writes back, then see if you can make use of views to get a matching database schema for your domain model. You do not have to use this strategy for the whole domain model. You can use it for part of the domain model, or even a single entity. Let's take a look at an example. We will use the same example that we used for joins earlier. In our domain, we have an `Employee` class which looks as follows:

```
public class Employee
{
  public virtual int Id { get; set; }
  public virtual string Firstname { get; set; }
  public virtual string Lastname { get; set; }
  public virtual DateTime DateOfJoining { get; set; }
  public virtual string AddressLine1 { get; set; }
  public virtual string AddressLine2 { get; set; }

}
```

Again, the situation in the database is similar to what we had with the join. We have an `Employee` table and an `Address` table. Since we only want to load the `Employee` entity and never insert or update it, we should decide to create a view to match our entity definition. Following is how that view could look:

```
CREATE VIEW [dbo].[EmployeeView]
AS
SELECT dbo.Employee.Id,
dbo.Employee.Firstname,
dbo.Employee.Lastname,
dbo.Employee.DateOfJoining,
dbo.Address.AddressLine1,
dbo.Address.AddressLine2
FROM dbo.Address INNER JOIN
dbo.Employee ON dbo.Address.Employee_Id = dbo.Employee.Id
```

The preceding view is just joining the `Employee` and `Address` tables, to return data combined from both tables. Once this view is in place, we can treat it like a table from an NHibernate point of view and map it just like that. The following code snippet shows the mapping for this view:

```
public class EmployeeMapping : ClassMapping<Employee>
{
  public EmployeeMapping()
  {
    Table("EmployeeView");
    Id(e => e.Id);
    Property(e => e.Firstname);
    Property(e => e.Lastname);
    Property(e => e.DateOfJoining);
    Property(e => e.AddressLine1);
    Property(e => e.AddressLine2);
  }
}
```

And we are done. This is exactly the same as mapping a usual table. The only additional thing is declaring a table name. Because view name is not the same as entity name, we need to tell NHibernate what the name of the table to which we want to map this entity is. As long as we only query the `Employee` entity and do not try to save or update it, this would work just fine. We can even mark the entity as read-only by adding the following lines of code to the mapping file:

```
public class EmployeeMapping : ClassMapping<Employee>
{
  public EmployeeMapping()
  {
    Mutable(false);
    //other mapping configuration
  }
}
```

This code will throw an exception when we try to modify the entity state. Even without the preceding code, we will get an exception when we try to update the entity, but for a read-only entity the exception will be thrown by NHibernate without hitting the database. Remember that we could still save a transient instance of the read-only entity. In that case, NHibernate would hit the database and come back with an error from database server that a record cannot be inserted in a view.

Before we close this topic, note that a view is a simple SELECT statement, at the end of the day. While defining a view you can use almost every SQL construct that is valid in a SELECT statement. So, if you want to sort or filter records within the definition of a view, you can do so.

This example is very close to the example we used during join. This may give you the impression that views can be substituted in situations where join is used. This is true, but the reverse is not true. There would be situations where you could use views but not joins. We used a familiar example to keep the discussion light. Do not mix these two concepts up. They stand on their own.

Using subselect instead of views

Views cater to the situation where we want to read data from multiple legacy tables and map it to a single domain entity. But under the hood, view is just a SELECT query. NHibernate offers another way to deal with the SELECT query directly, so that there is no need to have a view created in the database. This can be useful when you are not able to create views in the database for some reason. Some RDMBS have limited support for views, in which case we could use a subselect feature.

In a subselect feature, we would use the same query that we used to create the view, but this time, we will map to the entity directly. The following mapping definition demonstrates this:

```
public class EmployeeSubselectMapping : ClassMapping<Employee>
{
  public EmployeeSubselectMapping()
  {
    Subselect(@"SELECT dbo.Employee.Id, dbo.Employee.Firstname,
    dbo.Employee.Lastname, dbo.Employee.DateOfJoining,
    dbo.Address.AddressLine1, dbo.Address.AddressLine2
    FROM dbo.Address INNER JOIN
    dbo.Employee ON dbo.Address.Employee_Id = dbo.Employee.Id");
    Mutable(false);
    Synchronize("Employee", "Address");
    Id(e => e.Id, x => x.Column("Id"));
    Property(e => e.Firstname, x => x.Column("Firstname"));
  }
}
```

There are four important elements to understand here:

- **Subselect**: This method is used to declare the SELECT query that should be used to query the entity being mapped. We have got the exact same SQL here, that we used to create the view earlier.

- **Table synchronization**: Next we placed a call to the Synchronize method. This is to let NHibernate know about the tables which are referred to inside the SELECT query.

- **Mapping ID**: We also need to configure which column that was returned from the SELECT statement should be mapped to the identifier property of the entity. This is not required if the name of the identifier column in the SELECT statement matches the name of the identifier property on the entity. In the previous example, a call to the Id method is added to show the readers how to map an identifier.

- **Mapping properties**: An identifier property is mapped in the same way that other properties also need to be mapped, if their names do not match with the names of the columns returned by the SELECT statement. In the example, a call to the Property method shows how to do this.

Once this mapping is in place, we can query the Employee entity as we would query it normally. Internally, NHibernate would generate a subselect statement using the SELECT statement that we supplied in the mapping, and add any additional filtering criteria that we supply in our query. For instance, if we use ISession.Get<T> to query an entity instance with a particular ID, then NHibernate would generate the following SQL:

```
SELECT
   employee0_.id as id0_0_
FROM
   ( SELECT dbo.Employee.Id, dbo.Employee.Firstname,
     dbo.Employee.Lastname, dbo.Employee.DateOfJoining,
     dbo.Address.AddressLine1, dbo.Address.AddressLine2
FROM
   dbo.Address
INNER JOIN
   dbo.Employee
   ON dbo.Address.Employee_Id = dbo.Employee.Id ) employee0_
WHERE
   employee0_.id=@p0;
   @p0 = 1155
```

Notice how NHibernate has placed our SELECT statement as a nested SELECT inside the query that it generated.

Working with stored procedures

Stored procedure is a native way of interacting with most relational databases. Lot of legacy systems I have worked on used stored procedures extensively. On the application side, we would use ADO.NET to prepare SQL commands that execute stored procedures and return result sets. ADO.NET is well capable of executing any valid SQL that you send down the wire. So instead of sending commands to execute stored procedures, you can dynamically build a SQL and execute it. That is what NHibernate does. But most DBAs that I have come across prefer stored procedures. There were two main reasons for this preferred choice. They are as follows:

- Stored procedures let DBAs control access to databases in a better way. Instead of letting application users write over all database tables, and letting rogue users do anything with your data under the context of an application user, you can limit the access to only stored procedures and thus control the damage. If stored procedures are not coded to drop tables or delete records from database tables, then a rogue user with access to the database would not be able to carry out those activities.

- In the old days, lots of applications were vulnerable to SQL injection attacks. Companies with good reputations have lost critical data and dollars because of SQL injection attacks. We do not want to spend time discussing SQL injection attacks here, but this attack boils down to the application dynamically generating SQL commands, which use inputs from the end user in the final SQL without modification, thus opening the SQL to fudging by the end user. Parameterized SQL commands provided some relief against SQL injection attacks. But from a DBA's point of view, it is very difficult to ensure that developers are using parameterized SQL commands. Stored procedures, on the other hand, provide the same level of protection against SQL injection attacks, and are easier to enforce at the same time. Hence, a lot of DBAs insist on using stored procedures.

There may be other reasons why stored procedures are recommended even today, but these are the main ones that keep coming back in discussions that I have with DBAs.

Besides the preceding, a completely different scenario to consider is when you are working on a small application which is part of a bigger legacy application. You would obviously need to work with the legacy database of the old system. It is possible that this legacy database has some stored procedures already defined and you are asked to use those. It is also likely that stored procedures will contain business logic that you do not intend to duplicate in your application. Having business logic in stored procedures is not ideal, but you need to work with what is available. This situation is entirely different from the previous situation I described. In the previous situation, you will be most likely to get 4 stored procedures per database table, one each to insert, update, delete, and read a record from the table.

That is your only interface to database tables. In the second situation, you may be allowed to use a tool such as NHibernate to carry out database interaction, but you need to make use of the existing stored procedures wherever appropriate. NHibernate supports executing any kind of stored procedure and hydrating entities using the result sets that are returned. Let's first look at the most simple way of executing stored procedures.

Executing a stored procedure is same as executing any valid SQL command. Suppose you have got a stored procedure named [dbo].[Get_Employee] that looks like the following code:

```
CREATE PROCEDURE [dbo].[Get_Employee]
   @id int
AS
BEGIN
   SET NOCOUNT ON;

   SELECT Id, Firstname, Lastname
   FROM Employee
   WHERE Id = @id;
END
```

This stored procedure takes identifier value as input and returns the Id, Firstname, and Lastname column values from the Employee table for the record that matches the supplied identifier. In order to execute the preceding stored procedure, you would need to write the following SQL command:

```
EXEC [dbo].[GetEmployee] @id = 55;
```

Since the preceding line is a valid SQL query we could just use the ISession. CreateSQLQuery method to build a SQL command, and have it executed. We could even use parameter binding for the @id parameter, so that there is no scope for SQL injection attacks under any circumstances. Following is how that code looks:

```
var query = Database.Session.CreateSQLQuery(@"EXEC
[dbo].[Get_Employee] @id = :id");
query.SetInt32("id", 55);
var result = query.UniqueResult();
```

Calling the UniqueResult method on IQuery would execute the SQL and return the results in object array. This gets the work done but is not very elegant. You would want to be able to parse the returned data into an instance of Employee entity. You can do that by using something called result transformers. Result transformers are quite a useful set of tools if you are using raw SQL or HQL. We did not cover result transformers in great detail because our recommendation is to stay away from SQL and HQL if you can. In this example, we can use a result transformer named

`AliasToBeanResultTransformer`, which takes the result set coming from the database and transforms it into an entity that you specify. Let's use this transformer to make the preceding code return us a list of `Employee` instances:

```
var query = Database.Session.CreateSQLQuery(@"EXEC [dbo].[Get_
Employee] @id = :id");
query.SetInt32("id", 55);
query.SetResultTransformer(Transformers.AliasToBean<Employee>());
var employees = query.List<Employee>();
```

This is better than the previous version but still lacks the elegance of NHibernate's object oriented way of querying data. What would happen if the returned `Employee` instance has a collection of `Benefit` entities on it? Obviously, it would not be populated automatically for us. We would need to write plumbing code to do that.

There are two other ways in which stored procedures can be used. The first one is **named queries**. Named queries let you declare queries in your mapping files and then refer to them using a specified name. This makes queries reusable. The second way is to use a custom SQL to create, update, and delete. Usually NHibernate dynamically generates a SQL for inserting, updating, and deleting entities. But if, for any reason, you want to be able to use your own SQL, then you are allowed to do that. We will look into both of these in the next chapter. Both of these features support stored procedures in place of custom SQL.

Before we move on to the next topic, a word of caution—NHibernate's support for stored procedure is not extensive. Use it if it's your only option. If you are using it because DBAs in your team have a rule that any access to data must go via stored procedures, then try to bring them to the ORM camp. If not, you might find that using ADO.NET directly may be better, even though you would end up writing a lot more code.

Using custom DTOs

Sometimes, the difference between the domain model and database schema is so great that using NHibernate features to patch the gaps becomes a painful and buggy process. In such a situation, it is best to use custom **Data Transfer Objects (DTOs)** that are designed to match the database schema. Adding custom DTOs creates an additional layer in your architecture, which comes with its own overheads, and, if not designed with care, may lead to code that is inefficient and difficult to maintain. There is no magic formula to work with DTOs so that your persistence layer becomes more bearable. Fortunately, there is some common wisdom shared by veterans in the field, and a few tricks that I have learned from my experience that should help. This section is divided into two parts.

In the first part, we will cover basic areas such as: At what level should we add DTOs in the context of onion architecture and how to accommodate DTOs into an existing domain and domain service layers? Use of DTOs nullifies the effect of lazy loading. In the second section, we will see how that happens and go over an experiment that I have carried out to address this issue.

Right place for DTOs

The most appropriate place for DTOs is close to the database. This makes the persistence layer a natural choice for placing the DTOs into. You can either make DTOs an independent layer, or make them a part of the persistence layer.

 When I say an independent layer, I am really referring to the layer being "code in its own DLL or its own Visual Studio project". I do not mean a layer in the traditional sense, where it can be deployed independently and can be called into remotely.

The only time I would create a separate layer out of DTOs is when DTOs need to be shared beyond one application. Otherwise, I would just stick to adding DTOs under the existing persistence layer. If I had to add DTOs into the persistence layer of the employee benefits application, then the onion architecture, with DTOs included, would look like the following diagram:

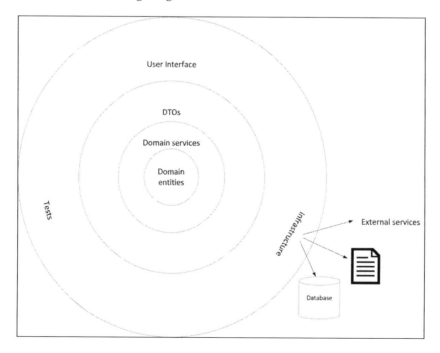

In terms of runtime dependency, the following diagram depicts that DTOs are at the bottom, and all other layers depend on it:

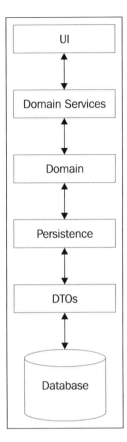

The conversion layer

Though we introduce DTOs in the solution, the domain layer still uses its own domain entities for everything. All the capabilities, such as `IRepository<T>` or `IRunQuery<T>`, that we saw in the previous two chapters continue to return domain types. But we load DTOs from the database and hence a conversion layer is required to convert from DTOs to domain entities. This conversion layer could be very simple, as we will see next, or you can make use of a third-party library called `AutoMapper`.

Let's assume that we have got the following DTOs defined to match to our legacy database:

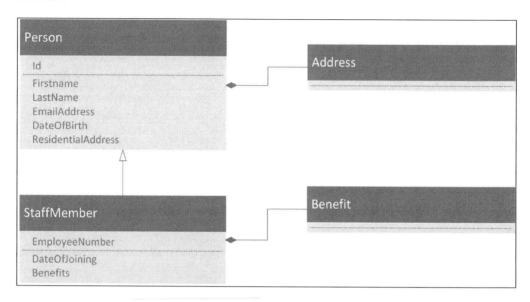

In the preceding figure, we have a Person class which holds the personal details such as name, email address, and so on, of any person in the company. We then have another class named StaffMember, which has other properties about the employment of that person. There are other sub-classes at this level, but we will ignore them as we are not interested in them. StaffMember has a collection of Benefits on it. Let's say that a set of tables that model benefits more or less match our domain model. Now, if we have got a repository interface like the following, defined within the domain layer:

```
public interface IRepository<T>
{
    T GetById(int id);
}
```

In the implementation of the GetById method of this interface, we will load a StaffMember instance from the database, but we cannot return this instance. We will need to convert that into an Employee instance.

The following code listing shows the implementation of `IRepository<Employee>`:

```
public class Repository : IRepository<Employee>
{
  private readonly ISession session;

  public Repository(ISession session)
  {
    this.session = session;
  }

  public Employee GetById(int id)
  {
    var staffMember = session.Get<StaffMember>(id);
    var employee = new Employee
    {
      Firstname = staffMember.Firstname,
      Lastname = staffMember.Lastname,
      //Initialize other properties here
    };
    return employee;
  }
}
```

After loading an instance of `StaffMember`, we will instantiate a new `Employee` instance and initialize properties on this instance from the `StaffMember` instance loaded from the database. Depending on the complexity of the domain model, the conversion code may grow big and complex. A lot of times, it becomes too repetitive as well. You can employ some design or refactoring patterns to avoid duplication, or you can use a library such as `AutoMapper`, which uses several default conventions to automatically map properties from DTOs to domain entities. You can find more details about `AutoMapper` by visiting its website at `http://automapper.org/`.

Downsides of using custom DTOs

DTOs solve an important and difficult problem for you but it all comes at a cost. Custom DTOs are obviously an overhead, because you need to maintain an extra set of classes and also keep converting from domain model to DTO and vice versa. But one of the major downsides of custom DTOs is that, during the mapping from DTO to domain model, you iterate over each and every property of the DTO, thus loading every association into the memory and making all the benefits of lazy loading go away. Let me use an example from our employee benefit domain to show you how bad it could be.

Suppose you are working on a feature which involves updating the residential address of an employee. So, you load the employee details using some filter, and then pass the loaded instance into the layer that converts from DTO into domain entity. But since `Employee` is the root entity and everything else hangs off it, what will happen during conversion is that every association from `Employee` to any other entity will be loaded. We only needed to load the `ResidentialAddress` property on `Employee`, but since the conversion layer has no knowledge of the context we are operating in, it just blindly converts everything. This results in other collections such as `Benefits` and `Communities` being loaded when they are not required. There is no easy solution to this problem. I have experimented with something I called "custom lazy loading retention" while I was working on a project that involved a legacy and completely disparate database schema. This was more of an experiment which seemed to address issues with lazy loading quite nicely. Let's see what exactly "custom lazy loading retention" is.

Custom lazy loading retention

Using NHibernate without lazy loading does seem a bit odd. While there are other benefits of using NHibernate, not being able to use lazy loading is a real handicap. On one of the projects I worked on, I had to face a similar situation and I experimented with this design construct that I called "custom lazy loading retention". This is basically about implementing part of NHibernate's lazy loading in our persistence layer. In *Chapter 6, Let's Retrieve Some Data from the Database*, we briefly discussed how lazy loading works internally. There is a lot that goes on, but if I had to explain the core of the lazy loading algorithm, then here is what it would be. Suppose we have the `Employee` class which has the `Benefits` collection on it as follows:

```
public class Employee
{
  public virtual ICollection<Benefit> Benefits {get; set;}
}
```

When our application starts, NHibernate will generate two classes dynamically. These classes are implemented as subclasses of `Employee` and `Benefit`, and override all properties that are present in base classes. For collection properties, there is a special code added that loads the property from the database. The following code listing tries to depict how that class could look:

```
public class EmployeeProxy : Employee
{
  public override ICollection<Benefit> Benefits
  {
    get
    {
```

```
        //load Benefits collection from database
        //set the loaded Benefits collection on base.Benefits
    }
  }
}
```

These classes are also called proxies. Note that the preceding code does not show actual proxy code; it is just a simplified version that shows how lazy loading works. If you look carefully, lazy loading is not very difficult to implement outside NHibernate. And by implementing custom lazy loading in our persistence layer, we can solve the problem introduced by DTOs. To see how this custom lazy loading works, let's refactor the preceding implementation of the repository to make use of custom lazy loading.

When repository loads StaffMember, instead of passing it through a conversion layer it creates a new instance of an EmployeeProxy class and returns it. EmployeeProxy class is the proxy that is implemented on the lines of proxy that NHibernate builds dynamically. The following code is how the EmployeeProxy class looks:

```
public class EmployeeProxy : Employee
{
  private readonly StaffMember staffMember;

  public EmployeeProxy(StaffMember staffMember)
  {
    this.staffMember = staffMember;
  }

  public override ICollection<Benefit> Benefits
  {
    get { return staffMember.Benefits; }
    set { staffMember.Benefits = value; }
  }

  public override Address ResidentialAddress
  {
    get { return staffMember.ResidentialAddress; }
    set { staffMember.ResidentialAddress = value; }
  }
}
```

The preceding code only shows a representative example of how a custom proxy can be implemented. Full implementation would involve overriding all the properties that are present on the base class `Employee`.

There are only two important things going on here that we need to understand. First of all, this class accepts an instance of `StaffMember` through the constructor. Second, it overrides all the properties from the base class `Employee`, and rewires those to return the appropriate property on the `StaffMember` instance that was passed into it. With this proxy available, the code in repository could be changed to look like the following:

```
public Employee GetById(int id)
{
   var staffmember = session.Get<StaffMember>(id);
   return new EmployeeProxy(staffmember);
}
```

The type returned by a call to `ISession.Get<StaffMember>`, is actually a proxy type dynamically generated by NHibernate. We pass that proxy instance into the constructor of `EmployeeProxy`, which is returned to the code that calls the `GetById` method. If you notice, none of the properties from the underlying `StaffMember` instance are converted to the `Employee` or `EmployeeProxy` class yet. As the calling code goes on interacting with the `EmployeeProxy` instance that was returned to it, the actual properties from the underlying `StaffMemberProxy` would be invoked, which would load the data on demand, using lazy loading offered by NHibernate.

This is a very simple example, used to show what is possible. If you want to use this in production code, then you might need to handle all the cases and do a thorough testing of your implementation.

Summary

Legacy databases do not refer to databases that are old. It is more of a situation that refers to when the mismatch between your domain model and the database schema is too great. This could happen on any database schema for a variety of reasons ranging from using existing database to build a new application, to strict rules around how the database schema must be designed. Working with legacy database situation is interesting and challenging at the same time. NHibernate has some features built-in that help with navigating through legacy databases. This makes working with legacy databases more fun.

In the old days, developers preferred using natural identifiers, and at times that led to composite identifiers. NHibernate supports composite identifiers to the extent of getting most common database operations done. Some features, such as identifier generation, would not work with composite identifiers. A single entity needing to be mapped to multiple tables, or multiple entities needing to be mapped to single tables, can be common occurrences with legacy database situations. NHibernate has you covered in both situations via support for components and joins. If you are working against a very complex database schema but all you need to do is read from the database, then you can use database views that match your domain model. As long as you are not saving or updating entities in your application, this would work just fine. It is possible that you will be asked to use stored procedure for a particular business operation or for usual CRUD operations. NHibernate's support for stored procedure works just fine in both the situations. You should let NHibernate generate the SQL if you can, as that is what it does best. If none of the above helps, then you can use custom DTOs that match your database schema. In your application, you will then need to transform from DTOs to domain entities and vice versa. This will get the job done, but it comes with its own overheads. A flipside of using custom DTOs is that lazy loading might not work properly. The experimental implementation of lazy loading retention, that we saw in this chapter, should help.

With these tips at hand, I am sure you will find working with legacy databases interesting. We are coming close to the end of our NHibernate journey. There is another slightly disconnected chapter next, which talks about important NHibernate features that we did not get a chance to talk about so far. The features covered in the next chapter are not used on a daily basis. They are there for rare occasions.

11
A Whirlwind Tour of Other NHibernate Features

In this last chapter, we are going to look at some of the important NHibernate features that we do not use on a daily basis. You may not find all of these features to be useful everywhere. So you might want to use your best judgement to choose appropriate features based on your requirements.

We would begin the chapter by talking about concurrency control, how it is important, and what NHibernate offers out of the box to deal with concurrency issues.

We would then touch upon event system of NHibernate and find out how to listen to different events and plug in our own logic when a particular event is about to happen or has happened. We would also look at a practical example that utilizes the event system of NHibernate to simplify a cumbersome and repetitive business requirement.

Next feature we would look into is different levels of support for caching available in NHibernate. We would try to go a bit deep into different types of caches to understand why there are multiple cache implementations and learn how to choose the right caching strategy.

NHibernate sessions are usually quite fast, but internally a lot goes on when even a simple entity is persisted to or loaded from the database. These internal operations make use of system resources such as memory and CPU. If you try to load thousands of entities from the database, then the response from the session may get slowed down due to the high usage of system resources. You may even run out of application memory. That is where the lightweight sibling of the session called the stateless session comes in handy. Stateless sessions are light and fast version of the session, which is implemented by turning off some features that we would be happy to use otherwise.

We would close the chapter by talking about user defined types. User defined types is another tool provided by NHibernate for greater control over how data is converted from database types to .NET types, and vice versa.

Concurrency control

At the heart of it, concurrency control is about working out which of the two concurrent database operations win. NHibernate's concurrency control goes beyond that and offers prevention against mistakenly updating stale data. This mostly applies to update operations. Select, insert, and delete operations can happen concurrently without any problem. Before we look into this feature, let's take a moment to understand what kind of problems we can face in absence of concurrency control for update operations. Let's assume that our employee benefits management system has a feature where in HR staff can update personal details of the employees. In a rare situation, it may happen that two HR staff members open the personal details of the same employee and try to update two different fields on their profile. Let's say that the first staff member updates the employee's last name, whereas the second staff member updates the employee's mobile number. Following is the sequence of events as it happens:

1. Staff 1 opens the personal details page of employee A

2. Staff 2 opens the personal details page of employee A

3. Staff 1 updates the last name of employee A

4. Staff 2 updates the mobile number of employee A

In *Chapter 5, Let's Store Some Data into the Database*, we learned about the `dynamic-update` setting which controls whether NHibernate generates the `update` statement for all properties on the entity or only the changed property. If we assume that `dynamic-update` is turned off, then the update made by staff 2 in the previous example would overwrite the last name updated by staff 1. When staff 2 opened the personal details page of employee A, she/he was working on the latest data. But by the time staff 1 updated the last name of employee A, that data had become stale. Effectively, Staff 2 updated stale data. You could argue that if we turn on dynamic updates then this problem would go away. Yes it would, as long as the second update does not involve any property that was modified in the first update. If staff 2 had updated the last name and mobile number of employee A, then changes made to the last name by staff 1 would have been overwritten even if dynamic update was on. Working with stale data is almost always dangerous.

Concurrency control features in NHibernate provide ways to detect if we are working with stale data and abort the update operation if that is the case.

There are two types of concurrency controls that NHibernate offers:

- **Optimistic concurrency control**: If the database record that is being updated is being changed by some other transaction, then do not proceed with the current update

- **Pessimistic concurrency control**: This involves locking the database record that is to be updated so that any other transaction cannot modify the record in the meantime

Let's take a look at how to work with both types of concurrency controls in NHibernate.

Optimistic concurrency control

Optimistic concurrency control boils down to validating that the record that is being updated is not modified by other transaction since it was loaded by the current transaction. NHibernate provides two different ways of performing this validation. First one is using a setting called `optimistic-lock` and second is using a special column called `version` to track the version of each record as it is updated by different transactions.

Using optimistic-lock

Optimistic-lock is a setting that can be applied on an entity during its mapping. As of version 4.0 of NHibernate, this setting can only be applied through XML mapping. Support for mapping by code is still being built and is expected to be out in version 4.1. Optimistic-lock takes two values – `Dirty` and `All`. Let's jump into an example to see what these mean. Following is a partial XML mapping for `Employee` that shows how to specify the `optimistic-lock` setting:

```
<class name="Employee"
optimistic-lock="dirty"
dynamic-update="true">
```

Note that besides setting the `optimistic-lock` attribute, we have also set the `dynamic-update` attribute to `true`. For optimistic locks to work, it is required to turn on the dynamic updates. With the preceding mapping in place, let's say we execute the following code:

```
using (var tx = Database.Session.BeginTransaction())
{
  var emp = Database.Session.Get<Employee>(id);
  emp.Firstname = "Hillary";
  emp.Lastname = "Gamble";
```

```
    tx.Commit();
}
```

In the preceding code, we are updating `Firstname` and `Lastname` on the `Employee` instance. Following SQL is generated by the preceding code:

```
UPDATE
  Employee
    SET
      Firstname = @p0,
      Lastname = @p1
    WHERE
      Id = @p2
      AND Firstname = @p3
      AND Lastname = @p4;
      @p0 = 'Hillary', @p1 = 'Gamble', @p2 = 10649600, @p3 =
      'John', @p4 = 'Smith'
```

The preceding update statement has used an additional WHERE clause to match the `Firstname` and `Lastname` column values of the record being updated to the original values that were loaded from the database. If some other database transaction has changed those values, then our update would not succeed and a `NHibernate.StaleObjectException` would be thrown. Also note that we have turned on the dynamic-updates. It makes sense to use dirty setting of optimistic-lock along with dynamic-updates. You are only validating and updating what has changed and not everything.

If you would rather validate all the columns of the entity instead of just the ones that are changed, then you can use the `optimistic-lock` setting to `all`, as shown next:

```
<class name="Employee" optimistic-lock="all"

dynamic-update="true">
```

Using this setting, the same previous code would generate the following SQL:

```
UPDATE
    Employee
  SET
    Firstname = @p0,
    Lastname = @p1
  WHERE
    Id = @p2
    AND EmployeeNumber is null
    AND Firstname = @p3
    AND Lastname = @p4
    AND EmailAddress is null
```

```
      AND DateOfBirth = @p5
      AND DateOfJoining = @p6
      AND IsAdmin = @p7
      AND Password is null;
  @p0 = 'Hillary', @p1 = 'Gamble', @p2 = 10682368, @p3 = 'John',
  @p4 = 'Smith', @p5 = 05/03/1972 00:00:00, @p6 = 28/05/2001
  00:00:00, @p7 = False
```

Using the version property

Another way to use optimistic concurrency control is to use a `Version` property on the entity which mapped using a special mapping construct. The `Version` property could be something simple similar to an integer, as shown in the following code snippet:

```
public class Employee : EntityBase<Employee>
{
  //other properties on Employee class

  public virtual int Version { get; set; }
}
```

And following is how we map this `Version` property:

```
public class EmployeeMappings : ClassMapping<Employee>
{
  public EmployeeMappings()
  {
    Version(e => e.Version, versionMapper =>
    {
      versionMapper.Generated(VersionGeneration.Never);
    });
  }
}
```

We have got a special method `Version` that takes in two lambda expressions as its input. First one expects a lambda to the property that is to be used for version tracking. Second lambda expression uses an instance of `NHibernate.Mapping. ByCode.IVersionMapper` to further configure the mapping of `Version`. There are several mapping options available here which I would like to leave to you to explore further. The only one that I have used and which is important is the `IVersionMapper.Generated` method. It is used to tell NHibernate whether we are expecting the database to generate the value for the version column or should NHibernate itself generate that value. This is specified by using enumeration `NHibernate.Mapping.ByCode.VersionGeneration`. A value of `Never` means that the database never generates this value and NHibernate should generate it instead.

Another value `Always` is used to tell NHibernate that it can leave the version generation to the database.

With this mapping in place, when we save a transient `Employee` instance, the following SQL is generated:

```
INSERT INTO Employee
            (
                        Version,
                        EmployeeNumber,
                        Firstname,
                        Lastname,
                        EmailAddress,
                        DateOfBirth,
                        DateOfJoining,
                        IsAdmin,
                        Password,
                        Id
            )
            VALUES
            (
                        @p0,
                        @p1,
                        @p2,
                        @p3,
                        @p4,
                        @p5,
                        @p6,
                        @p7,
                        @p8,
                        @p9
            );
@p0 = 1, @p1 = NULL, @p2 = 'John', @p3 = 'Smith', @p4 = NULL,
@p5 = 01/01/0001 00:00:00, @p6 = 01/01/0001 00:00:00,
@p7 = false, @p8 = NULL, @p9 = 11
```

Note that NHibernate has automatically generated and inserted a value for the `Version` column. If the preceding record is updated, then NHibernate would generate the following SQL:

```
UPDATE Employee
SET Version = @p0,
    Firstname = @p1,
    Lastname = @p2
WHERE Id = @p3
```

```
AND Version = @p4;@p0 = 2, @p1 = 'Hillary',
@p2 = 'Gamble', @p3 = 11, @p4 = 1
```

When this record was loaded from the database, `Version` had a value of 1. The `Update` statement generated by NHibernate increments that value to 2. At the same time, a check is being made that the version column in the database still has a value of 1. If some other transaction had updated the same record in the meantime, then the `Version` column would have had a different (incremented) value and the update statement would have failed, resulting in a `NHibernate.StaleObjectException`. When this update succeeds, then any other transaction that holds stale record would fail with `NHibernate.StaleObjectException`.

Using a numeric value for version tracking works nicely. But if there are database inserts happening that are not going to through NHibernate then you need to make sure that version is correctly inserted and updated. A database such as MS SQL offers a special column of type `ROWVERSION` which is automatically generated every time a new record is inserted and updated when the record is updated. You can make use of this feature of MS SQL Server and extend your concurrency control beyond NHibernate. NHibernate supports this native database feature via its user defined version type feature.

 User-defined version type is an extension of user-defined types feature that we would cover in this chapter.

In order to make use of MS SQL's timestamp-based versioning of the database records, we would need to declare a version property of type `byte[]`, shown as follows:

```
public virtual byte[] RowVersion { get; set; }
```

We then map this property as a `version` property, as shown in the following code snippet:

```
Version(e => e.RowVersion, versionMapper =>
{
  versionMapper.Generated(VersionGeneration.Always);
  versionMapper.UnsavedValue(null);
  versionMapper.Type<BinaryTimestamp>();
  versionMapper.Column(v =>
  {
    v.SqlType("timestamp");
    v.NotNullable(false);
    });
  });
```

We are telling NHibernate that versions are always generated by database. We are also telling NHibernate that the database type of the version column on database side is timestamp. The most important bit is the declaration of `BinaryTimestamp` as the type to be used for conversion from database's timestamp value to `byte[]` used in code. You can find the code for the `BinaryTimestamp` class in the accompanying code for this chapter.

Pessimistic concurrency control

Pessimistic locking works on the principle of "whoever gets there first, gets a chance to update the record". This is achieved by using row-level locks offered by most leading RDMBS. A row-level lock, as the name suggests, locks down the access of a row to a transaction on "first come first serve" basis. This lock comes in multiple different flavours, each defining a level of access of the locked row. For example, a write lock can be acquired when you intend to insert/update a row so that no other transaction can access this row. Locks work hand in hand with isolation levels which define access at transaction level. Every RDMBS has its own implementation of locks but NHibernate makes it easy to work with any of these by defining a common semantics defined via an enum `LockMode`.

This enum defines the following lock modes:

- `Write`: A transaction intending to insert a new row or update an existing row would automatically acquire this lock.

- `Upgrade`: This lock mode can be acquired explicitly by the user when a record is selected with the intention of updating it. We are going to use this in the next example where we would discuss this in more detail.

- `UpgradeNoWait`: Similar to upgrade lock with one difference – if the row is already locked by other user, then the database does not wait and returns immediately with a message that the lock could not be acquired.

- `Read`: A read lock is acquired automatically when NHibernate reads any data.

- `None`: Absence of a lock.

Pessimistic concurrency control is not set globally as part of mapping; it is instead set either on session or can be declared while loading an entity. Following code snippet would set the lock while the `Employee` entity is being loaded:

```
using (var tx = Database.Session.BeginTransaction())
{
    var emp = Database.Session.Get<Employee>(id, LockMode.Upgrade);
```

```
      emp.Firstname = "Hillary";
      emp.Lastname = "Gamble";
      tx.Commit();
}
```

You can notice in the following code that the SELECT statement generated by the preceding code has a row-level upgrade lock:

```
SELECT  employee0_.Id            AS  Id0_0_,
        employee0_.Firstname     AS  Firstname0_0_,
        employee0_.Lastname      AS  Lastname0_0_,
        employee0_.EmailAddress  AS  EmailAdd5_0_0_,
        employee0_.DateOfBirth   AS  DateOfBi6_0_0_,
        employee0_.DateOfJoining AS  DateOfJo7_0_0_,
        employee0_.IsAdmin       AS  IsAdmin0_0_,
        employee0_.Password      AS  Password0_0_
FROM    Employee employee0_ WITH (updlock, rowlock)
WHERE   employee0_.Id=@p0;@p0 = 3465
```

The lock ensures that the row remains locked as long as the transaction in which the lock was issued is either committed or rolled back. This lock prevents other transactions from updating this record while the current transaction is still working on it. When the current transaction is done with the record, which is often indicated via commit of the transaction, then the lock is released. If the current transaction does not acquire a lock immediately, then it will wait.

Eventually, it will time out and throw an exception, in which case the session object would become unusable and we would have to start all over again.

If you want to acquire the row level lock in a separate statement, then the following is how you can do it:

```
using (var tx = Database.Session.BeginTransaction())
{
  var emp = Database.Session.Get<Employee>(id);
  Database.Session.Lock(emp, LockMode.Upgrade);
  emp.Firstname = "Hillary";
  emp.Lastname = "Gamble";
  tx.Commit();
}
```

In a nutshell, the preceding does the same thing, but instead of issuing a single SELECT statement, it issues two SELECT statements. One to load the entity and the other to lock the row explicitly.

You may have guessed that an explicit row level lock would keep other threads waiting, which is not ideal. Under heavy load, you may end up getting too many database transactions waiting to acquire a lock, eventually timing out, and giving a bad user experience.

Event system

We have learned that entity state in the memory is synchronized to the database either when session is flushed or transaction is committed. All the calls we made to `ISession.Save` or `ISession.Update` till that point do not send any changes to the database. Instead, what they do is create an event and push it into the events array maintained by the session. When the session is flushed (explicitly or via committing the transaction), then NHibernate goes through each of the events and executes them one by one. As usual, I am making it easy by giving you a 10,000 feet view of how events work. Exact working of the events is more complex in reality. Intent of this section is not to understand how the events work internally. This section is more about how to listen to NHibernate's internal events and how to be notified so that we can execute our own code in response to a particular action that NHibernate carries out internally. Event listener is the mechanism that we would use for this purpose.

Event listeners

Event listener is the mechanism that lets us hook into the eventing system of NHibernate and execute our custom logic at various times during the execution of events. The way event listeners work is very simple. You build an event listener by implementing one of the several event listener interfaces and then hooking your implementation into the configuration object via appropriate event handler. There are several event listeners available to implement. Following table lists the event listeners that can be useful in most situations:

Event listener name	When is it triggered?
`IPreLoadEventListener`	Before injecting property values into a newly loaded entity instance
`IPreUpdateEventListener`	Before updating an entity in the database
`IPreDeleteEventListener`	Before deleting an entity from the database
`IPreInsertEventListener`	Before inserting an entity in the database
`IPostLoadEventListener`	After an entity instance is fully loaded
`IPostUpdateEventListener`	After an entity is updated in the database
`IPostDeleteEventListener`	After an entity is deleted from the database
`IPostInsertEventListener`	After an entity is inserted in the database

All the preceding event listeners are available in the `NHibernate.Event` namespace. Next we would implement one of the event listeners to see how to work with them.

Adding the audit trail for entities

We would implement an audit trail feature by making use of event listeners. Audit trail is information associated with every instance of entity that tells us more about how the entity instance has changed over time. Audit trail is very important in some business domains such as finances, trading, insurance, and so on. I would say, no matter what business domain you are working in, audit trail is an important piece of information that you should always try to maintain. It is useful in debugging data issues when the wrong data gets updated or even worse, when critical data gets deleted. Audit trail comes in different varieties, from most basic to most extensive. In the most basic form, it would consist of only the following information:

- When was the instance created?
- Who created the instance?
- When was the instance last updated?
- Who updated the instance last?

On the other hand, an extensive audit trail would try to capture original and modified values of every property on the entity, as and when the entity instances are modified. It is possible to implement the extensive audit trail by using event listeners but we would only look at a simple implementation to see how the event listeners work. You are encouraged to explore this topic more if you want to build a complete audit trail. The audit trail that we would implement would only record when the entity instance was created.

Let's begin by adding a `DateTime` type of field on `EntityBase<T>` to capture this information. We want audit trail for all our entities and hence have chosen to add this field on `EntityBase<T>` so that it is accessible to all of the entities. Following code listing shows the definition of this new property:

```
public virtual DateTime CreatedAt { get; set; }
```

We now need to map this property. Since we have not mapped `EntityBase<T>` explicitly, we need to map this property in every entity individually. Let's map it inside the `EmployeeMappings` class, as shown next:

```
Property(e => e.CreatedAt);
```

You may find that it is repetitive to map this property in mapping of every entity. This would become even more frustrating when you would have a full list of audit trail properties that need to be mapped in every entity. To avoid this, you can map the audit trail properties as components. Basically, you define a separate `AuditTrail` class that holds all the audit trail properties. Add a property of type `AuditTrail` in `EntityBase<T>` and then map that property as a component. You still need to map this component in every entity mapping but you are at least not repeating the mapping of a bunch of properties everywhere.

Let's now turn our attention to implementing the event listener. We want to set the `CreatedAt` property before the entity is saved in the database. So a preinsert event listener is the best choice. This event listener can be implemented by extending `IPreInsertEventListener`, as shown next:

```
public class AuditableEventListener : IPreInsertEventListener
{
  public bool OnPreInsert(PreInsertEvent @event)
  {
    var auditInfo = @event.Entity as IAmAudited;

    if (auditInfo == null) return false;

    var createdAtPropertyIndex =
    Array.IndexOf(@event.Persister.PropertyNames, "CreatedAt");

    if (createdAtPropertyIndex == -1) return false;

    var createdAt = DateTime.Now;
    @event.State[createdAtPropertyIndex] = createdAt;
    auditInfo.CreatedAt = createdAt;

    return false;

  }
}
```

There is a lot going on in the preceding code, with a lot of things that look new and strange. Let's dissect it so that it no more remains a magic. First of all, as part of implementing `IPreInsertEventListener`, we have implemented a method named `OnPreInsert`.

This method takes `PreInsertEvent` as an input and returns a Boolean as output. The `PreInsertEvent` object holds information about the entity being inserted. The Boolean value that this function returns is used to determine whether to go ahead with insert operation or not. This is called veto internally. So if you return a true from this function, you are effectively telling NHibernate to veto the operation (reject insert operation). Since we do not want to cancel the insert operation, we return false from all the return points in this function.

In the first line of the function, the `Entity` property on event object is typecast to an interface named `IAmAudited`. The `Entity` property holds the actual instance of the entity that was passed to the `ISession.Save` method. Since our event listener is a generic implementation for any entity, we do not know the type of the entity that we are dealing with here. We need to know the type in order to access the `CreatedAt` property on the entity. Hence, we have performed a little trick. We moved the `CreatedAt` property declared in `EntityBase<T>` into an interface named `IAmAudited`. Following is how the interface looks:

```
public interface IAmAudited
{
   DateTime CreatedAt { get; set; }
}
```

We then implemented this interface on `EntityBase<T>`. That is why we can now typecast any entity that we receive inside the event listener to `IAmAudited`. Next line is just a safety check to make sure that we have got an instance of `IAmAudited`. If not, we return a false without doing anything. The line after that uses the `Array.IndexOf` method to find out index of the `CreatedAt` property in the `PropertyNames` array. This is where things get interesting.

There are three properties on `PreInsertEvent` that are useful to us. First one is `Entity` that we just looked at. Second one is `Persister`, which holds information about mapping of the entity. `Persister` holds the list of mapped properties on the entity inside an array named `ProprtyNames`. Third is the `State` array, which holds the values of each property in the `PropertyNames` array. Our intention is to set correct value for the `CreatedAt` property inside the `State` array. That is why we first get the index of that property, and then using that index we set the value in the `State` array. We then also set the `CreatedAt` property on the `IAmAudited` instance that we typecast. We have to do this because the `State` array is populated using information from `Entity` before control was passed to the event listener. If we alter the `State` array at this stage then the entity instance tracked by the session and the `State` array goes out of sync, leading to subtle issues that could be very difficult to track down.

We now need to let NHibernate know of our little event listener. We do that by hooking our event listener into NHibernate configuration using the appropriate event handler. Following code snippet shows how to do that:

```
config.EventListeners.PreInsertEventListeners = new
IPreInsertEventListener[] {new AuditableEventListener()};
```

The `Configuration` class has an `EventListeners` property, which has further properties to hold event listeners for all types of supported events. We are creating an array of `IPreInsertEventListener` containing only the instance of `AuditableEventListener` and assigning it to the `PreInsertEventListeners` property on `EventListeners`.

For the sake of simplicity, we set `PreInsertEvenListeners` to a brand new array of the `IPreInsertEventLister` instances. It is possible that `PreInsertEventListeners` already had other event listeners assigned to it, either by NHibernate itself or our own code. If that is the case then it is best to add the new even listeners to the existing array instead of overwriting it.

That is all. The event listener is wired up and it is ready to roll. We can use the following test to verify that the `CreatedAt` property is actually set when an `Employee` instance is saved:

```
[Test]
public void CreatedAtIsSetWhenSavingNewInstance()
{
  object id = 0;
  using (var tx = Session.BeginTransaction())
  {
    id = Session.Save(new Employee
    {
      Firstname = "John",
      Lastname = "Smith"
    });

    tx.Commit();
  }

  Session.Clear();

  using (var tx = Session.BeginTransaction())
  {
```

```
var employee = Session.Get<Employee>(id);
Assert.That(employee.CreatedAt,
            Is.Not.EqualTo(DateTime.MinValue));
tx.Commit();
}


}
```

The preceding test should not need much explanation.

Other event listeners work almost the same way as pre-insert event listener works. So you can take this understanding and apply it to most of the other event listeners with little modification. The way we used pre-insert event listener to set audit trail before any entity was inserted into the database, in the same way we can use pre-update event listener to set audit trail around the modification of entity instance. For a complete audit trail implementation, you may even store the original entity instance into some shadow database table or a completely different datastore. There are numerous options as long as you are willing to experiment.

We used the auditing of entities as an example to learn how to use event listeners. Our implementation was quite simple but a complete implementation would be slightly complex to implement. If you need such sophisticated implementation of audit trail but do not want to invest into building every moving part yourself, then take a look at a third-party library based on NHibernate, called **Envers**. Envers makes it very easy to audit changes to the entity instances without you having to write much code. You can find more about Envers at `http://envers.bitbucket.org/`.

Caching

We have briefly touched the topic of caching in multiple places earlier. Caching support in NHibernate is more extensive than most of the frameworks that I have come across so far. Following are the three different types of caches available in NHibernate:

- **Session level cache**: `ISession` caches every entity that it loads from the database. This is default behavior and cannot be changed or turned off.

- **Query cache**: At individual query level, you can specify if the output of that query needs to be cached. This cache is shared across sessions.

- **Second level cache**: This is similar to session level cache but it is shared across all the sessions in a session factory. Due to its shared nature, this cache is most complex of all and comes with settings that you can use to fine tune use of second level cache in your application.

Let's dive into each type of cache in more detail to understand how to enable, disable, and make use of each cache.

Session level cache

We have come across references to session level cache on more than one occasion in the previous chapters. Session level cache, as the name suggests, is scoped to a session. You may hear some people refer to it as first level cache. Every new ISession instance that we create would have a cache associated with it. There is no way to enable or disable this cache. This is always enabled and it works transparently to our data access code. This has a huge benefit as we do not need to do any setup or write our code in a particular way to make use of this cache. Every time NHibernate loads any entity instance, it is kept in the session level cache. Next time you try to retrieve the same instance using its identifier, NHibernate would return it from the cache instead of going to the database.

Sometimes it is confusing to understand how the session level caching works in different situations. For example, in the following code listing, the first call to ISession.Get<Employee> would be returned from the cache but the second query would hit the database:

```
[Test]
public void SessionLevelCacheIsUsedOnlyForGet()
{
  object id = 0;
  using (var tx1 = Session.BeginTransaction())
  {
    id = Session.Save(new Employee
    {
      Firstname = "John",
      Lastname = "Smith"
    });

    tx1.Commit();
  }

  using (var tx2 = Session.BeginTransaction())
  {
```

```
    var employee = Session.Get<Employee>(id);
    Assert.That(employee.CreatedAt,
                Is.Not.EqualTo(DateTime.MinValue));
    tx2.Commit();
}

using (var tx2 = Session.BeginTransaction())
{
    var employee = Session.Query<Employee>().
    First(e => e.Firstname == "John");
    Assert.That(employee.CreatedAt,
                Is.Not.EqualTo(DateTime.MinValue));
    tx2.Commit();
}
}
```

A rule of thumb to remember with this caching behavior is that only ISession. Get<T> and ISession.Load<T> would go via this cache; custom queries written using any of HQL, Criteria, QueryOver, or LINQ would always hit the database. This is because the session level cache holds the entity instances against their identifiers, so if you are retrieving entities by their identifiers, only then it is possible to use the session level cache. Since the session level cache is a map of identifiers, it is also called identity map. There are times when NHibernate would internally make use of this identity map to lazily load some entities.

Second level cache

Fundamental difference between the session level cache and second level cache is the scope in which they operate. While the session level cache is only limited to a single session object, the second level cache spans across all the sessions created from a session factory. Scope of the second level cache extends until the session factory. This extended scope means that NHibernate has to carefully handle multithreaded and concurrent cache accesses.

To that end, NHibernate's second level cache provides a setting called cache usage strategy, which dictates how a cache can be accessed by different sessions. We would look into different cache usage strategies but before that, let's look into enabling second level cache. To enable second level cache, we need to configure a caching provider that we want to use. Caching provider is a class that implements the NHibernate.Cache.ICacheProvider interface. Out-of-the-box NHibernate provides an in-memory, hashtable-based implementation of this interface named NHibernate.Cache.HashtableCacheProvider.

This is not meant to be used in production but feel free to use it in development and test environments. Other than this, there are community implementations of `ICacheProvider` based on ASP.NET cache, Redis, memcached, AppFabric caching, NCache, SysCache, and the like. If you search using the term `NHibernate.Caches` on NuGet package repository then you would find all the available implementations of the second level cache provider. Readers are encouraged to do their own research before they decide on a particular cache provider. Following code shows how to configure a caching provider using programmatic configuration:

```
public class SqlServerDatabaseConfiguration : Configuration
{
  public SqlServerDatabaseConfiguration()
  {
    this.Cache(cache =>
    {
      cache.Provider<HashtableCacheProvider>();
    });
  }
}
```

Note that there usually is lot of other configuration in the preceding code. To save space, we are only showing the configuration of the caching provider. Once the caching provider is configured, we need to specify the cache usage strategy. This needs to be specified at individual class or collection level. Following are the three strategies available:

- **Read only**: Use this strategy if your application only needs to read the data from cache but never write it back. This is simplest to use, most performant, and is cluster-safe.

- **Read write**: If your application needs to update the data, then the read-write strategy is more appropriate. Second level cache provides a reliable world-view of data to your application. It is important that updates to the cache are aligned with updates to the database. Updates to the database happen when transaction is committed. Isolation level of a transaction has an impact on the behavior of commit and the end result overall. This also has an indirect effect on the caching provider's ability to work with particular isolation levels. This is a complex topic to understand but the point to note here is that the read-write strategy does not work if serializable transaction isolation level is used.

- **Non-strict read write**: If your application updates data very rarely and most of the time just reads the data, then it is highly unlikely that two transactions would update the same data concurrently. In such s situation, the caching provider does not need to lock items during updates, which provides some freedom to the caching provider while working with transaction isolation level. A non-strict read write strategy does not put any restriction on what isolation level you can use for your transactions.

Following code snippet shows how to specify the cache usage strategy during mapping of an entity:

```
public class AddressMappings : ClassMapping<Address>
{
  public AddressMappings()
  {
    //Mapping of other properties
    Cache(c =>
    {
      c.Usage(CacheUsage.Transactional);
      c.Region("AddressEntries");
    });
  }
}
```

We have used enumeration `NHibernate.Mapping.ByCode.CacheUsage` to specify what cache usage strategy we want to use. We have also specified a name for the region in the cache where instances of this entity should be cached. This is handy if you want a better organization of entities in the cache.

Usage strategy can also be specified on collections of an entity. In the next code sample, we specify cache usage strategy on the `Benefits` collection of the `Employee` entity:

```
Set(e => e.Benefits, mapper =>
{
  mapper.Key(k => k.Column("Employee_Id"));
  mapper.Cascade(Cascade.All.Include(Cascade.DeleteOrphans));
  mapper.Inverse(true);
  mapper.Lazy(CollectionLazy.Extra);
  mapper.Cache(c =>
  {
    c.Usage(CacheUsage.ReadWrite);
    c.Region("Employee_Benefits");
```

```
        });
    },
    relation => relation.OneToMany(mapping =>
            mapping.Class(typeof(Benefit))));
```

 In theory, the second level cache is scoped to a session factory but it really depends on the implementation of the cache provider. A distributed cache provider such as NCache can be configured to provide a second level cache that can be shared between multiple session factories belonging to multiple applications.

Query cache

Query level cache, as the name suggests, can be enabled on individual queries. Below you will see a query that we have used in one of the chapters in this book. We have turned on the query cache for this query by calling `Cacheable` at the end.

```
var employees = Database.Session.Query<Employee>()
                .Where(e => e.Firstname == "John")
                .Cacheable();
```

Before we can cache the results of any query into query cache, it must be turned on in the NHibernate configuration. Following code snippet shows how to turn on the query cache using loquacious configuration:

```
var config = new Configuration();
config.Cache(cache =>
{
    cache.UseQueryCache = true;
});
```

After caching the query, you might expect that the next time this same query is executed then NHibernate would not need to go to the database and the results would be returned from the query cache. That is partially true and that is where the query cache gets interesting. Query cache in reality only caches the identifiers of the entities that form the result of the query. For the actual entity state, the query cache relies on the second level cache. So this is how it works internally – we execute a query that is marked `Cacheable`. For the first time, this query is executed against the database. Identifiers of all the entities returned from the database are stored in cache. Next time the same query is executed, NHibernate loads the identifiers from the query cache and retrieves the entity instances corresponding to those identifiers from the second level cache. If the entity instances are not present in the second level cache for any reason, then NHibernate goes to the database to load those entities.

There are two important things coming out from the previous discussion. One, in order for the query cache to work, the second level cache must be turned on. Second, if you use the query cache without the second level cache, then you may end up making the queries slower than they would normally run. This happens because of the way cached queries are executed. If you have got a cached query that returns 50 records which we expect to be present in second level cache. If they are not, then NHibernate would make 50 database trips to bring each record individually, after it has loaded the identifiers for each of those 50 records from the query cache. In such instances, if we disable the query cache then NHibernate would only make one database trip to fetch all the 50 records every time we run that query. This approach may be faster than hitting the database 50 times.

Now that you know the different caching mechanisms offered by NHibernate, you may be tempted to turn on caching at every level to get a performance boost. But my advice to you would be to use caching as a last resort and use it selectively. If you encounter a slow running query then try to fix that query first. See if the query is written in a wrong way and check if we can make use of other features such as join fetching, batch fetching, and so on, to get better SQL commands or better utilization of the database roundtrips. It is very easy to hide the underlying issue in queries by using caching to make everything look faster. Also, make sure that you do not cache entities that should not be cached. If there are other applications that are connecting to the same database as yours, then it is possible that the entities cached by your application are updated by other applications, making the cache entries in your application stale. Changes made by one application would not be visible to the other application. Situations like these and many more determine how to best use caching or whether to use it at all. Make sure you have ticked all the boxes before you turn on caching.

Stateless sessions

NHibernate sessions are stateful by default. In other words, they maintain the state of the entities that pass through them. During the course of execution of any functionality, following is what usually happens if you are using a NHibernate session:

1. You open a new session.
2. You begin a transaction on this session.
3. You load some entities from the database using the session.
4. The entities loaded are tracked in the identity map (session level cache), in case they are queried again.
5. The entities are also kept in the second level cache if it is configured.

6. You then update few properties on the entities.

7. You then commit your NHibernate transaction to signal to NHibernate to persist your in-memory changes to the database (remember transitive persistence?).

8. NHibernate uses dirty checking to find out which of the entities in the session have changed and only persists the changes to the database.

9. As part of above, NHibernate also cascades the database operations down to the collections/associations as per mapping configuration.

10. NHibernate updates the copies kept in the second level cache.

Rather NHibernate is doing a lot of maintaining and tracking of entity instances internally. This heavy-lifting done by NHibernate means that we do not have to write extensive code to track the state of each entity and maintain entities already loaded from the database in the same transaction. But this also means that querying or persisting data gets slowed down. This is obvious. More work NHibernate does while loading or persisting data, the longer it is going to take to do the actual work. For usual business operations, this overhead is acceptable. So that, the advantages of this internal working of NHibernate greatly outweighs the overhead introduced.

But if you are required to load a large number of entities from the database, perform some operations on them, and save them back to the database, then above does not scale well. We have discussed the batching techniques in *Chapter 7, Optimizing Data Access Layer*, which we might want to use here. But even those solutions do not scale well when it comes to big numbers. OutOfMemoryExceptions would be too common if we try to use ISession to deal with thousands of entities at the same time. NHibernate team recognized this problem and they have provided an alternate, stateless implementation of ISession, aptly named IStatelessSession. Stateless session works exactly the same way as a normal session except for the lack of some features described as follows:

- No identity map leading to the data aliasing effect. If the same entity is retrieved twice, two copies of it are created in memory. There are cases when stateless session maintains a temporary identity map to de-duplicate entities, for example, when eager fetching is used. It would be useful to assume that we may end up with duplicate entity instances in memory if we are using stateless session.

- No write-behind or dirty checking. You need to explicitly tell NHibernate which entities to save/update/delete.

- No interaction with the second level cache. Also means that you cannot use query caching.

- Operations are not cascaded down to associations or collections. Any changes made to the parent entity that need to be cascaded down to associations or collections have to be done manually and explicitly.

- No automatic deletion of the orphan child records.

- Event system of NHibernate is completely bypassed. So if you are hooking into events to add audit information then make sure you have alternatives in place to work with the stateless sessions.

This absence of features is what gives the stateless session its performance and memory boost.

In order to open a stateless session, you can call the `ISession.OpenStatelessSession` method. Rest of the semantics around using a stateless session are the same as normal session except for the following two:

- There is no `Save` method. In order to persist a transient entity instance, we can use the `Insert` method.

- There is no notion of a transitive persistence as change tracking does not work. So for any updates to the persistent entities, the `Update` method has to be called explicitly.

In a nutshell, keep in mind that you need to explicitly specify how you want to add/update/delete the entities. NHibernate is not doing anything for you. So use it but with extreme care and make sure you test your code thoroughly.

> Most likely scenarios where you would want to use the stateless session is bulk import kind of scenario where you are being asked to load thousands of records in to the database at one go. Ideally, you should be using bulk import features natively supported by your database. The only reason you might need to use a stateless session is when the import process involves executing domain logic which you do not want to duplicate in the native import process of your database. But remember that stateless sessions, though faster than the normal sessions, are still slower than executing a stored procedure or native bulk import. So choose the right tool for the job.

User-defined types

For every property on the entity that you map, NHibernate uses its own defaults to determine the right database column type. On most occasions, this just works. If it does not and you need minor changes to type, for example, instead of Int32 you want Int64, you can do it via entity mapping. But if you need to map a database column to a property of a completely unrelated type, then you can define your own type for NHibernate to work with. This obviously assumes that your code knows both the type in the database and the type in the code. Your code also should know how these two types convert from each other.

Consider for example, you are working on a legacy database situation. You have got an Employee table which has a NVARCHAR(1) type of column named IsEmployed. A value of Y in this column means that the employee is still part of the organization. A value of N in this column means that the employee has left the organization. Now, while building the domain model for this domain, you may not want to use a string type to designate whether the employee is still part of the organization or not. You would rather use a Boolean. This conversion from a string type to Boolean is something NHibernate cannot do out of the box and we would need to define a type that can do the conversion for us. Let's see how we can handle this situation using a user-defined type.

> Situations like this, where you use a Boolean type on the application side and best suitable type on the database side, can also be handled using query substitutions. Query substitutions would let you use Boolean types in a database independent way. Readers are advised to explore this option before making the final choice.

A user-defined type is any class that implements the NHibernate.UserTypes. IUserType interface. Once this class is defined, we can use it during mapping of a property to tell NHibernate that it should use this class whenever it is dealing with that particular property. Let's see how this works by implementing a type to handle conversion from string to Boolean type we just discussed. Following code listing shows a class YesNoType that implements IUserType:

```
public class YesNoType : IUserType
{
  public bool Equals(object x, object y)
  {
    if (ReferenceEquals(x, y))
    {
      return true;
    }
```

```csharp
    if (x == null || y == null)
    {
      return true;
    }

    return x.Equals(y);
}

public int GetHashCode(object x)
{
  return x.GetHashCode();
}

public object NullSafeGet(IDataReader rs, string[] names, object
owner)
{
  var value = rs[names[0]] as string;

  if (value == @"Y") return true;
  return false;
}

public void NullSafeSet(IDbCommand cmd, object value, int index)
{
  var parameter = (DbParameter)cmd.Parameters[index];

  if (value == null)
  {
    parameter.Value = DBNull.Value;
  }
  else
  {
    var bValue = (bool) value;
    if (bValue)
    {
      parameter.Value = "Y";
    }
    else
    {
      parameter.Value = "N";
    }
  }
}
```

```
public object DeepCopy(object value)
{
  return value;
}

public object Replace(object original, object target, object
owner)
{
  return original;
}

public object Assemble(object cached, object owner)
{
  return cached;
}

public object Disassemble(object value)
{
  return value;
}

public SqlType[] SqlTypes
{
  get
  {
    return new[]
    {
      new SqlType(DbType.String),
    };
  }
}

public Type ReturnedType
{
  get { return typeof (bool); }
}

public bool IsMutable
{
  get { return false; }
}
}
```

There is a lot of code in the above implementation. But on careful observation, you would realize that some of the methods are not new and are clearly needed for NHibernate to do its job.

Let's go over the important methods to understand their role in the process:

Method name	Purpose
NullSafeGet	This is where the conversion from the database type to domain type happens. The instance of IDataReader that holds the result set returned from the database is passed into this method. We can then retrieve the column we want to convert and run the custom conversion logic. You can see that here we return a true if IDataReader contains a string Y, otherwise we return false.
NullSafeSet	This is exactly opposite of NullSafeGet. This is on the way to the database. IDbCommand containing the details to build the result SQL is passed into this method. Here we update the value for the IsEmployed parameter after converting it using the custom conversion logic.
DeepCopy	Returns a deep copy of the persistent state. The persistent state is passed in as object. Persistent state in our case is a simple Boolean so that we return the passed object as is.
Replace	This method is used during Merge to replace the value of persistent entity with the value from detached entity. Recommended practice is to return the first parameter passed into this function in case of immutable objects, and return a (recursive) copy otherwise. Again, in our example, Boolean is a value type and hence we can return the first parameter without any issues.
Assemble	A cacheable representation is passed into this function and a reconstructed object is expected to be returned. NHibernate recommends that this method should return a deep copy in the least.

Method name	Purpose
Disassemble	Exactly opposite of Assemble but goes with the same recommendation.
SqlTypes	An array of types on the database column side.
ReturnedType	Type of the property on the domain entity.
IsMutable	This tells whether the property is mutable.

Let's tell NHibernate to use this type. If I had a Boolean property named IsEmployed on the Employee entity, then following is how I would map it to make use of YesNoType:

```
public class EmployeeMappings : ClassMapping<Employee>
{
  public EmployeeMappings()
  {
    Property(e => e.IsEmployeed, mapper =>
                  mapper.Type<YesNoType>());
  }
}
```

Now you can use the IsEmployed property on the Employee entity as a normal Boolean property. Every time the property value needs to be updated into the database or needs to be read from the database, NHibernate would handle the conversion.

In the beginning, when I said that NHibernate does not support the preceding conversion out-of-the-box, I lied. In reality, the example we used is so common that NHibernate has a built-in type to support this. It is called NHibernate.Type.YesNoType. The built-in type is not implemented as a user-defined type but does exactly the same thing. If you come across a similar situation then you can avoid implementing a user defined type by making use of this build-in type. There are several such built-types to support commonly occurring legacy database situations.

Other user-defined types

IUserType is the most basic form of a user defined type. NHibernate has defined interfaces to represent more specific user defined types. These types can be used instead of IUserType if the latter cannot handle the situation sufficiently. Following table describes these additional user defined types:

Type	Purpose
ICompositeUserType	A custom type which can have its own properties. These properties may be mapped to a different table and can be referenced while querying the parent entity. This gives an effect similar to components.
IUserCollectionType	A user-defined collection type.
IEnhancedUserType	A custom type that may function as an identifier or discriminator type, or may be marshalled to and from an XML document.
IParameterizedUserType	A parameterizable user-defined type. This lets you parameterize values for properties on the type through mapping. It is useful when the same type is used in multiple places with minor changes in its behavior. These changes can be driven by the values of the parameterized properties.
ILoggableUserType	Can be used by the user-defined types that want to perform custom logging of their corresponding values.
IUserVersionType	A user defined type that may be used for a version property.

Examples or detailed explanation of each of these types is beyond the scope of this book. If you ever need to use one of the above types, feel free to ask for a helping hand on NHibernate user group.

Summary

This chapter has covered some of the most powerful features of NHibernate that we may not need to use on daily basis.

We started the chapter with concurrency control. Concurrency control is very critical from a business point of view as it helps with preventing corruption of data due to multiple writes to the same data at the same time. NHibernate mainly provides two ways of concurrency control.

Optimistic concurrency control is a database technology agnostic. This is built entirely within NHibernate and you can use it with any database. Pessimistic concurrency control, on the other hand, makes use of database locks to make sure that only one transaction can update a database record at any point of time. Event system of NHibernate is carefully designed to make sure that enough extension points are provided for the users of NHibernate to plug in their own code at multiple different times during the commit of a transaction. What you can do with these hooks is only limited by your creativity. The most common use of these hooks is to audit entities transparently and from one place. Next, we touched upon the different types of caching implementation that NHibernate offers. Session level cache is scoped to a session and cannot be disabled. Second level cache is shared across multiple sessions created from the same session factory. Query cache is shared across multiple sessions but is applied to specific queries and works in conjunction with the second level cache. Session level cache and dirty checking make the normal session a bit slow and consume more memory. These attributes do not have significant impact when working with small number of entities at a time. But if you are loading thousands of entities in memory then the session starts slowing down with its burgeoning memory footprint. At this point, a lightweight stateless session may come in handy. Stateless sessions perform faster and use less memory at the cost of disabling a lot of features we would normally use. In the end, user defined types provide you a tool that can be used when NHibernate fails to handle conversion of SQL column type to .NET type automatically for you. User defined types is an important feature that can come in handy when dealing with legacy database situations.

Though we do not use these features on a daily basis, these features are very important. Knowledge of these features may save you hours of efforts when you need them.

Index

A

ACID properties
about 137
Atomic 137
Consistency 137
Durability 137
Isolation 137
action filter
of ASP.NET MVC, using 272, 273
of Web API, using 272, 273
ADO.NET batching
limitation 223
memory consumption 223, 224
used, for batching write queries 220-222
architectural principles
about 246
anaemic domain model, defining 247
capabilities, declaring 253-256
dependency inversion principle 250-253
onion architecture 247-250
unit of work, defining 256-258
architecture diagram, NHibernate 173
association mappings
about 86
and database tables 57, 58
many-to-many 67-71, 88, 89
many-to-one 55-62, 87
mapping 54-56
one-to-many 55-60, 86
one-to-one 55-66, 87, 88
attribute/property 36

B

baseline
determining 218, 219
batching
about 220
lazy collections 227-229
reading, with future queries 224-226
batching settings 204
bidirectional associations
about 161-163
cascade 165
inverse 165
ownership 161-163
ownership, in many-to-many
associations 164, 165
building blocks, NHibernate
about 12
configuration 12, 13
mappings 12
Session object 13, 14

C

cache
about 353
query cache 353-359
second level cache 354-357
session level cache 353
cascade options
all 153
all-delete-orphan 153
delete 152

implementing, contextual
  sessions used 270
WCF 273
single-ended lazy associations
  about 198-200
  Proxy, versus NoProxy 201
single responsibility principle (SRP) 291
software
  optimizing 218
specification pattern
  about 292
  chaining 299, 300
  for NHibernate 297-299
  in original form 292-296
  limitations 301, 302
SQL injection attack 180
SQLite 21
SQL Server 2012 Express
  about 19
  URL 19
stateless sessions
  using 359-361
storage mechanism
  CallSessionContext 269
  ThreadStaticSessionContext 270
  WcfOperationSessionContext 270
stored procedures
  named queries 329
  working with 327-329
subselect
  mapping ID 326
  mapping properties 326
  table synchronization 326
  using, instead of views 325, 326

T

Test-driven Development (TDD) 15
theta style joins 194
transaction
  about 137, 138
  explicit transaction 139
  implicit transaction 139

transitive persistence
  associations, updating on persistent
    entity 158-160
  bidirectional associations 156-158
  implementing 154
  implementing, with cascade
    styles 149-153
  persistent entity, deleting 161
  transient entity, saving to other transient
    entities 154-156
  used, for updates 278, 279

U

unit of work
  about 137, 138, 245, 264
  contextual sessions 266-268
  CurrentSessionContext,
    configuring 269, 270
  defining 256-258
  implementation 274
  scope, for web applications 265
  session per request 266
  spanning whole HTTP request 274, 275
  with custom scope 276
user-defined types
  about 362-366
  Assemble method 365
  DeepCopy method 365
  Disassemble method 366
  ICompositeUserType 367
  IEnhancedUserType 367
  ILoggableUserType 367
  IParameterizedUserType 367
  IsMutable method 366
  IUserCollectionType 367
  IUserVersionType 367
  NullSafeGet method 365
  NullSafeSet method 365
  Replace method 365
  ReturnedType method 366
  SqlTypes method 366

V

Visual Studio 2013 19

W

WCF 273
web application
  building 246
workflow
  querying 176, 177
write queries
  batching, with ADO.NET
      batching 220-222

X

XML configuration 112, 113
XML mappings, Employee class
  about 39-41
  development environment, creating 42
  mappings 48
  mappings, verifying with
      unit tests 44-47
  working, with IntelliSense 42, 43

Thank you for buying
Learning NHibernate 4

About Packt Publishing

Packt, pronounced 'packed', published its first book, *Mastering phpMyAdmin for Effective MySQL Management*, in April 2004, and subsequently continued to specialize in publishing highly focused books on specific technologies and solutions.

Our books and publications share the experiences of your fellow IT professionals in adapting and customizing today's systems, applications, and frameworks. Our solution-based books give you the knowledge and power to customize the software and technologies you're using to get the job done. Packt books are more specific and less general than the IT books you have seen in the past. Our unique business model allows us to bring you more focused information, giving you more of what you need to know, and less of what you don't.

Packt is a modern yet unique publishing company that focuses on producing quality, cutting-edge books for communities of developers, administrators, and newbies alike. For more information, please visit our website at www.packtpub.com.

About Packt Open Source

In 2010, Packt launched two new brands, Packt Open Source and Packt Enterprise, in order to continue its focus on specialization. This book is part of the Packt Open Source brand, home to books published on software built around open source licenses, and offering information to anybody from advanced developers to budding web designers. The Open Source brand also runs Packt's Open Source Royalty Scheme, by which Packt gives a royalty to each open source project about whose software a book is sold.

Writing for Packt

We welcome all inquiries from people who are interested in authoring. Book proposals should be sent to author@packtpub.com. If your book idea is still at an early stage and you would like to discuss it first before writing a formal book proposal, then please contact us; one of our commissioning editors will get in touch with you.

We're not just looking for published authors; if you have strong technical skills but no writing experience, our experienced editors can help you develop a writing career, or simply get some additional reward for your expertise.

NHibernate 3.0 Cookbook

ISBN: 978-1-84951-304-3   Paperback: 328 pages

70 incredibly powerful recipes for using the full spectrum of solutions in the NHibernate ecosystem

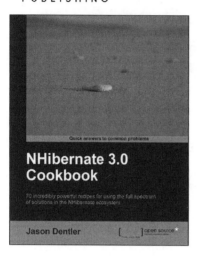

1. Master the full range of NHibernate features.

2. Reduce hours of application development time and get better application architecture and performance.

3. Create, maintain, and update your database structure automatically with the help of NHibernate.

NHibernate 3 Beginner's Guide

ISBN: 978-1-84951-602-0   Paperback: 368 pages

Rapidly retrieve data from your database into .NET objects

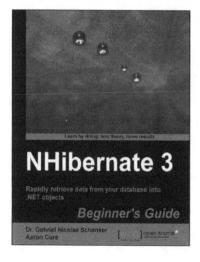

1. Incorporate robust, efficient data access into your .Net projects.

2. Reduce hours of application development time and get better application architecture and performance.

3. Create your domain model first and then derive the database structure automatically from the model.

Please check **www.PacktPub.com** for information on our titles

NHibernate 2 Beginner's Guide

ISBN: 978-1-84719-890-7 Paperback: 276 pages

Rapidly retrieve data from your database into .NET objects

1. Incorporate robust, efficient data access into your .Net projects.

2. Gain database independence, not tied to any particular technology.

3. Avoid spending countless hours developing data access layers.

4. Eliminate writing stored procedures.

ASP.NET Site Performance Secrets

ISBN: 978-1-84969-068-3 Paperback: 456 pages

Simple and proven techniques to quickly speed up your ASP.NET web site

1. Speed up your ASP.NET website by identifying performance bottlenecks that hold back your site's performance and fixing them.

2. Tips and tricks for writing faster code and pinpointing those areas in the code that matter most, thus saving time and energy.

3. Drastically reduce page load times.

Please check **www.PacktPub.com** for information on our titles